# Microsoft® Outlook® 2000

**SAMS**

A Division of Macmillan Computer Publishing, USA
201 W. 103rd Street
Indianapolis, Indiana 46290

*Dave Johnson*

# How To Use Microsoft® Outlook® 2000

Copyright © 1999 by Sams Publishing

All rights reserved. No part of this book shall be reproduced, stored in a retrieval system, or transmitted by any means, electronic, mechanical, photocopying, recording, or otherwise, without written permission from the publisher. No patent liability is assumed with respect to the use of the information contained herein. Although every precaution has been taken in the preparation of this book, the publisher and author assume no responsibility for errors or omissions. Neither is any liability assumed for damages resulting from the use of the information contained herein.

International Standard Book Number: 0-672-31588-2

Library of Congress Catalog Card Number: 99-61032

Printed in the United States of America

This book was produced digitally by Macmillan Computer Publishing and manufactured using computer-to-plate technology (a film-less process) by GAC, Indianapolis, Indiana.

First Printing: May 1999

00  99  98        4  3  2  1

**Executive Editor**
Mark Taber

**Acquisitions Editor**
Randi Roger

**Development Editor**
Alice Martina Smith

**Managing Editor**
Lisa Wilson

**Project Editor**
Rebecca Mounts

**Copy Editor**
Tonya Maddox

**Indexer**
Greg Pearson

**Proofreader**
Mary Ellen Stephenson

**Technical Editor**
Sunil Hazari

**Interior Designer**
Nathan Clement

**Cover Designers**
Nathan Clement
Aren Howell

**Layout Technicians**
Brandon Allen
Stacey DeRome
Timothy Osborn
Staci Somers

# Trademarks

All terms mentioned in this book that are known to be trademarks or service marks have been appropriately capitalized. Sams cannot attest to the accuracy of this information. Use of a term in this book should not be regarded as affecting the validity of any trademark or service mark.

# Warning and Disclaimer

Every effort has been made to make this book as complete and as accurate as possible, but no warranty or fitness is implied. The information provided is on an "as is" basis. The author and the publisher shall have neither liability nor responsibility to any person or entity with respect to any loss or damages arising from the information contained in this book or from the use of the CD or programs accompanying it.

# Contents at a Glance

| | | |
|---|---|---|
| 1 | Getting Started | 2 |
| 2 | Working with Email | 30 |
| 3 | Getting Fancy with Email | 60 |
| 4 | Managing Your Inbox | 94 |
| 5 | Working with Contacts | 112 |
| 6 | Working with the Calendar | 144 |
| 7 | Managing Your Day with Notes and the Journal | 168 |
| 8 | Automating Your Email | 188 |
| 9 | Using Outlook with Other Computers | 202 |
| 10 | Customizing Outlook | 212 |
| | Glossary | 241 |
| | Index | 244 |

# Contents

## 1 Getting Started 2

How to Start Outlook 4

How to Create an Internet-Only Email Account 6

How to Create a Corporate Email Account 8

How to Change the Internet Connection for Your Account 10

How to Start Your Day with Outlook Today 12

How to Print the Outlook Today Summary 14

How to Modify Outlook Today 16

How to Start Outlook in Your Favorite View 18

How to Get Around in the Outlook Bar 20

How to Set Options for Outlook 22

How to Set Options for Outlook Continued 24

How to Get Help from the Office Assistant 26

How to Get Help from the Internet 28

## 2 Working with Email 30

How to Find Your Way Around the Inbox 32

How to Check for New Mail 34

How to Read a New Email Message 36

How to Reply to a Message 38

How to Forward a Message 40

How to Create a Mail Message 42

How to Check Your Spelling 44

How to Hide Your Mail Recipients 46

How to Attach a File to a Message 48

How to Open a Mail Attachment 50

How to Use Word to Write Mail Messages 52

How to Print an Email Message 54

How to Check Mail Automatically 56

How to Send Mail from a Specific Mail Account 58

## 3 Getting Fancy with Email 60

How to Resend a Message 62

How to Create a Signature 64

How to Add Fancy Formatting to Email Messages 66

How to Send Mail in Plain-Text Format 68

How to Create Messages with Stationery 70

How to Send Contact Info Automatically 72

How to Add Personal Info to Contacts Automatically 74

How to Get a Digital ID 76

How to Send Secure Email 78

How to Add Words to the Spelling Dictionary 80

How to Format Message Replies 82

How to Display Messages with AutoPreview 84

How to Request a Read Receipt 86

How to Leave Messages on the Mail Server 88

Project 1: Creating an Attractively Formatted Message 90

## 4 Managing Your Inbox 94

How to Find a Message by Subject or Sender 96

How to Find a Message by Keyword 98

How to Mark Messages for Later Action 100

How to Mark a Message as Read or Unread 102

How to Organize Mail in Folders 104

How to Use the Organize Button 106

How to Sort Email Using Categories 108

How to Display All the Messages in the Same Conversation 110

## Working with Contacts 112

How to Get Around in Contacts 114

How to Create a New Contact 116

How to Add a Contact from an Email Message 118

How to Find a Contact by Name 120

How to Find a Contact by Keyword 122

How to Find a Contact from Any View 124

How to Find Someone Using the Internet 126

How to Create a Distribution List 128

How to Use the Organize Button 130

How to Organize Contacts 132

How to View a Map to a Contact's Home or Office 134

How to Place a Call to a Contact 136

How to Link Contacts and Email Messages 138

Project 2: Mail-Merge Outlook Data 140

## Working with the Calendar 144

How to Find Your Way Around the Calendar 146

How to Set an Appointment 148

How to Create a Recurring Appointment 150

How to Make a Task 152

How to Create a Day-Long Event 154

How to Invite Someone to a Meeting 156

How to Delegate a Task 158

How to Change a Scheduled Appointment 160

How to Print the Calendar 162

How to Share a Calendar 164

How to Publish Your Calendar to the Web 166

## Managing Your Day with Notes and the Journal 168

How to Create a Note 170

How to Convert Notes into Email and Back Again 172

How to Modify the Look of a Note 174

How to Organize Your Notes 176

How to Turn On the Journal 178

How to Find Your Way Around the Journal 180

How to View Journal Entries 182

How to View the Journal in Contacts 184

How to Track Your Activities 186

## Automating Your Email 188

How to Create a Rule 190

How to Disable a Rule 192

How to Create an Autoresponder 194

How to Create a Rule That Moves Mail 196

How to Create a Rule That Assigns Messages to Categories 198

How to Avoid Junk Mail Without Reading It 200

## Using Outlook with Other Computers 202

How to Import Mail from Another Computer 204

How to Synchronize Outlook with Another PC 206

Project 3: Syncrhronize Outlook with a Palm PC 210

## Customizing Outlook 212

How to Customize Menus and Toolbars 214

How to Add Groups to the Outlook Bar 216

How to Add a File to the Outlook Bar 218

How to Configure Outlook to Find People 220

How to Switch Between Internet-Only and Corporate Mail Settings 222

How to Add a Corporate Mail Account 224

How to Add Folders to the Folder List 226

How to Archive Old Mail 228

How to Archive Old Mail Continued 230

How to Discard Old Mail 232

How to Create a Mail Template 234

How to Use a Mail Template 236

How to Detect and Repair Outlook 238

Glossary 241

Index 244

## About the Author

**Dave Johnson** writes about technology and small business from his home in Colorado Springs, Colorado. The author of 10 computer books, Dave's latest is *Digital Photography Answers* by Osborne McGraw-Hill. Dave writes frequently for magazines such as *Home Office Computing* and *PC Computing*, and he's the mobile computing editor at Planet IT.

Dave's ultimate ambition in life is to find a pair of those cool psychedelic glasses that every hip singer wore in the '60s and to play bass in a band. Until then, playing computer games when he should be working will just have to do.

## Dedication

*For everyone who tolerated me at Richardson.*

# Acknowledgments

Writing a book is rarely as easy as it seems at first blush. For one thing, publishers are rarely willing to accept a manuscript scrawled on the back of a Hard Rock Café T-shirt. Even when they are, they always insist on testing all the procedures you outline in the book, which means that you can't write from memory about what the program looked like the last time you sat in front of a computer. And screenshots? You have to actually capture them on the PC, not sketch them out in crayon.

And I'm thankful for that. The Sams team is outstanding. Many, many thanks to **Randi Roger**, **Jill Mazurczyk**, and **Alice Martina Smith**—three people who made this book one of the smoothest and least painful writing experiences in my entire life.

Thanks also go to **Neil Salkind** and the crew at Studio B. A better agent I won't find until I get that gig on Letterman.

I can't imagine writing a book without the sound of **Kristin Hersh** in the background. Kristin, thanks again for making such amazing music.

Finally, my friends and family deserve a medal. **Kris**, **Evan**, and **Marin**—I love you. **Rick**, **Shawna**, **Anne**, and **Kevin**—you guys are the best.

# Tell Us What You Think!

As the reader of this book, *you* are our most important critic and commentator. We value your opinion and want to know what we're doing right, what we could do better, what areas you'd like to see us publish in, and any other words of wisdom you're willing to pass our way.

You can fax, email, or write me directly to let me know what you did or didn't like about this book—as well as what we can do to make our books stronger.

*Please note that I cannot help you with technical problems related to the topic of this book, and that because of the high volume of mail I receive, I might not be able to reply to every message.*

When you write, please be sure to include this book's title and author as well as your name and phone or fax number. I will carefully review your comments and share them with the author and editors who worked on the book.

Fax: 317-581-4770

Email: **office_sams@mcp.com**

Mail: Mark Taber
Executive Editor
Sams Publishing
201 West 103rd Street
Indianapolis, IN 46290 USA

# How To Use This Book

## The Complete Visual Reference

Each part of this book is made up of a series of short, instructional tasks, designed to help you understand all the information you need to get the most out of Outlook 2000.

**Click**: Click the left mouse button once.

**Double-click**: Click the left mouse button twice in rapid succession.

**Right-click**: Click the right mouse button once.

**Drag and drop**: Position the mouse pointer over the object, click and hold the left mouse button, drag the object to its new location, and release the mouse button.

**Selection**: This circle highlights the area discussed in the step.

**Key icons**: The key icons clearly indicate what key combinations to use to accomplish the instructions in the step.

Each task includes a series of easy-to-understand steps designed to guide you through the procedure.

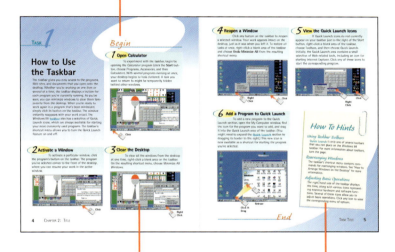

Each step is fully illustrated to show you how it looks onscreen.

Extra hints that tell you how to accomplish a goal are provided in most tasks.

Screen elements (such as menus, icons, windows, and so on), as well as things you enter or select, appear in **boldface** type.

*Continues*

If you see this symbol, it means that the task you're in continues on the next page.

# Introduction

*O*utlook 2000 is a Personal Information Manager (also called a *PIM* by people who like to use acronyms). Outlook ships with every version of Microsoft Office 2000, and it's also available on its own. The program is designed to manage almost every conceivable aspect of your daily agenda, much like a human assistant might do. Outlook receives, stores, and sends email; tracks your schedule and to-do tasks; keeps your address book; and much more.

Outlook goes beyond the capabilities of most PIM software. Although it's not hard to use, there's so much under the hood that a step-by-step guide is the best way to master the program. By the time you're done with this book, you should be able to do all of these things, plus much more:

- ✓ Craft elegantly formatted email messages
- ✓ Create mass-mailing lists to send a message to many people at once
- ✓ Automate your Inbox so that messages are handled without your direct supervision
- ✓ Use the contacts list to track friends and business associates
- ✓ Send messages to or call your contacts with a single click
- ✓ Invite co-workers to meetings using Outlook
- ✓ Find documents you created on a specific date or sent to a particular person

Welcome to *How to Use Microsoft Outlook 2000*. This book assumes that Outlook is already installed on your PC and that you have Internet access already working. In most cases, your company's IS department or your Internet software has already helped you establish an email account. Most people connect to the Internet using a *dial-up account*, which means that you use an analog modem to connect to the Internet.

Your Internet service provider (ISP) should provide you with a phone number, as well as connection instructions. The ISP should also provide you with an email address and should give you detailed instructions for setting up your email account. For instance, you'll need a username, a password, and server names. Most ISPs use a kind of email server, called *POP3*. Your incoming mail is delivered to a POP3 server, and the outgoing mail is sent using an *SMTP* server. Why they're referred to by these names is unimportant, although you do have to know the names of your POP and SMTP servers to configure email accounts.

If you already have Internet mail working, don't worry—just dive into the book.

*How to Use Microsoft Outlook 2000* is written so that you can get the most out of this amazing program. There are over 100 tasks in these pages, and each task explains how to accomplish a specific goal in short, simple steps. A screenshot accompanies each step, so you can never get lost.

If you run into problems that aren't addressed in this book, you can always contact me for additional information. Visit my Web site at **http://www.radioguys.com** or email me at **questions@radioguys.com**. I'll do my best to answer your questions—and comments may be integrated into the next version of this book.

Good luck with Outlook!

# Task

1. How to Start Outlook  4
2. How to Create an Internet-Only Email Account  6
3. How to Create a Corporate Email Account  8
4. How to Change the Internet Connection for Your Account  10
5. How to Start Your Day with Outlook Today  12
6. How to Print the Outlook Today Summary  14
7. How to Modify Outlook Today  16
8. How to Start Outlook in Your Favorite View  18
9. How to Get Around in the Outlook Bar  20
10. How to Set Options for Outlook  22
11. How to Get Help from the Office Assistant  26
12. How to Get Help from the Internet  28

## PART 1

# Getting Started

In the world of computer software, Outlook 2000 is known as a *Personal Information Manager*, or a *PIM*. Most PIMs allow you to keep an address book (for your frequent contacts) as well as track your schedule and daily tasks. Outlook goes far beyond these basic features, however, by also providing such tools as an *integrated mail client*—that means you can send and receive email from within the program. Because the program has so many features, Microsoft sometimes refers to Outlook as a *desktop information manager*.

Whatever you choose to call it, Outlook has a lot of capabilities. Before you dive into the many facets of this program, let's take a casual stroll around. Outlook has a daily summary view, called *Outlook Today*, that you should get acquainted with. You should also learn how to establish new mail accounts and switch views so that you can visit the Inbox, contacts list, calendar, and other views whenever you want.

These are exactly the sorts of things you're going to learn in this part of the book. Welcome to Outlook!

## TASK 1

# How to Start Outlook

Outlook is a multifaceted program you can use to manage almost every aspect of your working day. Before we dive in and tackle your email, appointments, contacts, and other topics, however, we should start by looking at the program's basic operation. Start by learning how to open Outlook, move around in the program, and close the program when you are done.

## *Begin*

### *1* Open the Start Menu

Choose **Programs, Microsoft Outlook** from the **Start** menu. If you don't see Outlook in the Start menu, it's possible that it's in a folder called **Microsoft Office** or **Office**. Look there instead.

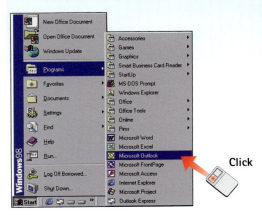

### *2* Welcome to Outlook 2000

When you start Outlook, you'll probably see a view called **Outlook Today**. This view provides a summary of your upcoming appointments, outstanding tasks, and new messages. If this is the first time you've opened the program, this view will be relatively empty.

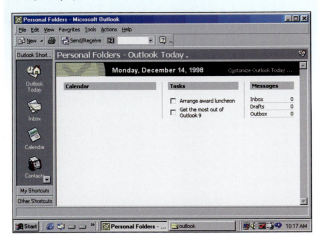

### *3* Moving Around the Outlook Bar

Outlook is a single program that has many views. Each *view* is designed to manage a different aspect of your day (such as email, contacts, appointments, and notes). You switch among these views by clicking the desired view in the **Outlook bar**, which is the vertical strip of icons on the left side of the Outlook window. Switch to the Inbox by clicking the **Inbox** icon.

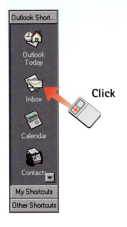

**4**   PART 1: GETTING STARTED

## 4 Turn On the Folders List

One of the ways Outlook helps you manage and organize your information is with *folders*. For example, you can file new mail in a folder instead of leaving it in the Inbox, where it can get lost among all the other new mail. You can display these folders and switch among them using the **Folder List**. Turn it on by choosing **View, Folder List**.

Click

## 5 Examine the Outlook Window

Outlook's appearance changes slightly depending on which view you select. All views share several features: Use the Outlook bar to change views; use the Folder List (if you turn it on) to view the contents of a folder; the main window displays the contents of the selected view; and the toolbar provides access to features for that view.

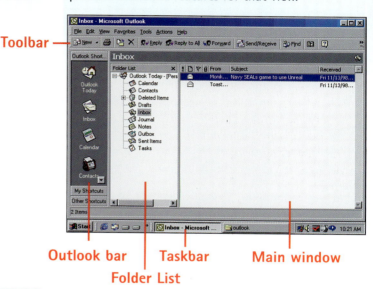

Toolbar — Outlook bar — Taskbar — Main window — Folder List

## 6 Close Outlook

To close Outlook, choose **File, Exit** from the menu bar or click the **Close** button (the **X**) in the upper-right corner of the screen. Remember that if you close Outlook, it cannot receive email or notify you about upcoming appointments. It's usually a good idea to leave the program running in the background as you work.

Click

*End*

## How-To Hints

### Start Outlook Automatically

Outlook is such a useful program that you may want it to start when you turn your PC on in the morning. Right-click the taskbar at the bottom of the Windows desktop and choose **Properties** from the pop-up menu. Click the **Start Menu Programs** tab and click **Advanced**. Drag the icon for Outlook into the **Startup** folder in the **Programs** list. Now Outlook will begin automatically when you start your PC.

## Task 2

# How to Create an Internet-Only Email Account

Before you can use Outlook to send and receive email, you need to set up one or more mail *accounts*. These accounts correspond to electronic mailboxes on your Internet service provider's (ISP's) mail server. When someone sends you mail, the message is stored on the ISP's server until you use Outlook to retrieve the message. Likewise, when you send mail from Outlook, it first goes to your personal mail account on the mail server and then goes off through the Internet to the recipient.

Outlook can manage not just one mail account but as many accounts as you have access to. That means you can check the mail account you use at work, the account you use at home, and any other accounts used by members of your family.

## Begin

### 1 Open the Accounts View

Because you can set up as many mail accounts as you want, the **Internet Accounts** dialog box displays all your account information. To open it, choose **Tools, Accounts** from the menu bar.

Click

### 2 Create a New Account

The **Internet Accounts** dialog box has three tabs at the top. Click **Mail** to see only your mail accounts. (We'll talk about the **Directory Services** later.) Choose **Add** to start creating a new account.

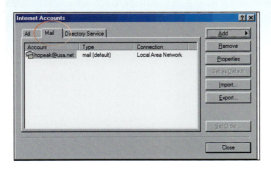

### 3 Answer the Wizard's Questions

Answer the questions on each page of the Internet Connection Wizard, choosing the **Next** button to move from one question to the next.

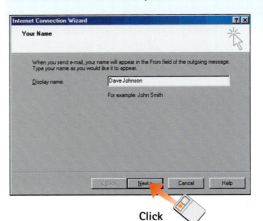
Click

Part 1: Getting Started

## 4 Enter Your Server Names

You may have to verify some of the wizard's questions with your ISP. In particular, you may have to find out what your POP server and SMTP server names are. This information is essential if Outlook is to properly connect to your mail account for sending and retrieving mail.

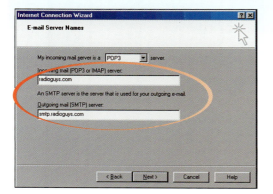

## 5 Enter Your Logon Name and

Your ISP should have given you a username with which you log on. It's usually the first part of your email address (for example, **myname** from **myname@myisp.com**). Outlook will remember your password if you select the **Remember Password** box; if you check this box, Outlook never asks again for a password to send or receive mail. Beware: Letting Outlook mind your password gives anyone with access to your PC the ability to send and receive email through your account.

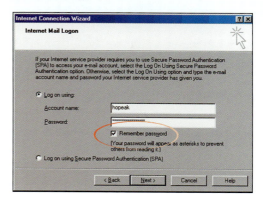

## 6 Choose a Connection

Select the kind of Internet connection that your computer uses. It's often convenient to select **Connect Using My Local Area Network**, even if you use a modem to connect to the Internet.

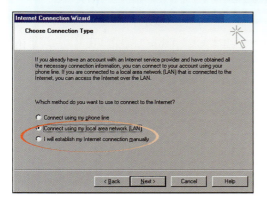

## 7 Set a Default Account

If you want to make your new account the default for sending email, select the account name and click the **Set as Default** button.

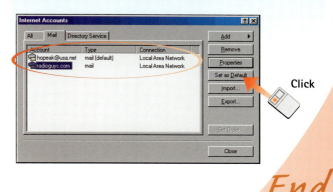

Click

*End*

HOW TO CREATE AN INTERNET-ONLY MAIL ACCOUNT   7

## Task 3

# How to Create a Corporate Email Account

Outlook can be configured to receive more than just Internet email. It can also send and receive Microsoft Mail, Lotus cc:Mail, and faxes, if it is configured for corporate email. Each *service* is a different kind of message, such as email, fax, or cc:Mail.

If the only kind of messaging you want to use is Internet email, you should reconfigure Outlook and set up your mail as described in Part 1, Task 2, "How to Create an Internet-Only Email Account." Learn how to switch between Internet-only and corporate email in Part 10, Task 5, "How to Switch Between Internet-Only and Corporate Mail Settings."

## Begin

### 1 Open the Services Dialog Box

To create a mail service in Outlook, you must first open the **Services** dialog box. Start by choosing **Tools, Services** from the **menu bar**. It doesn't matter which Outlook view you are in because they all share the **Tools** menu.

### 2 Add a New Service

To add Internet email to Outlook, you have to add the Internet Email service to your profile. Make sure that you are on the **Services** tab in the **Services** dialog box; click the **Add** button.

### 3 Choose Internet Email

The **Add Services to Profile** dialog box lists all the message services available in Outlook. (Unless you have access to a proprietary service such as Lotus cc:Mail, you probably don't need to worry about most of these services.) Double-click **Internet E-mail** in the list of available information services.

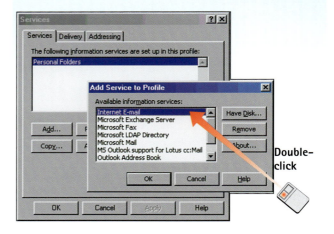

**8** PART 1: GETTING STARTED

## 4 Enter Email Information

Before you can get Internet email, you have to tell Outlook about your account using the **My ISP Properties** dialog box. Type your name and email address on the **General** tab. You can also give this service a nickname, which will later help you recognize it in Outlook's Options screens.

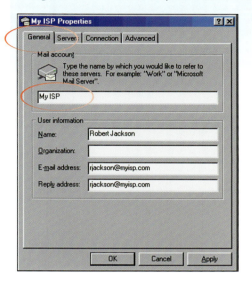

## 5 Enter Your Server Names

Click the **Servers** tab and enter the POP3 and SMTP server names for your account. Also type your mail account name and password. You may have to verify this information with your ISP before completing this step.

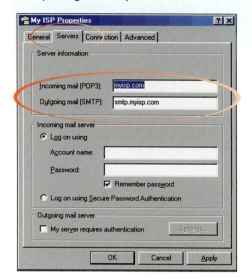

## 6 Specify a Connection

Click the **Connection** tab. Select the **Connect Using My Phone Line** option and choose the dial-up connection setting you want Outlook to use for this account. If it doesn't matter which you use to access your email, choose **Connect Using My Local Area Network**. In that case, Outlook will use whatever dial-up connection is currently active. Click **OK**.

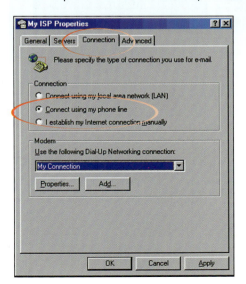

## 7 Restart Outlook

When you close the Services dialog box, Outlook warns you that the changes you made to Outlook won't take effect immediately. To use the new Internet email settings, close Outlook and restart the program.

*End*

HOW TO CREATE A CORPORATE EMAIL ACCOUNT

## Task 4

# How to Change the Internet Connection for Your Account

When you create an Internet email account, you have the opportunity to specify what kind of connection you will use. Later, you can change your dial-up access or decide to connect using a local area network.

Whatever the reason, you may want to change the way Outlook connects to the Internet to send and receive email. To make that change, simply edit the properties for your email account.

## Begin

### 1 Open the Accounts Dialog Box

To change the properties of your email account, choose **Tools, Accounts** from the menu bar. It doesn't matter which Outlook view you are currently in; this menu option appears in all views.

### 2 Select the Account

Click the **Mail** tab in the **Internet Accounts** dialog box. Outlook allows you to send and receive email from any number of email accounts. If you already have more than one account listed, click the desired account.

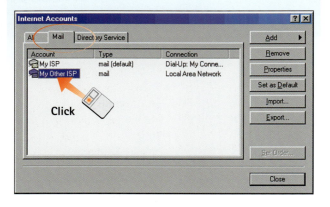

### 3 Edit Account Properties

To edit the properties of the selected account, click the **Properties** button.

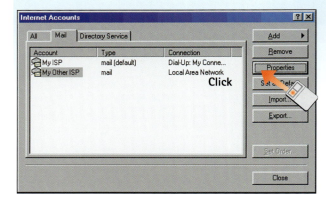

**10**  Part 1: Getting Started

## 4 Choose a Connection

In the **Properties** dialog box, click the **Connection** tab. You use the tab to specify the kind of connection you want to use. If you are connected to a local area network or you typically connect to your mail server using more than one dial-up connection, choose **Connect Using My Local Area Network (LAN)**. If you want to connect using a specific dial-up connection, click **Connect Using My Phone Line**.

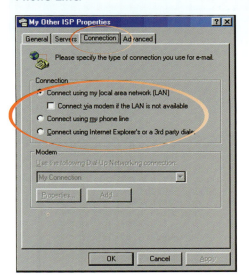

## 5 Select the Dial-Up Setting

If you choose to connect using a specific dial-up connection, choose the connection you prefer from the list in the **Modem** section of the **Connection** tab. You can also tell Outlook to try a specific dial-up if the local area network is unavailable. Click **OK** to close the dialog box.

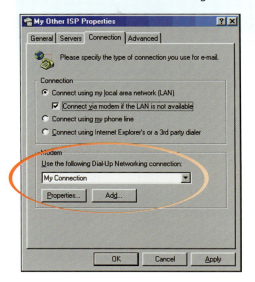

## 6 Close the Accounts

After you have made the appropriate changes to your email account, click the **Close** button to return to Outlook's main window.

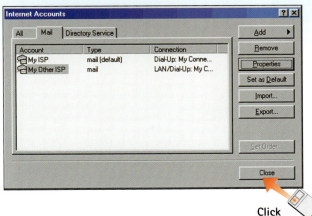

Click

*End*

## How-To Hints

### ISP Access Numbers

Some people check all their email accounts at once using the same access number. This often works just fine, but some ISPs do not allow you to send email through their mail server unless you dial in with their access number. This restriction prevents spammers from using the ISP's equipment without a proper account. If you have such an ISP, you should configure your email account to use that ISP's dial-up connection. Otherwise, you can use the same dial-up number to access all your mail at once.

# Task 5

## How to Start Your Day with Outlook Today

If you come to rely on Outlook for your messages and daily scheduling, you will especially appreciate its Outlook Today view. This view gives you an at-a-glance snapshot of your daily calendar as soon as you start the program—or at any time during the day.

You certainly don't have to use Outlook Today, but many people like to have the summary it provides just a single mouse-click away.

## Begin

### 1 Use the Outlook Bar

Outlook Today, like all the views in Outlook 2000, is only as far away as the Outlook bar. Switch to the Outlook Today view by clicking the **Outlook Today** icon.

### 2 Take a Look at Outlook Today

Outlook Today provides a quick snapshot of your day. It displays the current date as well as upcoming calendar events, scheduled tasks, and the number of messages waiting for you in the Inbox and other folders.

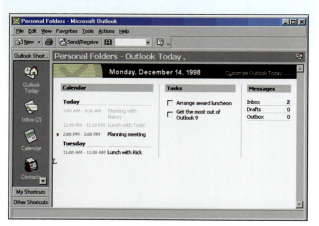

### 3 Click to Switch Views

The Outlook Today view doesn't just display your day's agenda—it allows you to switch directly to a specific entry for more information. Hold the mouse pointer over any entry in Outlook Today and notice that the pointer changes to a hand, indicating that you can click to change views. You can click the **Calendar**, **Tasks**, and **Messages** headings to go to those views, or you can click directly on a specific entry to open it. Click any entry on the screen to change views.

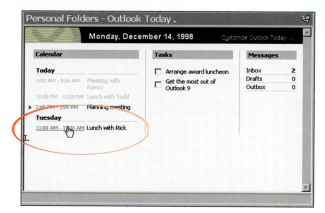

## 4 Switch Views

After clicking an entry in Outlook Today, the view changes to display whatever entry you selected. If you click an appointment or task, the dialog box for that entry opens. Click the **Close** box (the **X** in the upper-right corner) of the entry's dialog box to return to Outlook Today.

## 5 Complete Tasks

If Outlook Today shows *open* tasks (tasks yet to be completed), you can click the accompanying selection box to mark it as done. Completed tasks appear with a line through them.

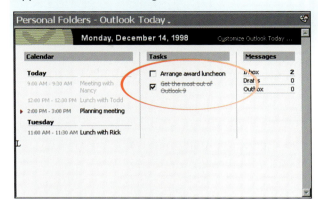

## 6 Go to Email

When you are done inspecting Outlook Today, you can switch to the Email view. In the **Messages** section of the window, click the folder you want to visit. You can choose the **Inbox**, **Outbox**, or **Draft** messages folder.

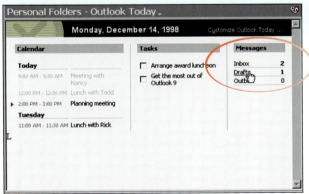

### How-To Hints

#### Understanding Appointments

Outlook Today displays appointments from your calendar for today and for several days into the future. Your next appointment is displayed with an arrow next to it; past appointments are displayed in lighter text. You learn how to set up and manage appointments in Part 6, "Working with the Calendar."

*End*

## Task 6

# How to Print the Outlook Today Summary

Not everyone spends all of his or her time chained to a PC. If you spend a lot of time on the go, you could benefit from printing the Outlook Today summary and carrying it with you. By referring to your Outlook Today summary throughout the day, you can make sure that you don't miss any meetings and that your tasks get done. Otherwise, you'll have to return to your computer to check your agenda.

## Begin

### 1 Start Printing

Make sure you that are in the Outlook Today view. (Click the Outlook Today icon in the Outlook bar.) Choose **File**, **Print** from the menu bar to display the **Print** dialog box. Alternatively, you can click the **Print** button on the standard toolbar.

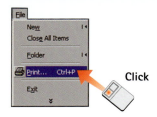
Click

### 2 Select a Printer

If your computer can print to more than one printer, the next step is to select the appropriate printer from the **Name** list in the **Print** dialog box.

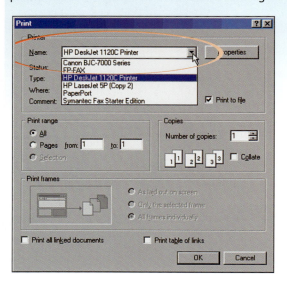

### 3 Set Print Options

Select the options you want to use when printing the Outlook Today page. Specify the number of copies you want to print and decide whether you want to print the entire document or—if the summary contains more than a single page—a particular page. You can configure the printer by clicking the **Properties** button.

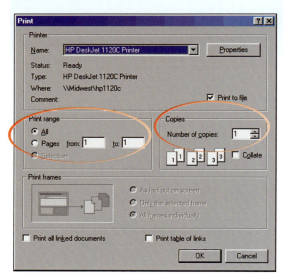

14  PART 1: GETTING STARTED

## 4 Configure the Printer

If you clicked the **Properties** button in step 3 to configure the printer, you can fine-tune the way your printer will operate. Note that printer properties vary from one printer to another. In general, the **Printer Properties** dialog box lets you change factors such as the print quality and paper size. Click **OK** to save your changes to the printer.

## 5 Print to File

You can select **Print to File** in the **Print** dialog box to save the print job to either a hard drive or to a floppy disk. You may want to do this if you don't have a printer connected to your computer but want to carry a floppy with the print job to a computer that does have a printer. When you click the **Print** button, Outlook presents the **Print to File** dialog box, where you specify the name of the print file. Take that file to a computer with a printer and print it.

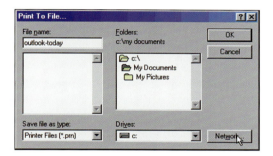

## 6 Print Outlook Today

On the **Print** dialog box, click **OK** to send your summary to the printer.

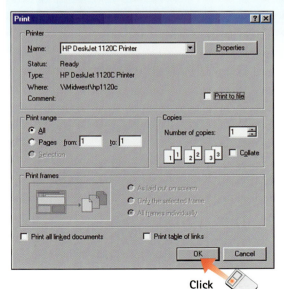

Click

## How-To Hints

### Choosing a Printer

If you have a choice of printers when printing the Outlook Today summary, choose a black-and-white laser. You don't gain anything by printing to a color printer, and inkjets are much slower at printing text than are lasers.

### How Do I Print the Print File?

If you print the summary to a file and later want to print that file, you must first open an MS-DOS prompt window. Choose **Start, Programs, MS-DOS Prompt**. Then type `copy filename.prn lpt1:`. Of course, be sure that you enter the correct `filename`.

*End*

## Task 7

# How to Modify Outlook Today

Outlook Today is useful from the moment you start scheduling your calendar activities and receiving email. You can take steps to modify the look and behavior of this view so that it's even more useful.

Although most Outlook options are controlled by choosing **Tools, Options** from the menu bar, Outlook Today has its own options settings accessible only from the Outlook Today view.

## Begin

### 1 Customize Outlook Today

Switch to the Outlook Today view by clicking the **Outlook Today** icon in the Outlook bar. Then click the **Customize Outlook Today** button at the top-right corner of the Outlook Today window.

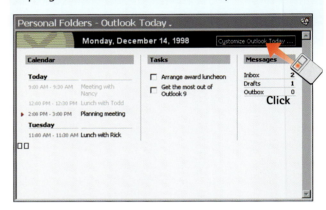

### 2 Change Settings

If you want Outlook Today to be the first thing you see when you start Outlook, click the check box next to **When Starting, Go Directly to Outlook Today**. To see more or fewer appointments in the Calendar section, change the number of days in the **Show This Number of Days in My Calendar** box. Set the other options to suit your taste.

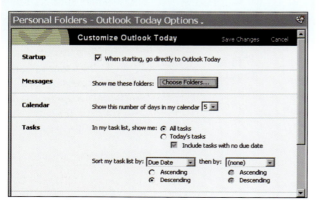

### 3 Show Email Folders

The default folders in Outlook Today are Inbox, Outbox, and Drafts. If you want to see how many email messages you have in other folders, click the **Choose Folders** button on the **Outlook Today Options** screen and select the folders you want from the **Select Folder** dialog box.

## 4 Change the Style

Outlook Today comes with several visual styles. If you don't like the standard style (which appears by default), you can choose others by clicking in the **Styles** list on the **Outlook Today Options** screen.

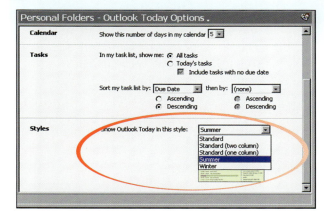

## 5 Save Your Changes

When you are satisfied with the changes you've made to Outlook Today, click the **Save Changes** button at the top-right corner of the screen. You can exit without making any changes by clicking the **Cancel** button.

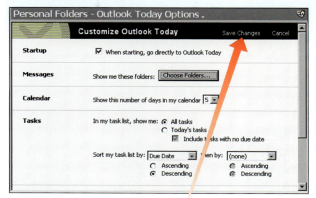

 Click

## 6 Display the Folder List

If you want to see the Folder List in the Outlook Today view (and in other views as well), choose **View**, **Folder List** from the menu bar or click **Personal Folder—Outlook Today** in the title bar. When the Folder List appears, you can make it stay onscreen by clicking the **push pin** button.

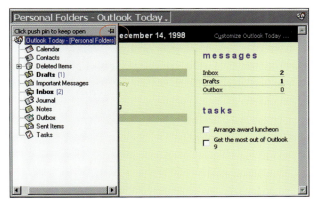

 End

# How-To Hints

### Avoiding Outlook Today

If you want to make Outlook start in a view other than Outlook Today (such as Inbox), disable the option to start in Outlook Today and specify the view you want Outlook to start in by selecting **Tools**, **Options** from the Outlook menu bar (see the following task for details).

### Setting Styles for Outlook Today

When customizing Outlook Today, you can choose from several styles. These styles affect the appearance of the entire Outlook Today window. Two styles—*Winter* and *Summer*—use colors and textures that evoke the feel of those seasons.

# TASK 8

## How to Start Outlook in Your Favorite View

Although Outlook ordinarily starts in the Outlook Today view, you may want it to open directly into the Inbox view or the Calendar view, depending on how you most frequently use the program.

You can actually configure Outlook to start in any view you prefer, but the setting is hidden in a hard-to-find location.

## *Begin*

### **1** Display the Options

The **Options** dialog box is where you choose what view appears when you start Outlook. Choose **Tools, Options** from the menu bar.

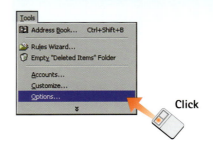

### **2** Select the Other Tab

Click the **Other** tab in the **Options** dialog box. This tab includes miscellaneous options for changing the way Outlook handles trash, archives old mail, and displays the Preview pane.

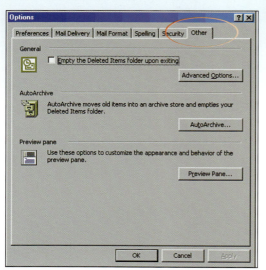

### **3** Enter Advanced Options

Click the **Advanced Options** button to open the **Advanced Options** dialog box.

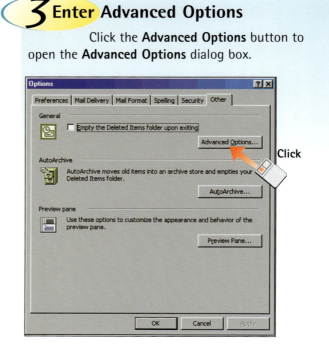

## 4 Choose a View

Click the **Startup in This Folder** list box to choose the view you want Outlook to open in. You can choose the **Inbox**, **Calendar**, **Journal**, **Contacts**, **Outlook Today**, or others. Click **OK** to close the **Advanced Options** dialog box.

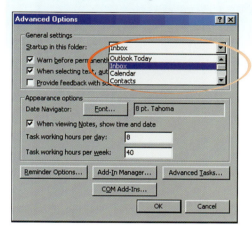

## 5 Save Your Changes

Click **OK** to close the **Options** dialog box. This action saves any changes you made in the **Options** dialog box, including the new startup view selection.

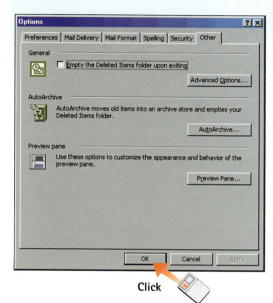

Click

## 6 Start Outlook

The next time you open Outlook, the program automatically displays the view you selected in step 4 instead of the default Outlook Today.

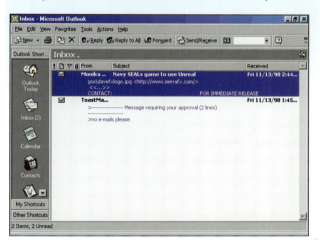

*End*

## How-To Hints

### Learn More About Options

Additional tasks in Part 1 dedicated to helping you understand how to set Outlook options. Look for these task titles:

Task 7, "How to Modify Outlook Today"

Task 10, "How to Set Options for Outlook"

HOW TO START OUTLOOK IN YOUR FAVORITE VIEW    19

## Task 9

# How to Get Around in the Outlook Bar

The **Outlook bar** is the primary way Outlook helps you switch among views. With the Outlook bar, no view is more than a single mouse click away. You can also use it to quickly switch to special folders and other applications.

## Begin

### 1 Welcome to the Outlook Bar

The Outlook bar is always available, no matter what view you have selected. It includes an icon for each view in Outlook.

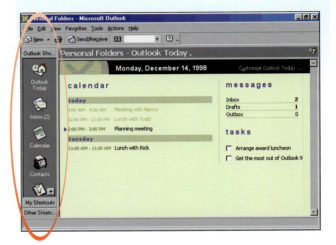

### 2 Scroll to See More

To view icons that aren't visible onscreen, use the up and down scroll buttons. These buttons disappear when you can't scroll up or down any further. You may not see any scroll arrows if you run Outlook on a very high-resolution monitor because all the view icons will fit on the screen at once.

### 3 Switch Views

To switch to the Tasks view, find the **Tasks** icon in the Outlook bar and click it. If necessary, use the up and down scroll buttons until you can see the icon. Notice that when you hold the mouse pointer over an icon, a box appears around the icon to indicate that it is selected.

## 4 Change Groups

The Outlook bar's icons are divided into groups. Each of the main Outlook views, for instance, are in the Outlook Shortcuts group, as indicated by the gray title bar at the top of the Outlook bar. Other groups, such as My Shortcuts and Other Shortcuts, also appear in the Outlook bar. Click the **Other Shortcuts** group to switch to that group.

Click

## 5 View Disk Folders

The **Other Shortcuts** group contains information about your hard disk. For example, click **My Computer** to see the contents of your hard disks in the main Outlook window.

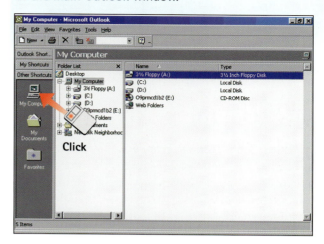

## 6 Switch to Outlook

Click the **Outlook Shortcuts** group bar to get back to the Outlook Shortcuts group. You can then click the **Outlook Today** icon to change the view from My Computer.

### How-To Hints

#### Modifying the Outlook Bar

If you spend a lot of time in Outlook, you may appreciate the fact that you can add items to the Outlook bar. Any program, folder, or document can be dragged directly into the Outlook bar from the Windows desktop, where you can launch it with a click. For more information, see Part 10, Task 2, "How to Add Groups to the Outlook Bar," and Task 3, "How to Add a File to the Outlook Bar."

## Task 10

# How to Set Options for Outlook

Outlook is a big program with lots of views, tools, and options. As you become more knowledgeable about how Outlook works, you can change the way it behaves to better suit your needs. Although you may be perfectly happy with Outlook to start with, there are many options to experiment with.

## Begin

### 1 Display Options

To open the **Options** dialog box, choose **Tools, Options** from the menu bar.

Click

### 2 Set Preferences

When the **Options** dialog box appears, there are many general settings you can modify on the **Preferences** tab. The options on this tab allow you to change the behavior of each of the major Outlook views.

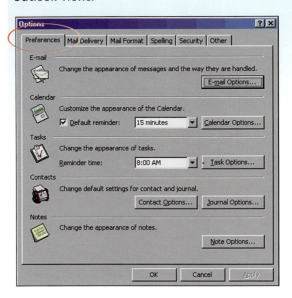

### 3 Set E-mail Options

Click the **E-mail Options** button on the **Preferences** tab to open a dialog box that provides more control over the Inbox. In the **On Replies and Forwards** section of this dialog box, you can specify what your email messages look like. For example, you can choose to display the original message marked with symbols when replying to messages.

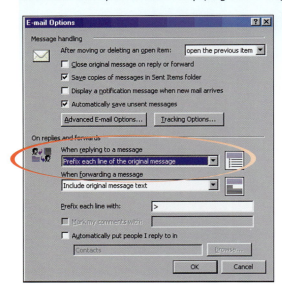

## 4 Save Email Addresses

If you want Outlook to automatically store the email addresses of those you correspond with in the Contacts view, select the option for **Automatically Put People I Reply In**. (A check mark appears in the box.) When you reply to an email, the recipient's name is automatically entered in the Contacts view, ensuring that you have that person's email address.

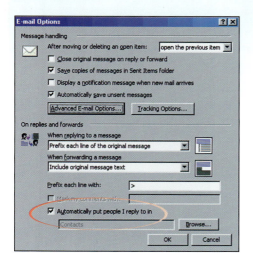

## 5 Set Calendar Options

Click the **Calendar Options** button on the **Preferences** tab of the **Options** dialog box. This opens a dialog box that provides more control over the Calendar view. Use this dialog box to specify which days Outlook treats as business days and to identify your typical work hours.

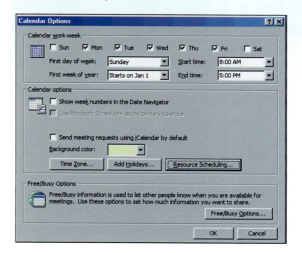

## 6 View More Mail Options

Click the **Mail Delivery** tab of the **Options** dialog box to change the way Outlook connects to your mail server. This tab allows you to modify your email accounts (although this feature is also available by choosing **Tools, Accounts** from the menu bar). More importantly, you'll find controls here for connection and dial-up options.

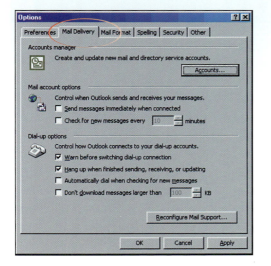

### How-To Hints

#### Mail Options

On the Mail Delivery tab of the Options dialog box, you can customize the way Outlook deals with your email messages. The Mail Format tab gives you options for how Outlook presents your messages. The Other tab lets you access dozens more options that you can use to set up Outlook to your liking.

*Continues*

## How to Set Options for Outlook Continued

### 7 Set Connect Options

If you want your mail to be transmitted as soon as your dial-up connection is established, select the **Send Messages Immediately When Connected** option. If you want Outlook to check your mail server for new messages automatically, select the **Check for New Messages Every** option and enter a time interval.

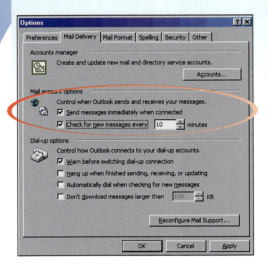

### 8 Set Dial-Up Options

Use the **Dial-Up Options** section to fine-tune Outlook's behavior as well as your modem's. You can select the **Warn Before Switching Dial-Up Connection** option if you have several email accounts and you don't want Outlook to disconnect you without warning. If you want to minimize your online time, select the **Hang Up When Finished Sending, Receiving, or Updating** option.

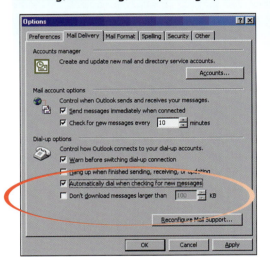

### 9 Set the Mail Format

Click the **Mail Format** tab to specify how your messages will appear. Because many recipients prefer their mail to arrive in text-only format, you may want to send all your messages in this format by default.

### 10 Empty the Trash

If you want messages that are placed in the **Deleted Items** folder to be discarded each time you close Outlook, click the **Other** tab and select the **Empty the Deleted Items Folder Upon Exiting** option.

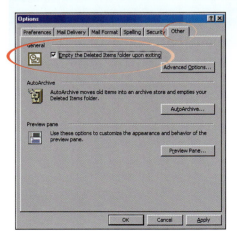

## 11 Set Trash Warnings

Click the **Advanced Options** button on the **Other** tab to display the **Advanced Options** dialog box. If you want to be warned before Outlook deletes email from the **Deleted Items** folder, specify that here. On the other hand, you may not want a warning—particularly if you set up Outlook to delete trash every time you close the program.

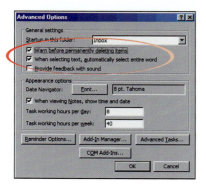

## 12 Save Your Options

When you are finished setting Outlook's options, click **OK** to save your work. If you want to discard all the changes you made in the **Options** dialog box, click the **Cancel** button instead.

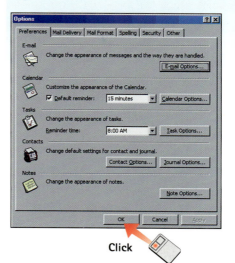

Click

## 13 View the Folder List

Another important option you can customize is whether Outlook displays the complete list of folders next to the Outlook bar. The folders make it easy to move messages out of the Inbox for safekeeping and to perform other file storage tasks. To display the Folder List, choose **View, Folder List** in the menu bar.

*End*

### How-To Hints

#### More About Mail Preferences

Email is the most common application on the Internet, and people take their messages very seriously. Consequently, you should strive to send mail that doesn't offend or annoy your recipients. Because most people prefer text messages over HTML or Rich Text messages, consider choosing the **Plain Text** option in the mail format options.

# Task 11

## How to Get Help from the Office Assistant

The **Office Assistant** is an animated character called an *avatar* (a graphical representation of a character; Microsoft uses avatars such as dogs, cats, and a fanciful Einstein to give the Help system a friendly face). The Office Assistant is your gateway to all the Help files stored within Outlook. The Office Assistant can interpret plain-English questions and can help you find the answers to questions that come up when you use Outlook on a day-to-day basis.

## Begin

### 1 Display the Office Assistant

To display the Office Assistant, choose **Help, Microsoft Outlook Help**. The Office Assistant appears, ready to provide support. The assistant will probably be Clippit, the paper clip; it might also be one of several other assistants that Microsoft designed for Office.

### 2 Type a Question

To get information from the Office Assistant, type your question in the yellow thought balloon that appears over the assistant's head. When you are done typing the question, either click the **Search** button or press **Enter**. Be as detailed as possible in your question; Outlook tries to correlate keywords in your question with Help topics in its database.

Click

### 3 Choose an Answer

Find the topic that best matches the topic you were hoping to find from the list of possible topics that the assistant displays. If necessary, click the **See More** arrow to display additional topics. If you don't see the answer you're looking for, there may be an answer to your question on the Web. See the next task, "How to Get Help from the Internet," for help.

## 4 Read the Answer

The Office Assistant opens the Microsoft Outlook Help window and displays the information you requested. You can read the Help file and print it by clicking the **Print** icon at the top of the window. If you want to search for related topics, click the **Expand** button at the top left of the Help window.

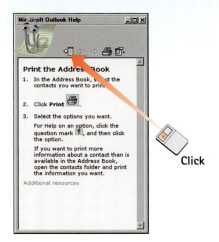

## 5 Get Related Information

If you clicked the **Expand** button in step 4, you can type keywords directly into the search engine and have Outlook look for related topics.

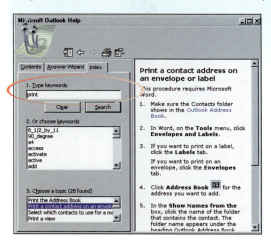

## 6 Hide the Office Assistant

When you're done with the Help system, you can hide the Office Assistant to get it off the computer screen. Choose **Help**, **Hide the Office Assistant**.

*End*

### How-To Hints

#### Changing the Office Assistant

If you want to change your Office Assistant's clothing, right-click the assistant and select **Choose Assistant** from the pop-up menu. You can change your assistant to a robot, a cat, a dog, or some other character.

#### Moving the Assistant

You can drag your assistant around if it is in the way of something onscreen. Just click the assistant and drag the mouse to move it to another location.

TASK 12

# How to Get Help from the Internet

Sometimes the Office Assistant can't give you all the information you need—particularly if you want to troubleshoot what appears to be a problem with the program. Perhaps you want information about a program add-on that the Assistant doesn't know anything.

In these (and other) cases, the easiest solution is to look on the Internet for answers. Microsoft has integrated the Office Assistant with its online Knowledge Base, so it's simple to see whether there's new or more detailed information on the Web.

## Begin

### 1 Display the Office Assistant

Getting help from the Internet begins the same way as getting information from the Office Assistant: Display the Office Assistant by choosing **Help, Microsoft Outlook Help** from the menu bar.

### 2 Type Your Question

Type your question in the yellow thought balloon, which appears over the assistant's head; click the **Search** button. Be as detailed as possible in your query.

### 3 Look for an Answer

Look for a topic in the list the assistant displays. Click the **See More** arrow if it's available to display more answer topics.

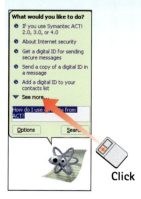

## 4 Look on the Web

If none of the assistant's suggested Help topics are what you need, look for the **None of the Above, Look for More Help on the Web** entry. Click this item.

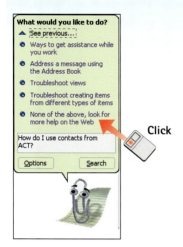

Click

## 5 Proceed to the Web

You can send a short note to Microsoft Technical Support about your problem. Enter the note and click the **Send and Go to the Web** button. Your Web browser will launch and take you to Microsoft's Knowledge Base Web site.

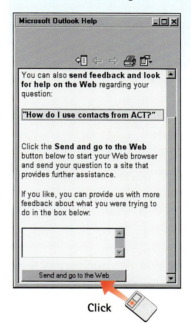

Click

## 6 Find an Article

Microsoft displays all the articles in its Knowledge Base that appear to match your query topic. Scroll through the Web page to locate an article that meets your needs. Click the article to load it into your browser and read it.

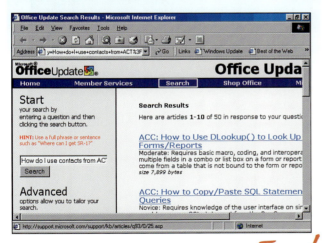

*End*

## How-To Hints

### Visit Office on the Web

Look on Microsoft's Web site for periodic program updates, bug fixes, and additional software designed to work with Outlook. An easy way to get to Microsoft's Web site is to choose **Help, Microsoft on the Web** from the Outlook menu bar.

# Task

1. How to Find Your Way Around the Inbox  32
2. How to Check for New Mail  34
3. How to Read a New Email Message  36
4. How to Reply to a Message  38
5. How to Forward a Message  40
6. How to Create a Mail Message  42
7. How to Check Your Spelling  44
8. How to Hide Your Mail Recipients  46
9. How to Attach a File to a Message  48
10. How to Open a Mail Attachment  50
11. How to Use Word to Write Mail Messages  52
12. How to Print an Email Message  54
13. How to Check Mail Automatically  56
14. How to Send Mail from a Specific Mail Account  58

# PART 2

# Working with Email

Despite Outlook's many views and modules, you'll probably spend most of your time sending, receiving, and managing your email messages. It's not surprising, then, that email is the first topic in this book covered in detail. Outlook is a very comprehensive mail program, offering nearly every tool and feature you're ever likely to need.

Before you get into advanced features, however, you'll want to learn the basics, which include retrieving mail, sending new messages, including file attachments with messages, and printing your mail. These are just some of the topics we'll discuss in this part of the book.

## Task 1

# How to Find Your Way Around the Inbox

The *Inbox* is the name Microsoft uses to describe the entire email portion of the Outlook program. From the Inbox, you can send, receive, and manage your email—as well as store it in an unlimited number of folders, only one of which is actually called Inbox!

The Inbox view is in all likelihood where you'll spend most of your time in Outlook. Managing email is typically the most common activity performed each day.

## Begin

### 1 Welcome to the Inbox

The Inbox view is where you manage all your incoming, outgoing, and stored messages. When you click the **Inbox** icon in the Outlook bar, Outlook switches to this view and displays the contents of the Inbox folder. This is where new email goes when it arrives.

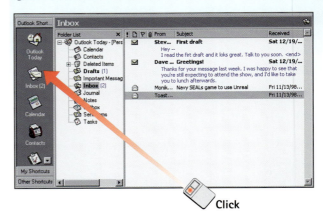

### 2 Using the Folder List

Activate the Folder List (a list of all the folders in which you can store messages) by choosing **View, Folder List**. To switch to a folder, just click that folder. You can move a message to a folder by dragging it from the folder contents pane on top of the folder name.

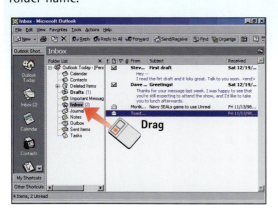

### 3 Toolbar Message Actions

The toolbar is where you'll find the most common commands for dealing with email. In particular, the **Reply** and **Reply to All** buttons let you respond to an email sender; the **Forward** button lets you send a message that you've received to someone else.

PART 2: WORKING WITH EMAIL

## 4 Toolbar Message Management

You'll also use a few other buttons on the toolbar frequently. Use the **Send/Receive** button to check for mail; use the **Find** button to search for a specific message by sender, date, keyword, or subject. The **Organize** button displays tools that make it easy to mark and move messages for easy reference.

## 5 Understand the Message Symbols

You can quickly assess the status of messages in the Inbox view by looking at the symbols in the folder contents window. The **Message Importance** icon indicates a sender-assigned status. The arrow's direction in the **Message** icon tells you whether a message has been replied to or forwarded. You can mark messages with the **Message Flag** icon as a reminder that some action is required. The **Attachment** icon indicates that a message has files attached to it.

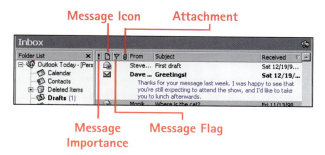

## 6 Switch Views

The **Outlook bar** is always available to allow you to change the view to another part of Outlook. Just click the icon in the Outlook bar that represents the view you want to switch to.

*End*

## How-To Hints

### Using ToolTips
If you want to determine what a toolbar button does, just hold the mouse pointer over the button. A ToolTip appears after a few seconds, describing the button's purpose.

### Finding Menu Items
Outlook 2000 uses *personalized menus*, which hide infrequently used commands from view. If you want to see all the items available in a menu, just click the double arrows at the bottom of the menu.

## Task 2

# How to Check for New Mail

When people send you email, it arrives at a special mail server at your Internet service provider (ISP). It waits there until your mail program actually downloads the messages. You can tell Outlook when to check for new mail. At the same time you check for new mail, any messages you've prepared to send out to others are transmitted.

You can configure Outlook to check for new mail on its own; see Part 2, Task 13, "How to Check Mail Automatically." Alternatively, you can follow these steps to manually check for mail any time you like.

## Begin

### 1 Prepare Outgoing Mail

The first thing Outlook does when you check for new mail is send any mail stored in the Outbox folder. You can tell what is waiting to be sent by inspecting the number in parentheses after the Outbox folder name.

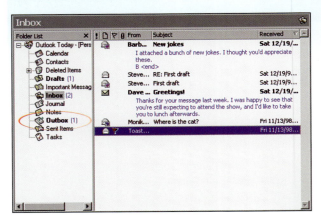

### 2 Check for New Mail

To check for new mail, click the **Send/Receive** button in the toolbar. The status dialog box opens and begins sending mail.

Click

### 3 Send Mail

The status dialog box shows the email transmission activity. The first thing Outlook does is send any messages currently in the Outbox folder. The status bar shows the progress of the message transmission.

**34** Part 2: Working with Email

## 4 Receive Messages

After Outlook sends messages in the Outbox folder, it checks your mail server and downloads any messages waiting for you. Again, the status bar keeps you informed of the transmission progress.

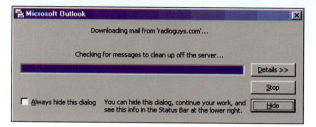

## 5 View Details

If you prefer to see more information about the progress of the mail transmission, click the **Details** button on the status dialog box. The dialog box expands to show more information about the transmission, including which email account is being checked.

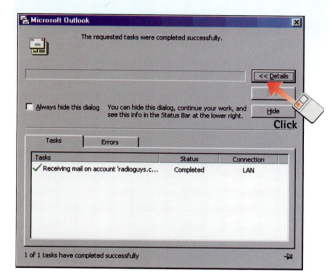

## 6 View New Messages

New messages are stored in the Inbox folder as they arrive. You can see how many unopened messages are stored there by inspecting the number in parentheses next to the Inbox folder name.

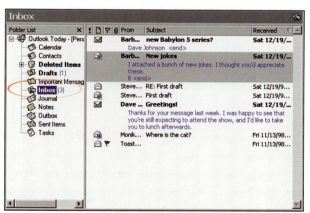

### How-To Hints

#### Troubleshooting Email Problems

If you're having trouble sending or receiving email, the Details section of the status dialog box can be invaluable. The dialog box shows which email account is being checked (especially handy if you have multiple accounts); any errors are logged to the Errors tab. When you call your ISP's technical support center, you can read the error details to more quickly determine where the problem lies.

**HOW TO CHECK FOR NEW MAIL** 35

## Task 3

# How to Read a New Email Message

After you've checked for new mail and the messages are in your Inbox folder, you'll probably want to read them. Email works just like any other kind of message: You can read it and throw it away, respond to the message, or send it to someone else. Let's start by reading the message.

## Begin

### 1 Get the Gist of It

Often, you can get the gist of the message without even opening it. Outlook's **AutoPreview mode** lets you see the first few lines of the message without ever opening it. If AutoPreview isn't activated on your PC, choose **View, AutoPreview** to turn it on.

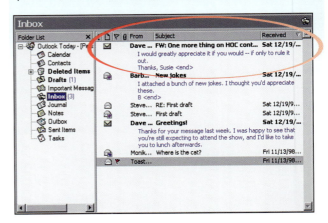

### 2 Open the Message

To read the entire message, double-click the message in the folder contents pane. The message opens in a new window. Alternatively, you can click the message and press the **Enter** key.

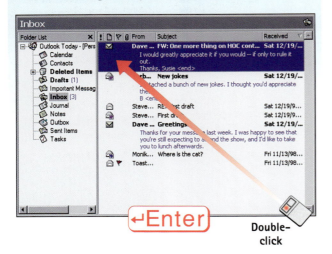

### 3 Read the Message

The message opens in its own window, where you can read the message in its entirety.

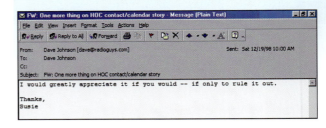

**Part 2: Working with Email**

## 4 Respond to the Message

After you read the message, you can use the toolbar to manage the message using the **Reply**, **Reply to All**, or **Forward** buttons. These buttons are explained in detail in Tasks 4, 5, and 6 of Part 2.

## 5 Restore Message's Unread Status

A message is no longer displayed in AutoPreview mode after it's read. Sometimes you'll want to restore a message to its unread status to remind yourself to deal with its subject later, or perhaps you will want to see the first few lines of the message in the Inbox. To restore a message to its unread status, right-click the message and select **Mark as Unread** from the menu.

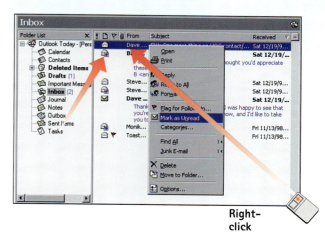

Right-click

## 6 Delete a Message

If you do not want to keep a message, you can delete it. Click the message you want to delete and click the **Delete** button in the toolbar, or press the **Delete** key on the keyboard.

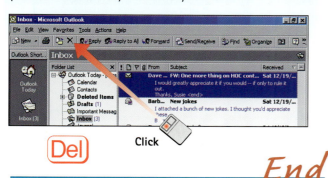

Del   Click

*End*

## How-To Hints

### Managing Your Inbox

Over time, your Inbox folder can get very cluttered with messages. You should store messages you plan to keep for a long time in another folder and delete the messages you no longer need from the Inbox folder. If you don't clean out your folder from time to time, it will get very difficult to find messages when you need them. See Part 4, "Managing Your Inbox," for a variety of tasks that help you keep things on the up-and-up.

## Task 4

# How to Reply to a Message

After you've had an opportunity to read an email message, you may want to reply to it. If you want to reply directly to the sender, you typically choose Outlook's Reply tool. If the message has been sent to a number of people at the same time and you want everyone to see your comments, choose Reply to All.

## Begin

### 1 Select the Message

Start by choosing the message you want to reply to. Select the message by clicking it.

### 2 Use the Toolbar

If you have previously read and closed the message window, you don't have to reopen the message to reply to it. Click the **Reply** button in the toolbar instead.

### 3 Open the Message

Alternatively, you can open and read the message before you reply to it. In that case, double-click the message in the contents pane. You'll have the option to reply to the message in the message window's toolbar.

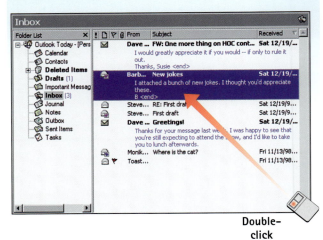

Part 2: Working with Email

## 4 Reply to the Open Message

If you've opened the message window, you have the same reply options from the toolbar in this view. Click the **Reply** button in the toolbar to reply to the sender. If you've already responded to this message, Outlook reports that in the header region of the message.

## 5 Type Your Reply

When you click the Reply button, Outlook opens a modified version of the message and places the cursor in the window so that you can type your reply. The exact appearance of this reply is determined by choosing **Tools, Options** and clicking the **E-mail Options** button in the **Preferences** tab.

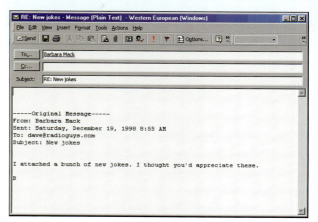

## 6 Send the Message

When your reply is complete, click the **Send** button in the toolbar. The message is sent to the Outbox folder, awaiting transmission.

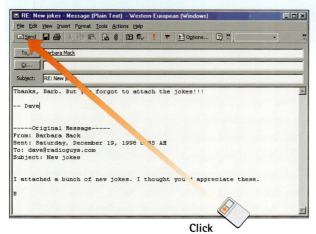

Click

*End*

## How-To Hints

### Beware of Reply to All

The Reply to All button is a great way to respond to lots of people all at once. But watch out—it's easy to direct a personal (and potentially embarrassing) reply, meant just for the original author of the message, to everyone in the message's recipient list. Click **Reply to All** only if you really want everyone to see what you have to say.

### Fine-Tune the Reply

As already mentioned, when you reply to a message, the email's appearance is determined by choosing **Tools, Options** and clicking the **Email Options** button in the **Preferences** tab. Choose the format you like best. I use the option called **Prefix Each Line of the Original Message** because it's easier to see what text is new and what text is old.

## Task 5

# How to Forward a Message

*Message forwarding* is the process of sending a message you received from one person to someone else. If someone sends you a document—such as a sales report or the latest email Dilbert newsletter—you can forward it to someone else you think needs to see it.

## Begin

### 1 Select the Message

Choose the message you want to forward. Just as you can with message replies, you can either forward the message from the Outlook main window or open the message and forward it from there.

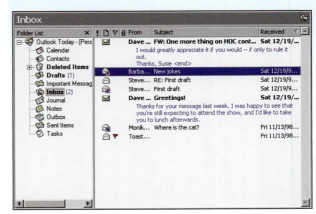

### 2 Use the Toolbar

If you have previously read and closed the message window, you don't have to reopen the message to forward it. Click the **Forward** button in the toolbar instead.

Click

### 3 Open the Message

There are situations in which you may want to reread the message before you forward it. In that case, double-click the message in the contents pane. You are given the option to reply to the message in the message window's toolbar.

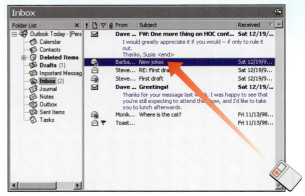

Double-click

40    PART 2: WORKING WITH EMAIL

## 4 Reply to the Open Message

If the message window is open, you can forward the message using the toolbar. Click the **Forward** button in the toolbar to send it to another person.

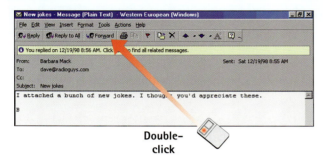

Double-click

## 5 Type Your Comments

When you click the Forward button, Outlook opens a modified version of the message and places the cursor in the window so that you can enter a message to the recipient. The exact appearance of this message is determined by choosing **Tools, Options** and clicking the **E-mail Options** button in the **Preferences** tab. Note that you can forward a message to many people at once by entering multiple names in the To or Cc box.

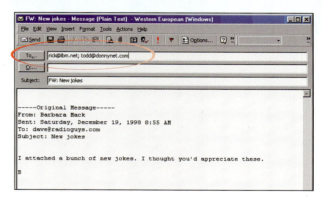

## 6 Send the Message

When you finish modifying the message you want to forward, click the **Send** button in the toolbar. The message is sent to the Outbox folder, awaiting transmission.

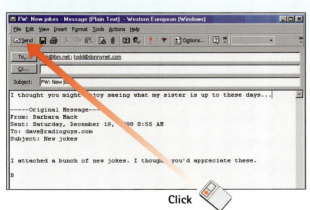

Click

*End*

## How-To Hints

### Don't Spam

Email makes it easy to send the same message to dozens, hundreds, or even thousands of people at once—at virtually no cost to you, the sender. If you send a message to recipients who didn't ask for it, it's called *spam*, and the action is universally despised on the Internet.

Think twice before you forward a message to your friends or co-workers. You may receive dire-sounding warnings about computer viruses or other general-interest messages that turn out to be false about 99.9 percent of the time. Don't spam people with such annoyances.

TASK 6

# How to Create a Mail Message

Creating an email message is one of the most basic tasks you can master when using Microsoft Outlook. There are many flourishes you can add to the process—such as applying fancy formatting, hiding the recipient list, and sending attachments—but first you have to learn how to create a message from scratch and get it into the Internet for delivery.

## Begin

### 1 Open a New Message Window

Make sure that you are in the Inbox view; a new message window appears when you click the **New** button on the toolbar.

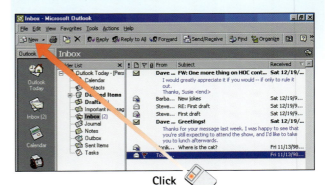
Click

### 2 Add Recipients

Click the **To** button at the top of the message window to add recipients to the message. *Recipients* are the people to whom the message will be sent; you can enter one or more names.

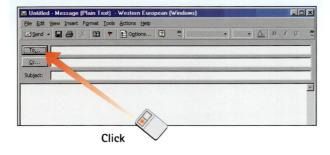
Click

### 3 Select Names

Double-click names from the Select Names dialog box to add them to the address list for your message. If you have not yet added any names to your Outlook address book, click the **Cancel** button to get rid of the Select Names dialog box; simply type the address you want to mail the message to (such as **jdoe@isp.com**) in the To line.

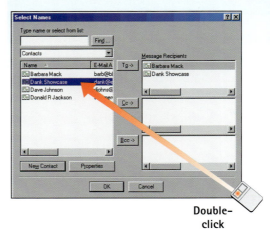
Double-click

42  PART 2: WORKING WITH EMAIL

## 4 Type Your Message

After you enter the recipients of your message, just type the *subject* (a brief synopsis of your message's topic) and the message *body* (the actual message).

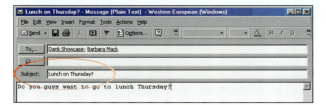

## 5 Send the Message

When you finish typing the message, you can send it by clicking the **Send** button in the toolbar. Alternatively, you can send the message from a specific email account—click the arrow next to the Send button in the toolbar and select the account from which you want to send the message. (See Task 14, "How to Send Mail from a Specific Mail Account," for details.)

## 6 View the Outbox

After you click the Send button, your message is stored in the Outbox folder until you click the Send/Receive button in the toolbar or wait for Outlook to send the message automatically. You can view the message in the Outbox by clicking **Outbox** in the Folder List.

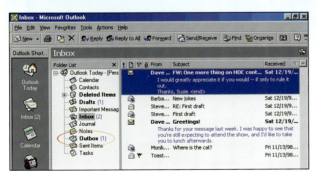

# How-To Hints

## Entering Multiple Recipients

If you want to send a message to more than one person at a time, you can type their email addresses in the message window's To or Cc line, separating them by semicolons, like this:

`davej@blackbox.net; edjackson@usa.net; pauls@ibm.net`

## Using the Courtesy Copy

Many people are confused about the difference between the To line and the Cc line. In reality, there's not a lot of difference. Either way, the recipient will get your message. It's more a matter of office protocol. The *primary recipient* should be placed on the To line; anyone who is getting the message for informational purposes should be listed on the Cc line, indicating that they're getting a courtesy copy.

## What's an Address Book?

The address book is Outlook's electronic phone book. It's another way to view your contacts, which are described in detail in Part 5, "Working with Contacts."

## Task 7

# How to Check Your Spelling

Even in email—arguably one of the most informal means of correspondence in use today—misspelled words are embarrassing. It's not a big deal if you're writing to a friend or a family member, but spelling is critical in business letters.

Thankfully, Outlook includes a spelling checker that works very much like the one in Microsoft Word. The spelling checker is not turned on by default, however, so you have to learn to activate it and use it for good-looking email messages.

## Begin

### 1 Open Outlook Options

You must turn the feature on before Outlook can check your spelling. Choose **Tools**, **Options** to open the Options dialog box.

### 2 Enable Spell Checking

In the Options dialog box, click the **Spelling** tab and select the **Always Suggest Replacements for Misspelled Words** and **Always Check Spelling Before Sending** options. Outlook won't check your spelling properly before sending messages if these options aren't selected.

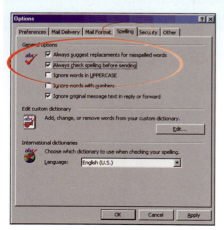

### 3 Send Mail

You can create a message after you set up the spelling options. When you're done writing the message, click the **Send** button in the toolbar. Outlook checks the spelling before sending the message to the Outbox.

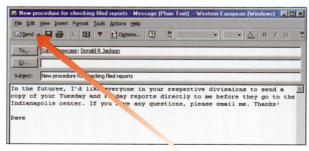

Click

**44** PART 2: WORKING WITH EMAIL

## 4 Change Misspelled Words

The Spelling dialog box automatically appears if Outlook encounters a misspelled word. It displays the incorrect word and suggests alternative spellings. If you see the correct word in the list of suggestions, double-click the correct word to change it. (Alternatively, select the appropriate suggestion and click the **Change** button.)

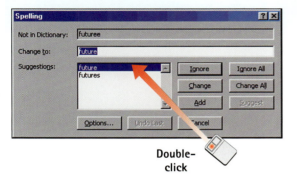

Double-click

## 5 Add New Words

If Outlook encounters a word it doesn't recognize, it automatically suggests a replacement. The word may be correct in some cases, but Outlook doesn't recognize it. You can bypass the word by clicking the **Ignore** button, which leaves the word unchanged. However, Outlook flags it as misspelled every time it sees it. On the other hand, you can click the **Add** button, which adds the word to the Outlook dictionary, ensuring that it'll never be identified as misspelled again.

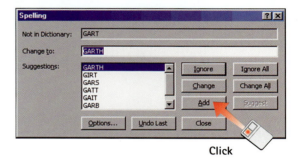

Click

## 6 Abort the Spelling Check

After you configure the spelling options, Outlook tries to spell check every message you send. Sometimes you don't want to bother checking the message; you just want to send it in a hurry. In this case, click the **Cancel** button in the Spelling dialog box. The spelling check is aborted, and Outlook asks whether you want to send the message even though it wasn't checked. Click the **Yes** button to send the message.

*End*

## How-To Hints

### Check Carefully

Be careful when using the spelling check feature; it's easy to get careless and accept whatever Outlook suggests, even if it's the completely wrong word. There's no substitute for careful proofreading.

### Using the Spelling Dictionary

For more information about adding words to the spelling dictionary, refer to Part 3, Task 10, "How to Add Words to the Spelling Dictionary."

TASK 8

# How to Hide Your Mail Recipients

You'll often find yourself sending the same message to several people at once. Usually, there's nothing wrong with all the recipients seeing who else got the message, but sometimes privacy becomes an issue—if you're sending the same message to individual clients, for example. In such a case, you need to send the message so that no one can see any other recipient's email address. In other words, you need to use a feature called Bcc, which stands for Blind Courtesy Copy.

## *Begin*

### *1* Start a New Message

Begin in the usual way; assuming that you are already in the Inbox view, click **New** in the toolbar to open a new message window.

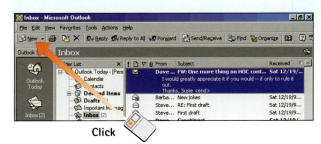
Click

### *2* Open the View Menu

The Blind Courtesy Copy option is found in the message window's **View** menu. Click **View** from the menu bar and then click the **arrow** at the bottom of the menu to expand the menu and show all the commands.

Click

### *3* Turn on the Bcc

Choose **Bcc Field** from the **View** menu. A new Bcc field will appear on the message window under the existing Cc field.

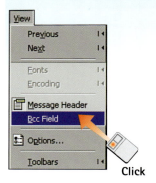
Click

46   PART 2: WORKING WITH EMAIL

## 4 Add Names to the Bcc Field

Enter recipients in the Bcc field the same way you add them to the To or Cc field. You can type email addresses directly or use the address book.

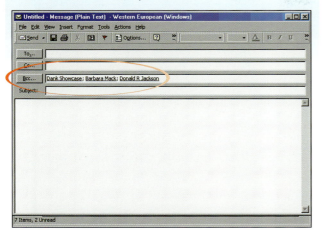

## 5 Send the Message

Finish filling in the message and then click the **Send** button in the toolbar to place the message in the Outbox.

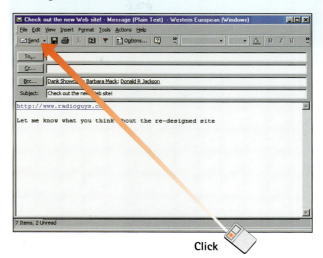

Click

## 6 Turn Off the Bcc Field

After you send the message, you may want to disable the Bcc field. Although you can leave it on all the time, it reduces the amount of screen space available for seeing messages. If you want to turn off the Bcc field when it's not in use, open a new message window and choose **View, Bcc Field** to remove the check mark.

*End*

# How-To Hints

### Privacy Is Important

In today's Internet climate, fewer and fewer people want their email addresses released to the general public. There are too many organizations out there who want to seize those addresses and send unsolicited email—*spam*. When in doubt about whether to use the Cc or Bcc field when emailing a group of people who don't know each other, choose Bcc.

### A Bcc Warning

After sending a message to a group of people using the Bcc field, Outlook cannot later display the email addresses of those who were listed in the Bcc field. That means you can't open a sent message from your Sent Items folder and find out what someone's address is. Instead, you have to store those addresses in your address book if you want to be able to use them again.

HOW TO HIDE YOUR MAIL RECIPIENTS 47

# Task 9

# How to Attach a File to a Message

Text messages are fine, but what if you want to send someone a picture from a digital camera, an Excel spreadsheet, or a formatted Word document? In those cases, there's only one solution: an email attachment.

With Outlook, you can attach almost any kind of file to an email message; when the other party receives your message, that person can save the file to a hard disk and edit, print, or otherwise use the file. In general, you can receive attachments in Outlook from any other mail program, and you can send attachments to anyone else.

## Begin

### 1 Create a New Message

If you want to add a file attachment to an email message, you must first create the message. Assuming that you are already in the Inbox view, click **New** in the toolbar to open a new message window.

Click

### 2 Insert a File

Choose **Insert, File** from the menu bar. The Insert File dialog box appears.

### 3 Find the File to Send

Navigate around your PC's hard disk and select the file you want to attach to the message. You can include more than one file in your message.

48   Part 2: Working with Email

## 4 Complete Your Message

The attached files appear at the bottom of the message window. Finish your message by entering the subject and message body. When you are done, click the **Send** button on the toolbar.

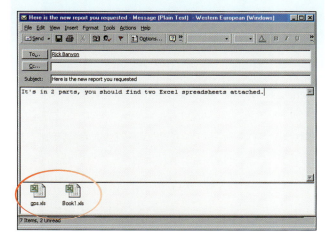

## 5 Show the Attachment Button

If you frequently send email with file attachments, you may want to place a button on the toolbar that you can click instead of selecting **Insert, File**. To add the button to your toolbar, open a new message window and click the **arrow button** in the standard toolbar. Click the **Insert File** button (the paper clip) to add it to the toolbar.

Click

## 6 Use the Attachment Button

From now on, the Insert File button appears in the toolbar. To insert a file in your message, just click this button.

Click

*End*

# How-To Hints

## Attachment Problems

If your attachments aren't arriving intact in the recipient's Inbox, you must modify Outlook's options. For example, your attachments may appear as scrambled text in the body of the message. If your recipients complain about this kind of behavior, choose **Tools, Options** and select the **Mail Format** tab. Click the **Settings** button and switch your mail format option from MIME to Uuencode (or vice versa).

HOW TO ATTACH A FILE TO A MESSAGE    **49**

## Task 10

# How to Open a Mail Attachment

Now you know how to include file attachments in a mail message. But how do you deal with an attachment when it arrives in your own Inbox? Typically, you can open an attachment (if you have the right application software) or save it to your hard disk.

Being able to use file attachments is one of the most important skills you can develop when dealing with Outlook's mail features. Most people deal with many file attachments in a typical day.

## Begin

### 1 Find the Mail Attachments

It's easy to see which messages in Outlook have attachments—even without opening the message. Look at the symbols to the left of the messages in the content pane. Messages with attachments have paper clip icons.

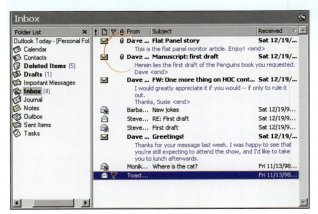

### 2 Open the Message

To deal with an attachment, you must first open the message window. Double-click the message you want to see.

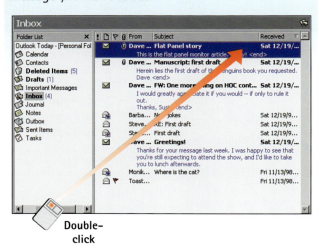

Double-click

### 3 Save the Attachment

If you don't want to immediately work with the attachment in its native application (for example, you don't want to open an attached Word document in Word), you can save the file to a location on your hard disk. To do that, right-click the file icon and choose **Save As** from the menu.

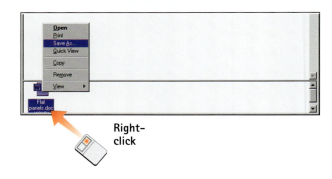

Right-click

## 4 Specify a Location

The Save Attachment dialog box opens. Choose the folder in which you want to store the file. You can either accept the original filename (the one it had in the email message) or you can specify your own filename. Click the **Save** button to finish.

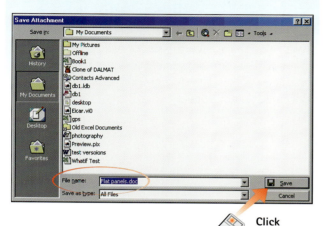

Click

## 5 Open the Attachment

Instead of saving your attached file to the hard disk, you can open it directly into its native application. To do so, double-click the icon in the mail message and click **Open It** from the Opening Mail Attachment dialog box. The file opens in its native application, where you can then edit, print, or save it.

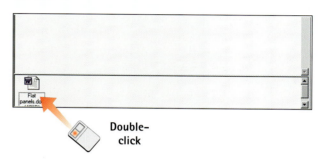

Double-click

## 6 Drag and Drop the Attachment

Another way to get the attachment out of Outlook and onto your hard disk is to drag and drop the file. To open an attachment on the Windows desktop, for example, just click the file's icon and drag it off the message window and onto the desktop. You can then open the document from the desktop.

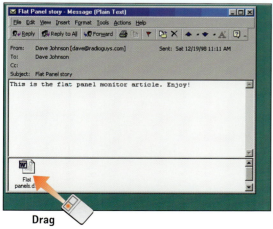

Drag

# How-To Hints

## More Attachment Problems

If you can't open a file attachment, it probably means that you don't have the right application. If someone sends you a Word file, for example, Microsoft Word must be installed on your computer before you can view and edit the Word file. Sometimes, however, a file's three-letter extension (such as .DOC or .XLS) can be scrambled in the transmission process. Ask the sender what file format the file was sent in and then rename the file with the appropriate extension and try to open it again.

End

## Task 11

# How to Use Word to Write Mail Messages

If you send messages primarily in text-only format, you're probably quite happy with the built-in message editor in Outlook. However, some people prefer to send messages with fancy formatting; if you're one of those people, you may want to use a message editor that has more formatting tools than does Outlook's. For example, you may want to create your messages with Microsoft Word. Outlook can be configured to use Word as its message editor, giving you all of Word's ordinary tools and features for use in your email messages.

## Begin

### 1 Open the Options Menu

To tell Outlook to use Word as its message editor, you must open the Options dialog box. Choose **Tools, Options** from the Outlook menu bar.

### 2 Switch to Mail Format Tab

Click the **Mail Format** tab on the Options dialog box. This tab contains options for changing the format of the mail messages, and it's where you'll enable Word as Outlook's message editor.

### 3 Select Word as Editor

Click the **Use Microsoft Word to Edit E-mail Messages** option so that a check mark appears in the box.

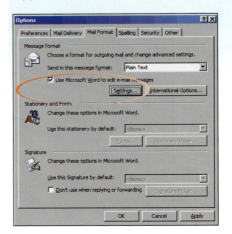

52  PART 2: WORKING WITH EMAIL

## 4 Save the Change to Options

Click the **OK** button to save the change you have made to the Options dialog box.

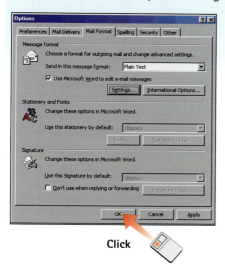
Click

## 5 Start a New Message

The procedure for creating a message using Word is identical to the way you ordinarily create a new message: Click the **New** button in the toolbar. You'll see the message window.

Click

## 6 Create the Email in Word

The message window has the same elements as before, but it also offers you access to all of Word's formatting tools, including fonts, text alignment, and tables, to name just a few. Create and send your message as you normally do.

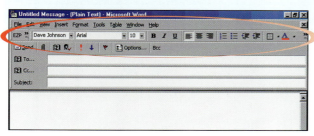

*End*

## How-To Hints

### Using Word in Outlook

Microsoft Word provides many formatting tools for creating fancy email messages, but it isn't the solution for everyone. Using Word in Outlook is a bit slower than using Outlook the ordinary way because it takes longer to launch Word than the default Outlook message editor. In addition, Word is generally useful only if you're creating email in Rich Text or HTML format, because these formats have fancy formatting capabilities. If you set Outlook to send messages in plain text, any formatting you include with Word will be lost as soon as the message is sent.

How to Use Word to Write Mail Messages    53

## Task 12

# How to Print an Email Message

Email messages are great because they save trees. They travel through the Internet ether electronically, and you can refer to them on your hard disk forever without resorting to paper.

That's great in theory, but there are always occasions when you have to print an email message and carry it around with you. Usually, the Print feature is never more than a single click away.

## Begin

### 1 Print from the Inbox

To print an email message, click the message you want to print and then click the **Print** button in the toolbar. The message prints to the default printer.

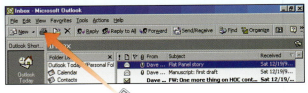

Click

### 2 Print an Open Email Message

If your message is already open, simply print it by clicking the **Print** button in the toolbar.

Click

### 3 Print Options

If you want to print a message, but first want to access the printer options, choose **File, Print** from the menu bar. This action opens the Print dialog box.

**54** Part 2: Working with Email

## 4 Choose Print Options

The Print dialog box has a number of options you can choose from. You can specify the printer you want to use and the number of copies you want of the message. You can specify whether you want to print a selected message or all the messages in the Inbox. To print the selected message, click **Memo Style**. To print the contents of the Inbox, click **Table Style**.

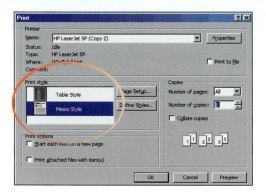

## 5 Printing Attachments

You can print just the selected message or the message and the contents of any attached files. To print file attachments, click the **Print Attached Files with Item(s)** option.

## 6 Print the Message

When you are ready to print the message, click the **OK** button on the Print dialog box. The Printing dialog box appears while the data is sent to the printer.

## How-To Hints

### Economy Printing

If you print a lot of messages (and other documents), you're probably always on the lookout for ways to save paper and toner cartridge costs. Here are a few suggestions:

✓ Use a printer that allows you to print more than one page per sheet. Many printers can shrink the page and squeeze two, four, or more pages onto a single piece of paper. The text can be a little hard on the eyes, but reducing print size can save you a ton of paper.

✓ Print on both sides. You can save old documents and load them into your printer upside down, doubling the life of your paper investment.

✓ When you're printing just for yourself, switch your printer to the economy toner-saver mode.

# Task 13

## How to Check Mail Automatically

Outlook is a very intelligent program. Although you can easily check for new email manually (as discussed in Part 2, Task 2, "How to Check for New Mail"), you can also configure Outlook to look for mail on its own, on a set schedule, without any intervention from you.

When Outlook checks for new email, it also sends any messages that are waiting in the Outbox. You can rely on Outlook's automated mail checking system to send and receive email messages on its own.

## Begin

### 1 Open the Options Menu

To configure Outlook to check mail automatically, you must open the Options dialog box. Choose **Tools, Options** from the menu bar.

### 2 Switch to Mail Delivery

When the Options dialog box opens, switch to the **Mail Delivery** tab. This tab has options for dial-up and mail account settings.

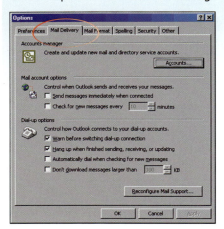

### 3 Check Mail Automatically

Configure Outlook to look for new mail automatically by clicking the **Check for New Messages Every** option. You may also want to make sure that **Send Messages Immediately When Connected** and **Automatically Dial When Checking for New Messages** are selected. These options make Outlook somewhat more autonomous.

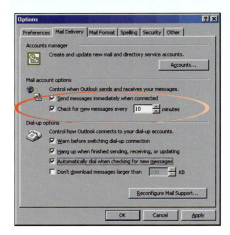

## 4 Specify the Frequency

When you first configure Outlook to check for mail, its default setting looks for new messages every 10 minutes. This interval may be too short or too long for you. If you depend on email throughout the day for your job, you may want to change the interval to 5 minutes. If you receive email only occasionally, 60 minutes may be a better interval for you.

## 5 Save Your New Options

When you finish configuring Outlook to check for mail automatically, click the **OK** button to save your changes.

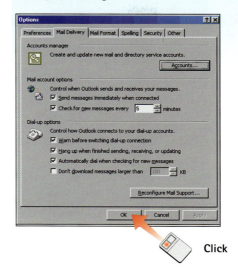

Click

## 6 Check Manually if Desired

From now on, Outlook checks for new messages without your direct input. If you want to check for mail immediately for some reason (for example, if someone calls to say they've emailed you an important file), you can click the **Send/Receive** button in the toolbar to check for mail manually.

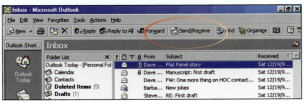

### How-To Hints

**Where Do Messages Go?**

After a message has been sent, Outlook moves it from the Outbox folder to the Sent Items folder. If you want to look up old messages or resend a previously sent email message, look in the Sent Items folder for it.

# Task 14

## How to Send Mail from a Specific Mail Account

If you have more than one email account set up in Outlook, one of those accounts is the *default*, which is used to send messages. You may occasionally want to send a specific message from a different account. You may want to do this so that replies are sent to a different email address, or perhaps so that you can keep business and personal email separate. In Outlook, it's easy to specify which email account sends which email message.

## Begin

### 1 View Your Internet Accounts

If you have only a single account, you have no choice about which account sends which email. To see your accounts, choose **Tools, Accounts** from the menu bar.

### 2 Specify a Default Account

If you have more than one account, decide which one you plan to use the most often. On the **Mail** tab in the Internet Accounts dialog box, select this account and click the **Set as Default** button. The account you select is the account used when you click the **Send** button.

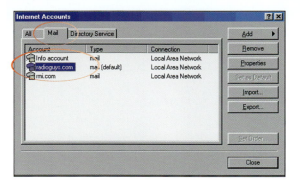

### 3 Add a New Account

If you want to add a new email account to Outlook, click the **Add** button and select **Mail** from the pop-up menu. Adding email accounts is described in Part 1, Task 2, "How to Create an Internet-Only Email Account."

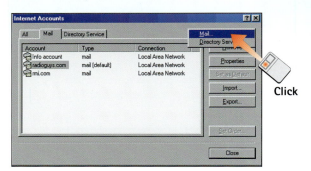

**58** Part 2: Working with Email

## 4 Create a New Message

To send a message from a specific account, start the same way as if you were sending it from the default account: Click **New** from the toolbar.

Click

## 5 Complete the Message

Create the message: Enter the recipient, subject line, and message body.

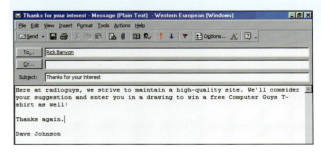

## 6 Specify the Account

When you're ready to send the message, click the **list arrow** next to the **Send** button in the toolbar. Select the account you want to use. The message is sent to the Outbox using that account information.

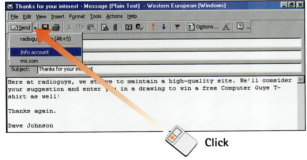

Click

*End*

## How-To Hints

### Finishing a Message Later

If you start a message but aren't ready to send it, you can save the message in its current form and finish it later. Click the **Save** button in the toolbar. This action puts a copy of the message in the Drafts folder; you can reopen the message later to complete and send at your leisure.

# Task

1. How to Resend a Message  62
2. How to Create a Signature  64
3. How to Add Fancy Formatting to Your Email Messages  66
4. How to Send Mail in Plain-Text Format  68
5. How to Create Messages with Stationery  70
6. How to Send Contact Info Automatically  72
7. How to Add Personal Info to Contacts Automatically  74
8. How to Get a Digital ID  76
9. How to Send Secure Email  78
10. How to Add Words to the Spelling Dictionary  80
11. How to Format Message Replies  82
12. How to Display Messages with AutoPreview  84
13. How to Request a Read Receipt  86
14. How to Leave Messages on the Mail Server  88

Project 1: Creating an Attractively Formatted Message  90

## PART 3

# Getting Fancy with Email

Once you've mastered the email basics, you'll soon discover there's a whole new world open to you. For instance, most people send messages in plain-text format, which doesn't allow for any fancy formatting. Perhaps you'd like to send messages with special styles, so that your message looks like a Web page. You can include different text styles, paragraph alignment, and even graphics in your email messages.

Perhaps you want to send encrypted messages so that only the designated recipient can read your mail; maybe you want to request a receipt so that you know when the mail you sent has been read.

All these things are possible with Outlook, and this part of the book explains how to do it.

## TASK 1

# How to Resend a Message

The beauty of email is that it's an electronic message you can reuse as needed. In the old days, when you had to send a copy of a letter, you had to photocopy the original or even re-create it from memory. With email, you can simply find the message in the Sent Items folder and reuse it however you see fit—with little effort on your part. That comes in handy when you want to send a message to someone a second time (perhaps he lost the original) or send it to another recipient.

## *Begin*

### *1* Switch to Sent Items

To send a sent message again, you must first locate the original message. Click the **Sent Items** folder in the Folder List to locate the message you need to resend.

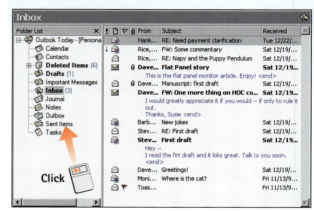

### *2* Open the Sent Message

Find the message you want to resend in the Sent Items folder and double-click to open it. If necessary, use the **Find** button to locate the message, as explained in Part 4, Task 1, "How to Find a Message by Subject or Sender."

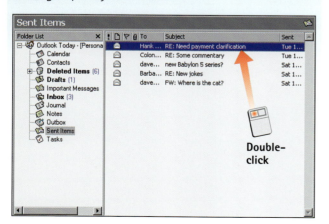

### *3* Work with Personalized Menus

Click **Actions** in the menu bar and look for **Resend This Message**. If you don't see that menu item, it's hidden from view thanks to the Personalized Menus. Click the **arrow** at the bottom of the menu to display the rest of the menu items.

**62** PART 3: GETTING FANCY WITH EMAIL

## 4 Choose to Resend

Click **Resend This Message** from the **Actions** menu. The message opens in a format ready to resend to the original recipient.

## 5 Modify the Message

You can modify the body of the message, change its subject, or even re-address it to other recipients. Make any changes you desire to the message.

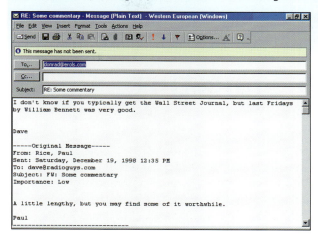

## 6 Send the Message

When you're ready, click the **Send** button in the toolbar to send the message to the Outbox.

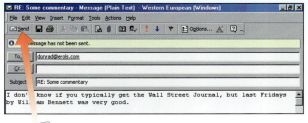

 Click

## How-To Hints

### Including Attachments

If you resend a message to the original recipient or a different set of people, any attachments that were part of the original message are automatically included in the new message. Make sure that you really intend to include attachments when sending this kind of email.

**How to Resend a Message** 63

# Task 2

## How to Create a Signature

If you've received very much email over the Internet, you've no doubt seen the *signature* many people attach to the end of their messages. Signatures identify the sender, often provide contact information, and can also say something unique about the sender. Some signatures include witticisms or provide a one- or two-line resume.

You don't have to re-create your signature each and every time you send an email. Outlook allows you to store one or more signatures and automatically attach them to your messages.

## *Begin*

### **1** Open the Options Dialog Box

Signatures are stored in the Options dialog box; open it by choosing **Tools, Options** from the menu bar.

### **2** Change Tabs

In the Options dialog box, click the **Mail Format** tab. The Signature section at the bottom includes all the tools you need to edit and manage signatures. If this is the first time you've used signatures, no default signature appears in the dialog box.

### **3** Open the Signature Picker

Click the **Signature Picker** button to open the Signature Picker dialog box. This is where you create your signature.

Click

**64** Part 3: Getting Fancy with Email

## 4 Create a Signature

The Signature Picker lets you choose and edit from a list of custom signatures you've created. If this is your first time here, the signature list is blank and the preview pane is empty. Click the **New** button to start the Create New Signature Wizard.

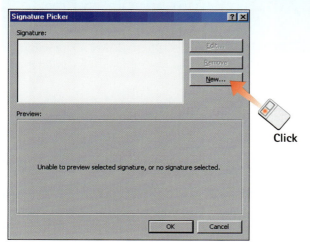

Click

## 5 Name the Signature

Your first step in the Create New Signature Wizard is to give your signature a name so that you can more easily select it from the signature list. If you plan to create only one signature and use it all the time, the name you give it isn't particularly important. Click the **Next** button to actually design the signature.

## 6 Design the Signature

Type your signature in the **Signature** text box. Add any elements you want, including your name, phone number, email, or Web address. When you're done, click the **Finish** button.

*End*

## How-To Hints

### Keep It Small

Although your signature is a way to express yourself in email, don't make it too long—four to six lines is about as lengthy as it should get. Gone are the days when people created intricate pictures in their signature using text characters laid out in interesting patterns. Many Internet users are sensitive to what they perceive as people wasting bandwidth with excessive signatures, and if yours is too long, you might hear about it!

### Including Links

Depending on the nature of your signature—personal or business—you may want to include contact information such as a phone number or Web page address. Most email programs automatically convert Web addresses into links, so the recipient of your message can click your signature to go to your Web site.

### Multiple Signatures

If you have more than one signature and want to send different ones to different people, you can choose the appropriate signature when sending email by clicking the **Signature** button in the toolbar in the message window.

How to Create a Signature  65

## Task 3

# How to Add Fancy Formatting to Email Messages

Traditionally, email messages were always sent in plain text, also known as *ASCII text*. This kind of message doesn't allow for any kind of formatting—you can't use this format to send a message with different fonts, large headlines, or integrated graphics.

Today, people want more control over the look of their email. Now you can choose to send traditional plain-text messages (which many people still prefer) or you can send a message using Hypertext Markup Language (HTML). HTML is the same language Web pages are made from, which means that you can send email messages featuring all the fancy formatting found on a Web page.

## Begin

### 1 Open the Options Dialog Box

To send messages with fancy formatting, you must first to enable HTML email. Choose **Tools, Options** from the menu bar to open the Options dialog box.

### 2 Choose Mail Format

Click the **Mail Format** tab. You can choose the default message format for all your email in the Message Format section of this page.

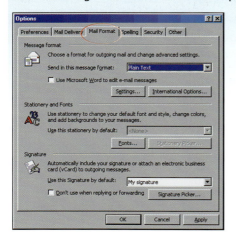

### 3 Choose HTML Format

Choose **HTML** from the **Send in This Message Format** list. If you later want to send plain-text messages, return to this dialog box and choose **Plain Text**. The Microsoft Outlook Rich Text option is useful only for people who have Microsoft mail programs, so you may want to avoid this option.

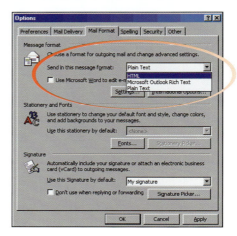

**66** Part 3: Getting Fancy with Email

## 4 Save Your Changes

After you've selected the mail format for your messages, click **OK** to save your changes to the Options dialog box.

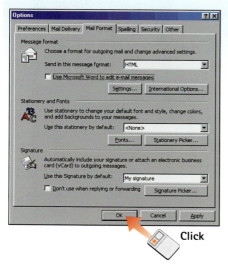

Click

## 5 Change the Background

Once you make the changes in the Options dialog box, you can create new messages with HTML formatting. You'll find you have additional formatting options available when you create a new message in the ordinary way. Give your message a colored background, for example, by choosing **Format, Background, Color** and picking the color you prefer.

## 6 Change Formatting

It's easy to change the formatting of text in your message. Just create the text, select it, and choose **Format, Paragraph**. Select the appropriate justification (left, right, or center) from the dialog box. For a detailed overview of fancy formatting, see Project 1 at the end of Part 3, "Creating an Attractively Formatted Message."

*End*

## How-To Hints

### HTML Isn't for Everyone

Keep in mind that not everyone has an email program that can interpret HTML. If you send email in HTML format to someone with a plain-text mail reader, the message is converted to an attachment, which the recipient must open in a Web browser to read. That's not particularly convenient for your reader, so use HTML with care.

How to Add Fancy Formatting to Email Messages

## Task 4

# How to Send Mail in Plain-Text Format

Although HTML offers you the ability to send messages with fancy formatting, there are disadvantages to using this kind of email. Task 3 mentioned some of those disadvantages: Some people just don't like HTML mail, and some email applications can't properly display HTML messages.

Those issues aside, HTML also makes even small messages take longer to send and receive because HTML pads the message with formatting information and graphics. For times when HTML mail is just not appropriate, you can send plain-text messages instead.

## Begin

### 1 Open the Options Dialog Box

If you want to tell Outlook to send all messages in text-only format, open the Options dialog box by choosing **Tools, Options**.

### 2 Choose Mail Format

Select the **Mail Format** tab. If your mail was previously set to send in HTML format, you should see that in the **Send in This Message Format** list box.

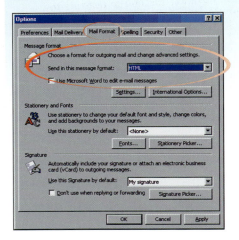

### 3 Choose Plain-Text Format

Choose **Plain Text** from the **Send in This Message Format** list. All email messages will now go out in plain-text format. Click the **OK** button to save your changes.

**68**   PART 3: GETTING FANCY WITH EMAIL

## 4 Specify Recipients of Email

Even if you decide to make HTML your default email format, you may know some people who prefer to receive mail in text-only format. If so, you can tell Outlook to send them text-only mail. Choose **Tools, Address Book** from the menu bar.

## 5 Choose a Recipient

In the address book, double-click the entry for a recipient to whom you always want to send messages in text-only format. The Properties dialog box for that recipient opens.

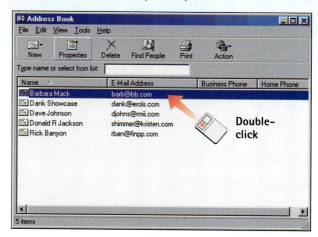

## 6 Specify Text Only

Click the **Personal** tab in the recipient's Properties dialog box and click the **Send E-Mail Using Plain Text Only** option. In the future, that person will get plain-text mail from you even if your default in the Options dialog box is to send HTML messages.

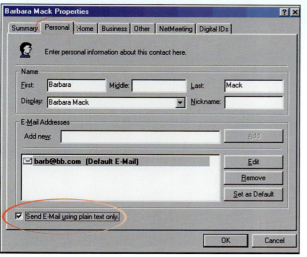

### How-To Hints

#### Change Format On-the-Fly

You can switch between HTML and plain-text formats even after you start creating a message. With the message window open, choose either **Format, Plain Text** or **Format, HTML** from the menu bar to change the message's style; complete the message and send it. You can even use this method to override the address book settings for plain-text messages.

# Task 5

## How to Create Messages with Stationery

If you create messages in HTML format—messages that can feature fancy formatting and embedded graphics—you may find that few things can energize an email message better than using Outlook's stationery. *Stationery* is simply a background image your message text is layered on top of. The effect is very much like typing on fancy stationery.

Microsoft starts you out with an assortment of stationery images you can incorporate into your email. Some images are generic; others are targeted at holidays and special occasions. If your email is configured for HTML format (see Part 3, Task 3, "How to Add Fancy Formatting to Email Messages"), then you should give stationery a spin.

## Begin

### 1 Change the Background

Assuming that you already have a new message window open and it's set to HTML format, you can change the background of the message by choosing **Format, Background**. You have two choices: Picture or Color. The Color menu item allows you to change the background to a solid color of your choice. Instead, choose **Picture**, which opens the stationery controls.

### 2 Choose Some Stationery

You can choose stationery from the Background Picture dialog box. Choose a stationery file from the **File** list box and click **OK**. Because there's no preview button, you may have to repeat steps 1 and 2 a few times to determine which stationery file you want to use.

### 3 Finish Your Message

Complete your message the way you ordinarily would. When you're ready, click the **Send** button in the toolbar to send the message to the Outbox.

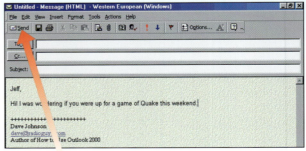

 Click

70 PART 3: GETTING FANCY WITH EMAIL

## 4 Set Your Default Stationery

If you like a particular stationery file, you can make it the default for all your email messages. You can specify the default stationery from the Options dialog box: Choose **Tools, Options** from the menu bar to open the dialog box.

## 5 Select the Mail Format Tab

Click the **Mail Format** tab on the Options dialog box. To select stationery, click the **Stationery Picker** button. Note that the Stationery list box is available only if the message format is set to HTML in the Send in This Message Format list box.

## 6 Choose a Stationery

Choose a stationery file from the Stationery Picker dialog box. You can see a preview of the currently selected image. When you have selected the file you want to use in most of your email messages, click the **OK** button.

## How-To Hints

### Get More Stationery

There are more stationery files available if you want to expand your library. You can use the **Get More Stationery** button on the Stationery Picker dialog box to download new images from Microsoft's Web site. In addition, some stationery files you select may have to be installed from the Outlook CD-ROM. Follow Outlook's instructions for installing the CD if you see a message that certain stationery isn't installed.

## Task 6

# How to Send Contact Info Automatically

A signature is a great way to keep others informed about your personal or business contact information—but wouldn't it be so much more convenient if your email contained all your contact information in a form that was ready to insert in Outlook's Contacts view?

Just such a feature exists. It's called a *vCard*, and if you include one in your email, your message recipients can save the vCard into their Contacts view, where they'll automatically have your name, email, and anything else you choose to send—without any typing at all.

## Begin

### 1 Set Up Your vCard

If you want to send messages with your vCard embedded in the email, the first stop is the Options dialog box. Choose **Tools, Options** to open the dialog box.

### 2 Switch to Mail Format

The vCard is actually a part of your signature. Click the **Mail Format** tab to switch to that tab. The bottom of the dialog box has the options for your signature.

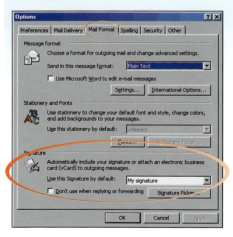

### 3 Choose a Signature

You must have a signature in order to use a vCard because you associate your vCard with a specific signature file. If you have more than one signature created in Outlook, choose the one you want to use by selecting it from the **Use This Signature by Default** list box.

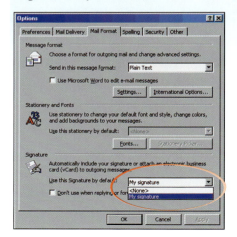

72  PART 3: GETTING FANCY WITH EMAIL

## 4 Go to Signature Picker

Now create your vCard. This is done from within the Signature Picker, so click the **Signature Picker** button on the Options dialog box.

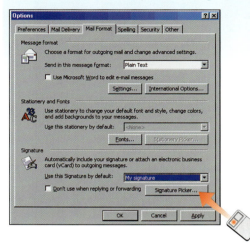
Click

## 5 Edit Your Signature

On the Signature Picker dialog box, select the signature you want to associate your vCard with (if you have more than one signature) and click the **Edit** button.

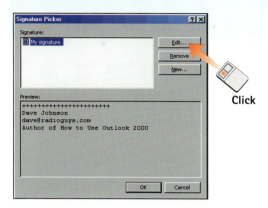
Click

## 6 Create a vCard

The bottom of the Edit Signature dialog box contains a section for vCard options. Click **New vCard from Contact**. A list of all the contacts in Outlook opens, from which you can choose your vCard information.

Click

## 7 Choose Your Contact

Double-click an entry from the left side of the dialog box to move it to the right side; click **OK** to close the dialog box. The selected entry becomes your vCard. In other words, whenever you send an email message with this vCard attached, the recipient will have immediate access to all the information in this contact entry in Outlook format. As a consequence, you should choose your own contact information from Outlook. If you haven't yet made a contact entry for yourself, do so by clicking the **New Contact** button.

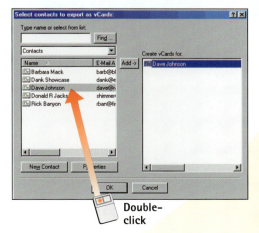
Double-click

*End*

HOW TO SEND CONTACT INFO AUTOMATICALLY

## Task 7

# How to Add Personal Info to Contacts Automatically

When you get an email message from someone who is not already in your contacts list, you can add his or her email and contact information to your list without a lot of effort. This technique can come in handy if you frequently add names to your address book and don't want to type lots of email addresses.

## Begin

### 1 Open the New Message

If you've received email from a new person and you want to add his or her email address to your contacts quickly and easily, start by opening the message: Double-click the message in the Inbox.

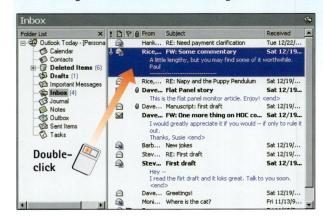

### 2 Use the Right Mouse Button

Place the mouse pointer directly over the individual's email address in the From field and click the right mouse button. Choose **Add to Contacts** from the menu. The Contact dialog box opens with the sender's email address already entered.

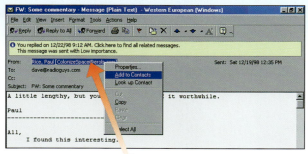

### 3 Enter More Information

Although the email address is already entered, you may want to add information, such as a phone number or address. If the sender included that information in the message, you can copy and paste it into the Contact dialog box.

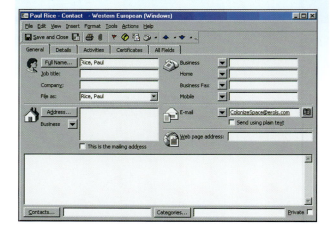

**74** Part 3: Getting Fancy with Email

## 4 Save the Contact

When you finish filling out your contact's information, click the **Save and Close** button in the toolbar.

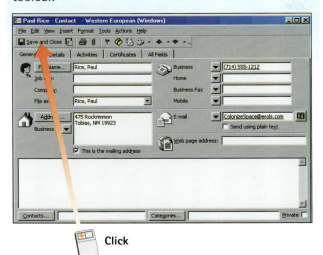
Click

## 5 Avoiding Duplicate Entries

Every once in a while, you may find that you accidentally used this method when, in fact, there was already an entry for this person in your address book. That's not a problem. Outlook warns you with a Duplicate Contact Detected dialog box. You can click the **Open Existing Contact** button to inspect the older entry.

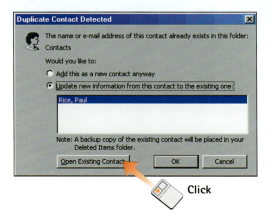
Click

## 6 Update the Original Card

If you have a duplicate entry, you can click the **OK** button. This action merges the old and new cards into a single entry. It's a good choice, especially if your new card has more information than the older card (for example, an extra phone number or secondary email address). The new card has all the information from both cards.

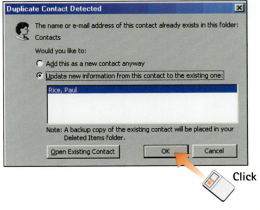
Click

## How-To Hints

### Automatic Addresses

If you know that you always want to add email addresses to Contacts whenever you reply to messages from new people, you can specify that option and never have to worry about losing an email address again. Choose **Tools, Options** from the menu bar and click the **E-mail Options** button on the **Preferences** tab. Then select the **Automatically Put People I Reply to In** option. Now, whenever you reply to email messages, Outlook creates a contact for the recipient.

*End*

## Task 8

# How to Get a Digital ID

Although most of your Internet activity is fairly safe from prying eyes, a little bit of paranoia can be good—especially if you're using email for critical business activities. In those cases, you may want to encrypt your messages so that only the right people can read them. Before you can send encrypted messages with Outlook, however, both you and anyone you want to send such emails to have to acquire a *digital ID*. You can get a free digital ID on a 60-day trial basis and you can purchase an annual subscription for about $10.

## Begin

### 1 Open the Options Dialog Box

To acquire and activate your digital ID, you must first have a connection to the Internet. Make sure that you have one and then choose **Tools, Options** from the Outlook menu bar.

### 2 View the Security Options

Click the **Security** tab on the Options dialog box. In the Digital IDs section at the bottom of the page, click the **Get a Digital ID** button. This action launches your Web browser and takes you to a digital ID Web site.

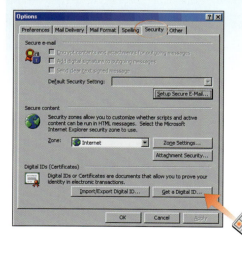

Click

### 3 Visit the VeriSign Site

Outlook takes you to a Web site that explains digital IDs in detail. Feel free to read as much about them as you like. *VeriSign* is the leading digital ID company today; it offers a 60-day free trial. Click the link for **VeriSign** to try it out.

 Click

## 4 Fill Out the Form

When you reach VeriSign's Web site, you are asked to complete a form to get your trial digital ID. Complete the form, remembering that at this stage you do not have to provide any credit card information. An email message is sent to your Outlook **Inbox**. Wait for the message to arrive before proceeding. The message should arrive almost immediately. Click the **Send/Receive** button on the Outlook toolbar to accelerate the process.

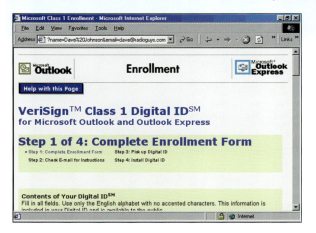

## 5 Process Your Email

After your email from VeriSign arrives, open the message and follow the instructions: Simply click the **Continue** button in the message. Your Web browser opens to complete the installation.

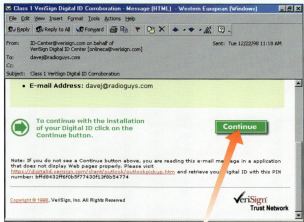

Click

## 6 Complete the Installation

When the digital ID page is loaded in your Web browser, click the **Install** button to complete the process. Your digital ID is automatically installed in Outlook. Now you're ready to start encrypting email messages.

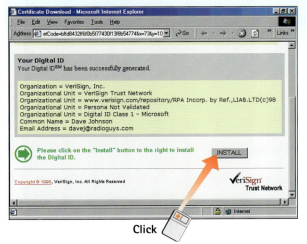

Click

*End*

## How-To Hints

### Internet Security

Do you need a digital ID? That depends. Most email is not at risk of being read or stolen, but the fact remains that email is not a very secure format. Messages are sent in "clear text" format over the Internet, which means that anyone can intercept and read them, particularly at your ISP or mail administrator's offices.

Mail is also kept in the form of back-up tapes at your mail server for a very long time, meaning that even now there's an electronic record of email you deleted from your PC long, long ago. That's why some people choose to encrypt their messages using digital IDs, which render your messages essentially unreadable by anyone except those with whom you intend to share the mail.

## TASK 9

# How to Send Secure Email

Armed with a digital ID, you can send encrypted messages to other people as long as the recipient is using Outlook, Outlook Express, or another program compatible with digital IDs. For encrypted email to work, you and the other party must both have records of each other's digital ID. Once that's done, messages can be encrypted strongly enough that no one short of the National Security Agency will be able to crack open your messages.

## Begin

### 1 Enable Secure Email

If this is the first time you're sending secure email after obtaining a digital ID, you have to set up Outlook accordingly. Open the Options dialog box by choosing **Tools, Options** and then switching to the **Security** tab. Click the **Setup Secure E-Mail** button and click **OK**.

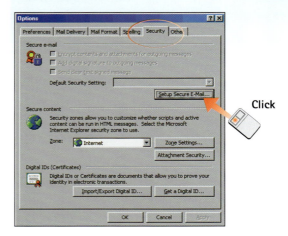

### 2 Exchange Digital IDs

Before you can send encrypted email, you must exchange digital IDs with the other party. It's important that both of you perform the next few steps; otherwise, Outlook won't allow you to use the secure email feature. Start by creating a new message and then click the **Options** button in the toolbar.

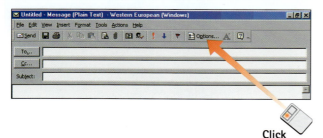

### 3 Send your Digital ID

Click the option for **Add Digital Signature to Outgoing Message**. This is your digital ID. Click **Close** to set that option for this email message and then send the message to the person with whom you want to exchange secure email. Make sure that the other person sends you a similar message.

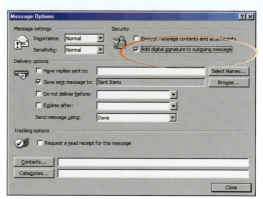

**78** PART 3: GETTING FANCY WITH EMAIL

## 4 Receive Digital ID

When you get the message from your email partner and it includes a digital ID, you'll see a special symbol in the Inbox. Open this message.

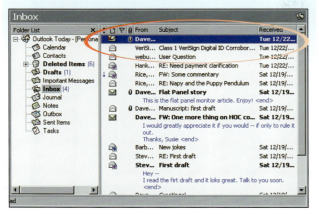

## 5 Add Digital ID to Contacts

After the message is opened, right-click the sender's name in the From field and choose **Add to Contacts** from the menu. You may have to update the contact using the Duplicate Contact Detected dialog box if this person is already in your Contacts list. This action adds the digital ID to the appropriate entry in your address book. You can send and receive secure email after both you and your email partner have performed this step.

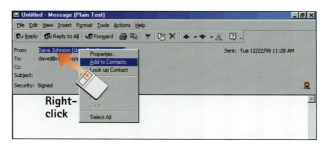

## 6 Send the Secure Message

To send a secure email, create a new message in the ordinary way; click the **Options** button in the toolbar.

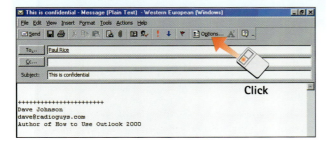

## 7 Enable Encryption

Click the **Encrypt Message Contents and Attachments** option to tell Outlook to send this message in an encrypted format. When the recipient receives this message, Outlook reports that the message is encrypted and opens it in a readable format. If it's intercepted and read on another system, however, the message appears as garbled text.

*End*

## How-To Hints

### Encrypting Automatically

Outlook can send all messages in secure format, but you can't encrypt messages for any recipients for whom you don't have a digital ID. To turn automatic encryption on, choose **Tools, Options**. Choose the **Security** tab and the **Encrypt Contents and Attachments for Outgoing Messages** option.

HOW TO SEND SECURE EMAIL    79

## Task 10

# How to Add Words to the Spelling Dictionary

Outlook's spelling checker uses the same spelling engine that other Microsoft Office applications such as Word and PowerPoint use. Consequently, it is good for general-purpose spelling tasks. If you use a lot of unusual words—particularly acronyms—in your email, however, you may want to add those words to Outlook's dictionary. You can either do this piecemeal as you work using the **Add** button on the Spelling dialog box, or you can enter them all at once and never worry about them again.

## Begin

### 1 Open the Options Dialog Box

You can add a lot of words at once to the spelling dictionary by entering some spelling options. Choose **Tools, Options** to open the Options dialog box.

### 2 Display Spelling Options

Click the **Spelling** tab to see the various spelling options. The top of the dialog box sets how Outlook checks your spelling. The Edit Custom Dictionary section of the tab is where you actually enter new words.

### 3 Edit the Dictionary

Click the **Edit** button on the dialog box to open a copy of Notepad. That's where you can type all the words and acronyms you want Outlook to remember.

Click

**80** Part 3: Getting Fancy with Email

## 4 Heed the Spelling Warning

Outlook indicates that any changes you make to the dictionary will not affect any open message windows you are currently working on. Click the **OK** button to proceed.

Click

## 5 Type New Words

Type each word you want to add to the dictionary on a new line, pressing the **Enter** key after each word. Add as many words as you want.

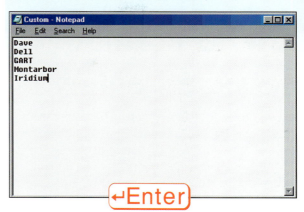

## 6 Save Your Changes

When you are done adding new words to the dictionary, click the **Close** button in the Notepad window. When Outlook asks if you want to save your changes, click **Yes**. Your new words will now be used when you spell check your messages.

Click

## How-To Hints

### Make Sure It's Enabled

Your spelling dictionary is useful only if you actually check your spelling. Make sure that you have Outlook configured to check spelling before every message is sent. Also realize that any words you add to the spelling dictionary are also used for other Office applications such as Word, Publisher, PowerPoint, and Excel. Make sure that you spell the words correctly when you enter them in the dictionary!

*End*

TASK 11

# How to Format Message Replies

When you reply to a message or forward an email to someone else, Outlook gives you several options for the overall appearance of the message. For example, you can choose to include the text of the original message in your reply message, or you can include only the text of your reply. If you include the original message, you can indent it, prefix it with a special symbol, or attach it as a file. It's up to you.

*Begin*

### 1 Open the Options Dialog Box

Message formatting is accessed from the Options dialog box. To get there, choose **Tools, Options**.

### 2 Display Email Options

Click the **E-Mail Options** button on the **Preferences** tab. This action displays the E-mail Options dialog box, which is where you can specify the formatting for messages.

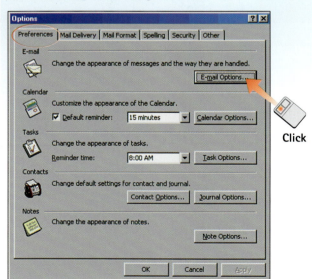

Click

### 3 Select a Reply Format

Choose a format for message replies from the **When Replying to a Message** list box. A small preview to the right of the list box shows what the message will look like when you select each option. Note that the original text appears below your reply text in all cases.

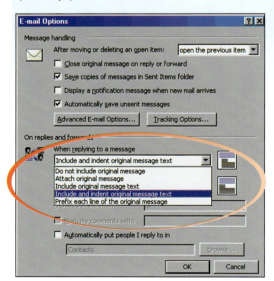

**82**  PART 3: GETTING FANCY WITH EMAIL

## 4 Choose a Prefix

If you select **Prefix Each Line of the Original Message**, you must specify a prefix symbol. The > is a common way to prefix original text in a message, but you can also use ¦, +, or any other symbol you choose.

## 5 Choose a Forwarding Style

You can specify a different format for messages you *forward* to others. People typically opt for the **Include and Indent Original Message Text** option because it leaves the original text unchanged and easy to read. Click **OK** to close the dialog box and save your changes.

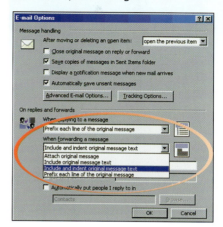

## 6 Heed the Spelling Warning

If you chose to display the original message text with a prefix character, Outlook warns you that it will spell check the entire message, including the original text. You may not want to spell check the original message every time you send a reply; if that's the case, click the **Cancel** button and select a different format. Otherwise, click **OK**.

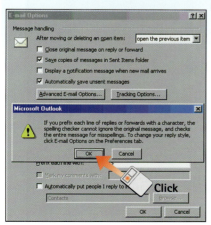

Click

*End*

# How-To Hints

### Try the Prefix Format

In many cases, the **Prefix Each Line of the Original Message** option is great for message replies. If you use this option, you can intersperse your own comments among the original message text, and it'll be obvious which is which because the original text has a prefix character at the beginning of each line.

## Task 12

# How to Display Messages with AutoPreview

One of the most convenient features in Outlook's Inbox view is called **AutoPreview**. With AutoPreview turned on, unread messages are displayed with their first few lines visible. That means you can often get the gist of a new email without even opening it—and thus decide whether to reply, discard, or save it for later.

Likewise, the Preview pane in the lower half of the Folder view shows the message in its entirety. You can use this pane to read an entire message without opening it. Together, these two tools help you manage your email more efficiently.

# Begin

## 1 Enable AutoPreview

You can toggle AutoPreview on and off by choosing **View, AutoPreview**. Note that AutoPreview can be independently turned on or off in each folder, which means that you can turn it on in the Inbox folder and turn it off in the Sent Items folder.

## 2 Use AutoPreview

After AutoPreview is enabled in a particular folder, any unopened messages appear with their first few lines displayed. The preview is deactivated after a message has been read, but you can get it back by right-clicking a message and choosing **Mark as Unread** from the menu.

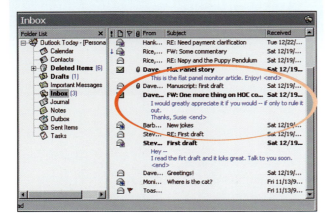

## 3 Enable the Preview Pane

You can toggle the Preview pane on and off by choosing **View, Preview Pane**. Just as with AutoPreview, the Preview pane can be independently turned on and off in each folder.

**84**  PART 3: GETTING FANCY WITH EMAIL

## 4 Use the Preview Pane

When you click a message in a folder view, the contents of the message are shown in the Preview pane. If the message is too long to fit in the pane, use the scrollbar to read the whole message.

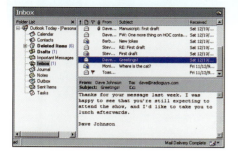

## 5 Access Preview Pane Options

You can change the way the Preview pane behaves. For example, you can let Outlook mark a message as read if you read it in the Preview pane. To get to these options, choose **Tools, Options**.

## 6 View Preview Pane Options

Select the **Other** tab and click the **Preview Pane** button to open options for the Preview pane.

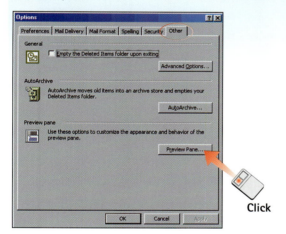

Click

## 7 View Preview Pane Options

If you want messages to appear as read after you read them in the Preview pane, click the **Mark Messages as Read in Preview Window** option. Also type a number for how many seconds you want Outlook to wait before marking the message as read. This way, if you put a message in the Preview pane for just a moment, it won't be marked as read. Click the **OK** button to close this dialog box.

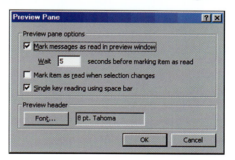

*End*

## How-To Hints

### Where to Preview

I recommend that you configure Outlook to use AutoPreview in the Inbox folder and to use the Preview pane in every other folder. That way, it's easy to see which new messages are unread; you can read messages in other folders more easily using the Preview pane. These settings create a less cluttered look in your folders.

HOW TO DISPLAY MESSAGES WITH AUTOPREVIEW     85

## Task 13

# How to Request a Read Receipt

Thanks to the magic of Internet mail, most people we work and play with are never more than a few minutes away, any time of day or night. In fact, you can exchange emails throughout the day with co-workers and get instant news, feedback, and assistance.

But the Internet isn't always as reliable as we'd like it to be, and sometimes you just don't know whether the recipient got your message. If you desire, you can send your email with a *read receipt request*; that way you get a verification that your message was opened.

## Begin

### 1 Create a Message

If you want to request a read receipt with your outgoing message, start by creating your message in the ordinary way: Click the **New** button in the toolbar to display a new message window.

Click

### 2 Display the Options

Create your message. Before you send the message, click the **Options** button in the toolbar to open the message's **Options** dialog box.

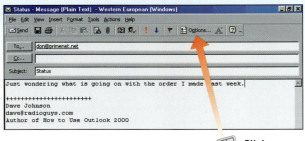

 Click

### 3 Request a Read Receipt

In the Tracking Options section of the dialog box, click the **Request a Read Receipt for This Message** option; then click the **Close** button to save these options for the message.

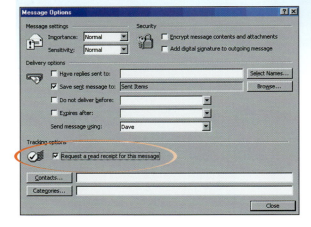

**86** Part 3: Getting Fancy with Email

## 4 Send the Message

When you finish writing your message, send it to the Outbox by clicking the **Send** button.

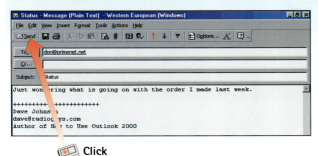
Click

## 5 Sending a Receipt

When the recipient opens the message, he or she sees a dialog box that asks whether he or she wants to send a receipt.

## 6 Read Your Receipt

After the recipient sends the read receipt, you'll get it in the form of a standard email message in your Inbox. The message reports when the message was read.

## How-To Hints

### Receipts Not Mandatory

It's important to realize that the recipient has the option of sending a receipt or ignoring the request, so if you are working with someone who doesn't send replies, you may still not know for certain when the message was opened. Don't rely on read receipts as your only way of knowing when a message was processed.

Also note that it may be perceived as bad form to send a read receipt to someone with whom you have not corresponded before.

## Task 14

# How to Leave Messages on the Mail Server

You may want to download your email on occasion, but you might also want to download it again later. That may sound odd, but consider a business trip in which you're checking mail on someone else's PC.

In an ideal world, you'd be able to go home when the trip was over and get that mail again so that you can deal with it more effectively than with the quick responses you were forced to give from the road. In that instance, you can configure Outlook to leave a copy of the mail you download on the remote server so that you can retrieve it later.

## Begin

### 1 Modify Your Account

First you must open your account settings. Choose **Tools, Accounts** from the menu bar.

### 2 View Account Properties

You have to create your account from scratch if you are using someone else's PC. If you already have your account information entered, all you have to do is modify it slightly. On the Mail tab, select the account you want to use and then click the **Properties** button.

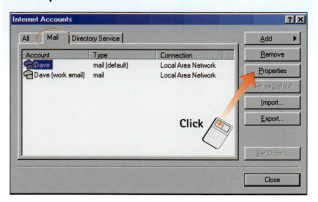

### 3 Switch to Advanced

The mail server settings are kept in the Advanced tab of the account's Properties dialog box. Click the **Advanced** tab to switch to that view.

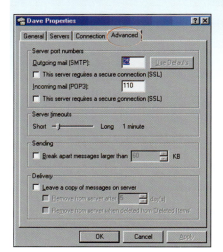

**88** PART 3: GETTING FANCY WITH EMAIL

## 4 Set Delivery Options

Click the **Leave a Copy of Messages on Server** option. This option allows you to download mail to one PC and later download it to another PC.

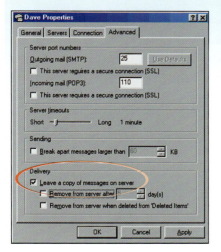

## 5 Delete Mail Automatically

You may want to let Outlook manage your mail for you. If you want mail on the server to be deleted after a certain period of time, select the **Remove from Server After** option and specify a time period. You can also let Outlook remove mail from the server if you discard the copy you downloaded into the Deleted Item folder. This technique can reduce the amount of mail you have to download again later.

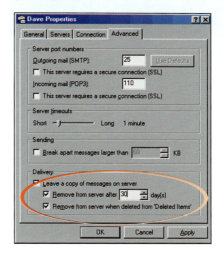

*End*

## How-To Hints

### Email Alternative: IMAP

Another way to leave mail on the server is to use an ISP that supports a mail standard called *IMAP*. Most mail systems today are POP3 compatible, and that's very likely what you already have. POP mail must be downloaded to your local PC before you can read, delete, or reply to it. IMAP mail servers move many of the mail management functions to your remote mail server. If you're interested in IMAP, ask your ISP whether it is supported. Outlook has built-in support for IMAP.

# Project 1

## Creating an Attractively Formatted Message

If you configure Outlook to create messages in HTML format, you can make messages that employ all the formatting tricks Web page designers use. You can create colored or textured backgrounds, bullets, tables, graphics, and more. To set Outlook to create these messages, see Part 3, Task 3, "How to Add Fancy Formatting to Email Messages."

### 1 Create a New Message

Start by creating a new message. Click the **New** button in the toolbar.

Click

### 2 Set the Background

Start by giving your message background an attractive color scheme. Choose **Format, Background, Picture** to choose a stationery. Alternatively, you can choose **Format, Background, Color** to specify a solid background color.

### 3 Choose Stationery

Pick a stationery file from the Background Picture dialog box. I chose the subtle Egg Shell pattern for this example.

### 4 Type a Headline

Enter a headline: Type **The Johnson's Open House** at the top of the message.

## 5 Change the Text Style

The headline should be much larger than the rest of the text. Outlook lets you choose from among standard HTML text sizes: Heading 1 is the largest and Heading 6 is the smallest. Pick **Heading 1** for this headline. Place the cursor in the headline you just typed and choose **Format, Style, Heading 1** from the menu bar.

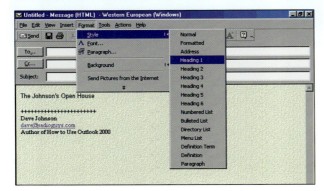

## 6 Center the Text

The headline should also be centered. With the cursor still in the headline text, choose **Format, Paragraph**. The Paragraph dialog box opens.

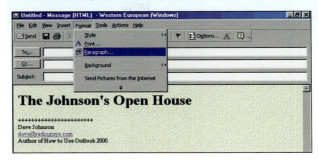

## 7 Select a Justification

From the Paragraph dialog box, click **Center** and then click **OK**. The headline appears centered on the page.

## 8 Enter Body Text

Type the body of your message. The message will appear in regular-size text.

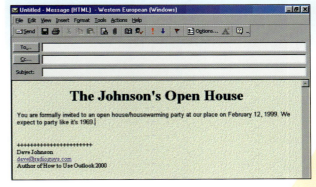

*Continues*

*Project 1 Continued*

## 9 Select Text for Editing

Let's make this body text a little more interesting; changing its color might be just the answer. Select the text you want to format by clicking the mouse at the start of the paragraph and dragging across the text until it is all selected.

Click & Drag

## 10 Select Font Options

With the text selected, choose **Format, Font**. The Font dialog box opens, providing you with options to modify many aspects of the selected text.

## 11 Change the Text Color

Choose an appropriate color from the Color list box. For this example, choose **Blue** because that color will stand out well against the Egg Shell background pattern.

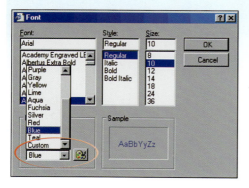

## 12 Add Text for Bullets

Now add some bulleted text to the message. Start by entering some text. Type **Games**, **Food**, **Music**, and **Quake and Total Annihilation multi-player tournaments**, each on its own line. Press the **Enter** key after each word or phrase.

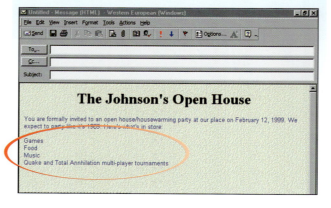

## 13 Select the Text

Before you can apply the bullet style to these words, you must first select them. Select the text you just entered.

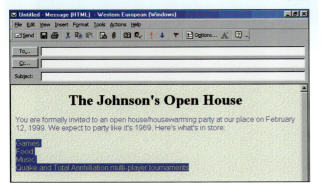

## 14 Apply Bullets to Text

With the text selected, right-click the text and choose **Bullets** from the menu. The text now appears prefixed with bullet symbols.

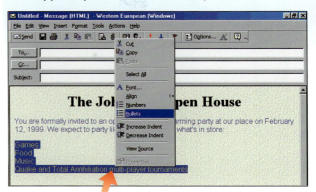

Right-click

## 15 Complete the Message

The message is taking shape. Add other elements as you see fit. When you're done, address the message and click the **Send** button in the toolbar.

*End*

## How-To Hints

### Sending Formatted Messages

I want to reiterate that not everyone can read messages with HTML formatting. If you send messages to someone who has a plain-text email reader, the message may arrive as an attachment or littered with HTML formatting codes. In addition, you should never send a message with HTML formatting to a Usenet newsgroup (with a program like Outlook Express); newsreaders do not generally deal with HTML very well. If you know that your recipient can handle fancy formatting, however, these techniques can really spruce up your email messages.

## Task

1. How to Find a Message by Subject or Sender  96

2. How to Find a Message by Keyword  98

3. How to Mark Messages for Later Action  100

4. How to Mark a Message as Read or Unread  102

5. How to Organize Mail in Folders  104

6. How to Use the Organize Button  106

7. How to Sort Email Using Categories  108

8. How to Display All the Messages in the Same Conversation  110

# PART 4

# Managing Your Inbox

Because you'll spend so much time in Outlook's Inbox view, it's just a matter of time before the program gets as cluttered as your kid's room in the middle of summer vacation. Email messages have a habit of accumulating; after you have generated enough messages, it becomes a chore to find important emails that came last week or last month.

With that in mind, Outlook includes a variety of tools that help you manage your Inbox. For example, Outlook provides search features that let you find messages by keyword or the sender's name. You can also store messages in a nest of folders, kind of like using an electronic filing cabinet.

Whether you get 10 messages a week or 10 messages an hour, you'll need to know how to keep your Inbox organized. In this part of the book you learn how to master the Inbox using these and other management tools.

## Task 1

# How to Find a Message by Subject or Sender

If your Inbox has just a few messages, it's easy to find what you're looking for. But, what if you have to locate a specific message among hundreds or thousands? My Sent Items folder has over 3,400 messages spanning a year's time. To locate a particular message in a box that crowded, you need a special tool designed for the job.

## Begin

### 1 Open the Find Pane

The Find tool is handy for quickly searching large numbers of messages. To open the tool, switch to the folder you are interested in searching (such as the Inbox folder) and click the **Find** button in the toolbar.

Click

### 2 Welcome to the Find Pane

You can use the **Find** pane at the top of the folder window to search the current folder for whatever word you want to locate. To use this feature, just type the word you want to find and click the **Find Now** button.

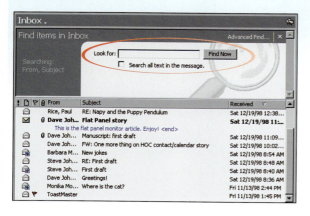

### 3 Enter the Search Word

To find a message, type either a word from the subject line or the name of the sender. You don't have to type the entire name; to find messages from Paul Rice, for instance, you can just type **Paul**. Click **Find Now**.

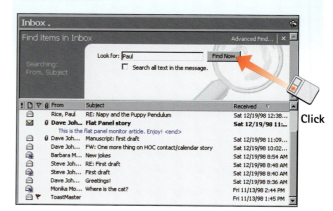
Click

96   Part 4: Managing Your Inbox

## 4 Start the Search

Outlook very quickly searches through the messages in the current folder and displays any messages that contain the search word.

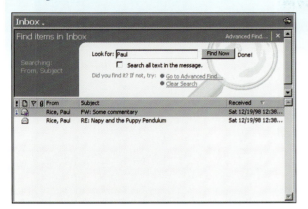

## 5 Scan with a Preview Pane

If you're not sure which message from your search results is the right one, you can speed your search by temporarily turning on the Preview pane: Choose **View, Preview Pane**.

## 6 Search Your Results

After you have the search results displayed and the Preview pane open, you can click a message and use the arrow keys on your keyboard to browse the results in the Preview pane and find the message you want.

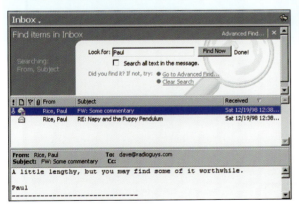

*End*

# How-To Hints

## Searching for Any Word

So far, you've searched messages based on a name or word in the subject line of your messages. To look for any word that may be somewhere in the message body, you can click the **Search All Text in the Message** option in step 3. This option generally works, but in my experience, it is not always 100 percent accurate. For an alternative way to search for text anywhere in a message, see Part 4, Task 2, "How to Find a Message by Keyword."

## Close the Find Pane

To close the Find pane and restore the full-length view of the folder contents, click the **X** in the upper-right corner of the Find pane. You can also close the Preview pane by selecting **View, Preview Pane** from the menu bar.

# Task 2

## How to Find a Message by Keyword

Often, searching for a specific message by the sender's name or the subject line is the best way to locate a message. What if you know a word that was used somewhere in the message (for example, *invoice*), but you don't know whether it's in the subject line or the message body? Then you need to perform a more general search and look for *keywords*.

## Begin

### 1 Open the Find Pane

Your keyword search of email messages begins in the same place as a subject or name search: the Find pane. Open the folder you want to search and click the **Find** button in the toolbar.

Click

### 2 Welcome to the Find Pane

You can enter a search word and click the **Search All Text in This Message** option to see whether that solves your problem. It has been my experience, however, that Outlook doesn't always perform a complete search. If you don't find what you want, click the **Advanced Find** button in the Find pane.

Click

### 3 Welcome to Advanced Find

The **Advanced Find** dialog box is a much more flexible search tool than is the Find pane, but it is somewhat less user friendly—and it's also slower. It has additional fields for specifying search words, time periods, folders, and more.

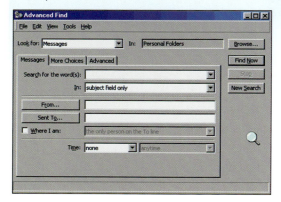

## 4 Generate the Search

To perform an advanced search, type the search word in the **Search for the word(s)** field and then specify **frequently-used text fields** in the **In** field. These options tell Outlook to look everywhere in a message for the search word.

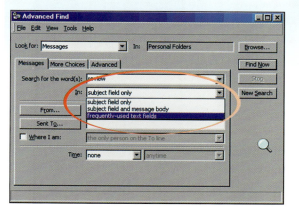

## 5 Start the Search

After you set up the search parameters, click the **Find Now** button. The search begins.

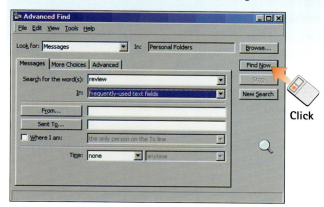

Click

## 6 Review Your Results

Messages that meet your search criteria are displayed at the bottom of the **Advanced Find** dialog box. Double-click the messages to open them.

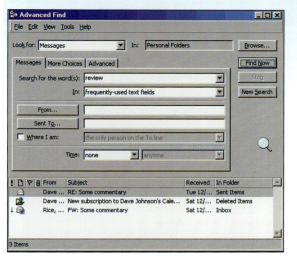

*End*

### How-To Hints

#### Other Advanced Searches

You can use the **Advanced Find** dialog box for other specialized search needs. The **More Choices** tab offers the capability to search for specific categories, as well as for messages with attachments or messages that have been read (or unread).

HOW TO FIND A MESSAGE BY KEYWORD  99

## Task 3

# How to Mark Messages for Later Action

Outlook includes a set of flags for marking your messages. *Flags* are simply visual cues and can be used to identify messages as needing follow up or some other label. It's up to you how you mark your messages. You can set a flag and change it later to suit your needs.

## Begin

### 1 Select a Message to Flag

Message flags are most useful as visual identifiers in the Inbox's folder view. Start by choosing the message you want to flag.

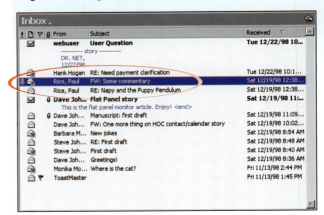

### 2 Mark the Message

Right-click the message you want to flag. Choose **Flag for Follow Up** from the menu. The **Flag for Follow Up** dialog box opens.

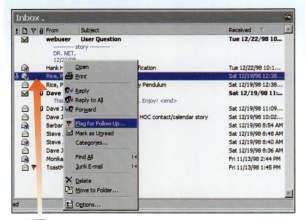

Right-click

### 3 Choose a Flag

Choose a flag from the **Flag to** list box in the **Flag for Follow Up** dialog box. You can choose from 10 flags, including Call, Follow Up, For Your Information, and Review.

## 4 Set the Flag

Click the **OK** button to close the dialog box and set the message to your selected flag.

Click

## 5 View the Flag

After you mark a message with a flag, you can see the flag in the Inbox folder view as well as in the message window. Open the marked message and you will see the flag details in the header region of the message.

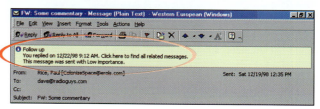

## 6 Marking a Flag Complete

You usually flag a message because the email requires some kind of action you can't complete right away. You can mark the message as complete after finishing the action, making it visually obvious that no further action is required. Right-click the flagged message and choose **Flag Complete** from the menu. The flag changes color to indicate that the action is complete.

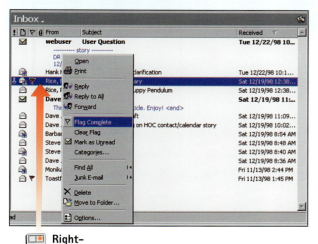

Right-click

### How-To Hints

#### Clearing Flags

You can remove a flag from an email message if you complete the action or mark it in error. Just right-click the message and choose **Clear Flag** from the menu.

End

## Task 4

# How to Mark a Message as Read or Unread

Like most mail programs, Outlook marks each message as read or unread to help you manage your Inbox more effectively. Unread messages must be dealt with; read messages have (at the very least) been reviewed and may not require any action. Most people tend to keep messages requiring action as unread, a reminder that action is required. You can switch messages between read and unread status easily with Outlook.

## *Begin*

### 1 Mark Read as Unread

If you want, you can make a previously read message revert to its unread status. That way, it is displayed in AutoPreview mode (if you use that feature) and sticks out as needing attention. Start by choosing the message you want to mark as unread.

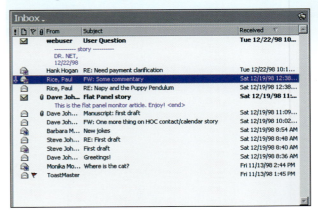

### 2 Mark the Message

Right-click the message you want to mark as unread and choose **Mark as Unread** from the menu.

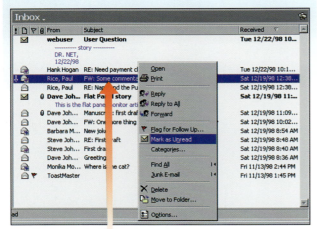

Right-click

### 3 View the Marked Message

After you mark the message as unread, Outlook treats the message as if you never read it. For example, the message is displayed with AutoPreview if you use that feature. (Note that marking a read message as unread does not affect any read receipts you've previously sent out regarding that message.)

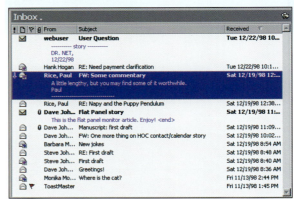

## 4 Mark as Read

You can also mark a message as read even if you haven't read it. Right-click the message and choose **Mark as Read** from the menu. This action has the same effect as if you double-click the message to open it and then close the message window.

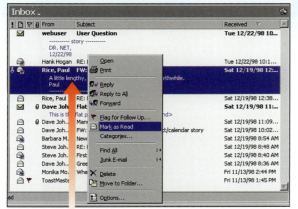

Right-click

## 5 View the Marked Message

With the message now marked as read, notice that AutoPreview no longer displays the first few lines of the message in the folder view.

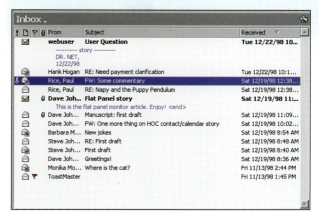

*End*

---

## How-To Hints

### Viewing Attachments

As you see, you don't have to open a message window to read a message or mark it as read. Likewise, you don't have to open a message window to view email attachments. If you are in a folder view with the Preview pane enabled, you can click the **Attachment** icon in the Preview pane to open the attached file. Alternatively, you can right-click a message in the folder view and choose **View, Attachments** from the menu.

# Task 5

## How to Organize Mail in Folders

The Inbox is a poor place to store your messages. The Inbox folder is ideally where new mail arrives; mail you've dealt with or want to save for future reference should be moved elsewhere. Otherwise, old messages can get in the way of new emails that you have to manage right away. Outlook provides a very flexible folder system for storing and retrieving messages.

## Begin

### 1 Open the Folder List

Before you begin creating folders and moving messages into them, you must first display the folders. If you don't already have the Folder List enabled, choose **View, Folder List**.

### 2 Create a New Folder

To create a new folder, right-click the **Outbox Today – Personal Folders** item in the Folder List and choose **New Folder** from the menu. This action creates a new folder in which you can store messages.

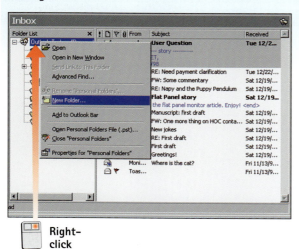

Right-click

### 3 Name the Folder

The Create New Folder dialog box appears. Give your new folder a meaningful name in the **Name** box and click the **OK** button.

Click

104   PART 4: MANAGING YOUR INBOX

## 4 Complete the New Folder

Outlook displays a dialog box that asks whether you want to add a shortcut for this new folder to the Outlook bar. Although a shortcut icon can sometimes be handy (particularly if you frequently access this folder), you don't want to clutter your Outlook bar right now. Click the **No** button.

## 5 Move Message to the Folder

To move files from the Inbox to your new folder, just click the file you want to move and then drag and drop it into the folder you just created. Repeat this action as often as necessary to move the appropriate files out of the Inbox. You can also use the **Shift** or **Alt** key to select more than one file at a time for moving.

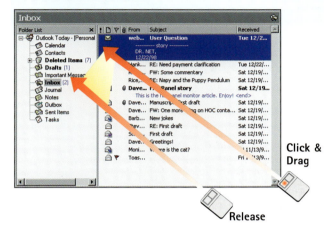

## 6 View the New Folder

After you've put a message in your new folder, you can view its contents any time you want. To switch to the new folder, just click it in the Folder List. A view of the selected folder immediately opens. Because this folder probably won't have unread messages, you may want to enable the Preview pane (see Part 3, Task 12, "How to Display Messages with AutoPreview").

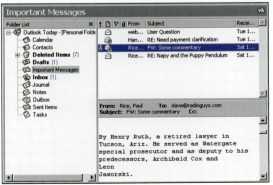

## How-To Hints

### Creating Nested Folders

When you create new folders, you can specify where they are located. It's easy to create *nested* folders, which are stored within other folders. Suppose that you created a folder called **Budget Stuff**. Right-click that folder and choose **New Folder**. Name the new folder **99 Budget**. Create another folder within Budget Stuff and call it **2000 Budget**. Nested folders are a great way to keep your messages in logical order.

## Task 6

# How to Use the Organize Button

The Inbox view is prone to massive levels of disorganization. There's no fundamental problem with Outlook, nor is it necessarily a problem with the way you work. It's just that you may get dozens of email messages each day; over time, it becomes difficult to keep them all organized. Outlook therefore provides the Organize button, which features a number of tools designed to keep your Inbox in shape.

## Begin

### 1 Open the Organize Pane

To get access to all of Outlook's semi-automated organization tools, click the **Organize** button in the toolbar.

Click

### 2 Welcome to the Organize Pane

The **Organize** pane opens at the top of the Inbox. The pane has four tabs: **Using Folders**, **Using Colors**, **Using Views**, and **Junk E-Mail**. Each of these tabs lets you move and organize your messages. From here, you can also open the Rules Wizard (discussed in Part 8, Task 1, "How to Create a Rule") and create new folders.

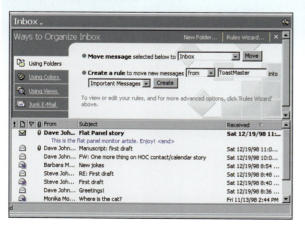

### 3 Moving Messages

If you want to move messages to a different folder, you can use the drag-and-drop method outlined in the preceding task. Alternatively, you can use the **Using Folders** tab in the **Organize** pane: Select the folder to which you want to move messages using the **Move message selected below to** list box.

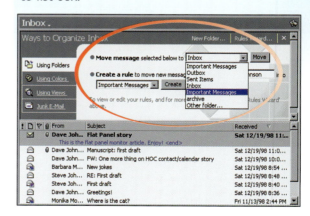

**106** Part 4: Managing Your Inbox

## 4 Select Messages to Move

To move messages to the selected folder, click them in the Inbox view and then click the **Move** button in the **Organize** pane. You can use the **Alt** or **Shift** key to select more than one message at a time.

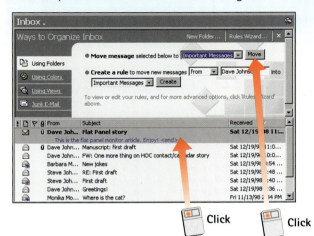

## 5 Flagging Messages by Color

You can use the **Organize** pane to mark specific messages in a certain color, making them easier to see in the folder view. Click the **Using Colors** tab and select a message. The **Color messages** option automatically changes to reflect the sender of the selected message. Select a color and click the **Apply Color** button to effect the change throughout the folder.

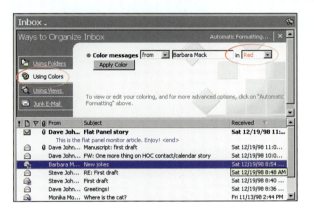

## 6 Organize Using Views

Outlook's views are a great way to add structure to your message lists. You can organize your messages according to the sender, the subject line, or some other criteria. To see messages by a specific view, click the **Using Views** tab and choose a view from the **Change your view** list box. If you want to return to the default view, choose either **Messages** or **Messages with AutoPreview**.

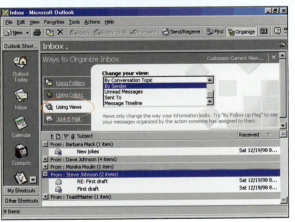

### How-To Hints

#### Customizing Folder Views

Each folder in Outlook has its own settings. That means you can configure one folder to show messages in timeline format, another by conversation, and still another in Message with AutoPreview format. Outlook is very configurable; you can take advantage of that to display messages just the way you want them.

*End*

How to Use the Organize Button   107

TASK 7

# How to Sort Email Using Categories

*Categories* are specialized labels you can assign to messages, contacts, notes, and other kinds of Outlook information. You can set up your own categories and make the labels more meaningful to the way you use the program. For instance, if your work is project based, you can create categories that represent your projects and assign messages to the appropriate project as the messages arrive. That will make it easier to find the right message later.

## Begin

### 1 Assign Categories

To sort and view messages by category, you first must make sure that the messages are assigned to the appropriate categories. To assign a message to a category, right-click a message and choose **Categories** from the menu. Assign a category from the **Categories** dialog box.

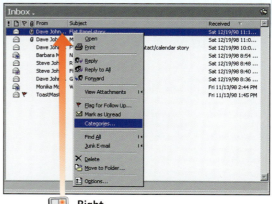

Right-click

### 2 Open the Organize Pane

After your messages are assigned to categories, click the **Organize** button in the toolbar to open the **Organize** pane.

Click

### 3 Change the Tab View

You have to customize the view in order to display messages by category. Click the **Using Views** tab to open these options.

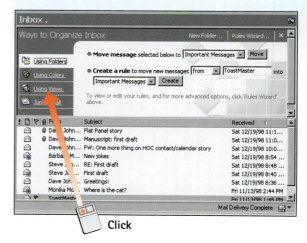

Click

108   PART 4: MANAGING YOUR INBOX

## 4 Customize the Current View

In the **Using Views** tab, click the **Customize Current View** button to open the **View Summary** dialog box. This dialog box contains options for customizing the view.

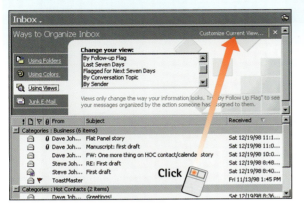

## 5 Group the Messages

Click the **Group By** button on the **View Summary** dialog box. This allows you to display the messages in a specialized way—for example, you can group them according to criteria such as categories.

## 6 Select the Group Criteria

In the **Group By** dialog box, select **Categories** from the **Group items by** list box. Click **OK** to save this change to the display options.

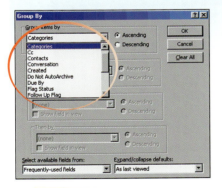

## 7 View the Grouped Messages

After you close the Organize dialog boxes, you can view your messages according to their assigned categories. This is a handy way to see all the messages related to a specific project—but this technique does require you to be diligent about assigning categories to new messages.

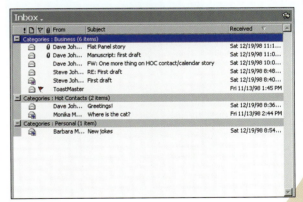

*End*

### How-To Hints

#### Drag and Drop Categories

If you use the **Group by Categories** scheme for displaying messages, you can easily assign new messages to existing categories. Messages are grouped in a category called **None** as they arrive in your Inbox. Simply drag and drop these new messages into one of the category groups in your Inbox to instantly relocate your messages in appropriate locations.

HOW TO SORT EMAIL USING CATEGORIES    109

## Task 8

# How to Display All the Messages in the Same Conversation

"How can I see all the messages related to the same topic?" is a common display problem people have when managing email. In other words, you want to see all the messages that follow the same topic, such as "Invoice Problems with New Freelancers." There are several ways to display exactly this kind of information in Outlook.

## Begin

### 1 View Conversations

The easiest way to find all the messages in the same conversation is to choose the appropriate option in the **Organize** pane. Click the **Organize** button in the toolbar.

Click

### 2 Select the View

Click the **Using Views** tab and select **By Conversation Topic** from the **Change your view** list box. The display switches to show you all the messages, organized into conversation threads. Click the **plus sign** next to the conversation heading to see the messages in the group.

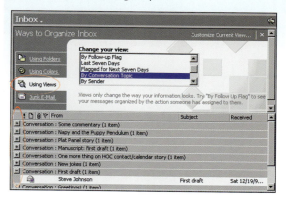

### 3 Find More Messages

The Organize pane sometimes doesn't display all the messages. If you've moved messages relating to that conversation to different folders, Outlook can't find them because it looks in only one folder at a time. Instead, open a message in the desired conversation and click the **Click here to find all related messages** option.

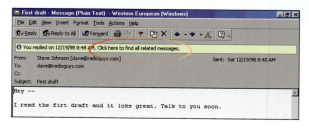

## 4 Select Folders to Search

The **Advanced Find** dialog box opens. Because you want to specify which folders to look in, click the **Browse** button.

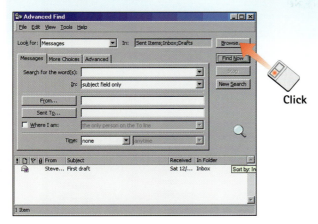

Click

## 5 Choose Folders

The **Select Folder(s)** dialog box appears. Click the check box for each folder through which you want Outlook to look for the messages. Remember that although selecting more folders results in a more thorough search, searching through more folders takes longer. Click the **OK** button to save these folders to the search.

## 6 Start the Search

When you finish setting search options, click the **Find Now** button. Outlook searches through the designated folders for messages related to the original email message.

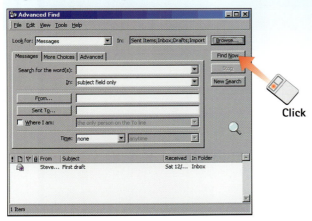

Click

## 7 View the Search Results

When the search is complete, Outlook displays all the messages that met the search criteria. Double-click messages to view them.

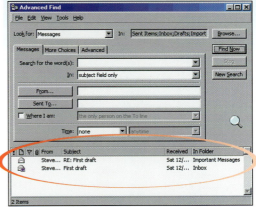

End

### How-To Hints

**Changing the Search Parameters**

To change a search, click **Stop** on the **Advanced Find** dialog and make changes. To reset the search rules, click **New Search**.

How to Display All the Messages in the Same Conversation

# Task

1. How to Get Around in Contacts  114
2. How to Create a New Contact  116
3. How to Add a Contact from an Email Message  118
4. How to Find a Contact by Name  120
5. How to Find a Contact by Keyword  122
6. How to Find a Contact from Any View  124
7. How to Find Someone Using the Internet  126
8. How to Create a Distribution List  128
9. How to Use the Organize Button  130
10. How to Organize Contacts  132
11. How to View a Map to a Contact's Home or Office  134
12. How to Place a Call to a Contact  136
13. How to Link Contacts and Email Messages  138

Project 2: Mail Merge Outlook Data  140

# PART 5

# Working with Contacts

Every home and office has an address book somewhere. Some address books are shining examples of organization and neatness, while most address books—probably including yours—are messy affairs that are rife with sticky notes and scrawls in the margins.

Forget about old paper-based address books. You can use the Contacts view in Outlook to store your contacts electronically, complete with street addresses, email addresses, phone numbers, and other vital information. You can use the information in the Contacts view to send postal letters, email messages, make phone calls, and even generate local maps.

The Contacts view is another important component that makes Outlook your one-stop shopping center for all your daily information needs. This part of the book shows you how to master the Contacts view and take charge of your information mess.

## Task 1

# How to Get Around in Contacts

The Contacts view is essentially a very elaborate address book. Contacts allow you to store email addresses, phone numbers, addresses, and lots of additional personal information for an almost unlimited number of people. Using the Contacts view, you can track email messages, place phone calls, and find Web pages. It's a very versatile part of Outlook, and you'll no doubt use this view often.

## Begin

### 1 Switch to Contacts View

You can switch to the Contacts view using the Outlook bar. If you're still in the Inbox view, click the **Contacts** icon in the Outlook bar. You'll switch immediately to Contacts.

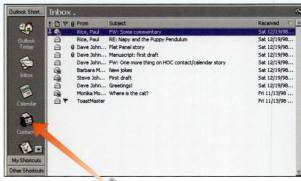

Click

### 2 Welcome to Contacts

The Contacts view has some elements in common with the Inbox. You'll recognize the Outlook bar on the left, the menu bar and toolbar across the top, and (if you have it turned on) the folder list next to the Outlook bar.

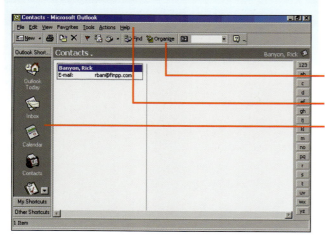

### 3 The Contacts Toolbar

You can create new contacts, print contacts, delete contacts, and mark contacts with the **toolbar** in the Contacts view. The toolbar also has the familiar Find and Organize buttons. Most importantly, you can send email and place phone calls to the selected contact with a single click.

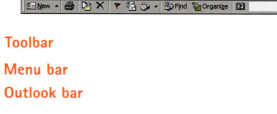

— Toolbar
— Menu bar
— Outlook bar

**114** Part 5: Working with Contacts

## 4 Browse with the Letter Tabs

The letter tabs on the right side of the Contacts view work like they do in any address book. To switch to a particular letter of the alphabet to find a contact, just click the appropriate letter tab.

## 5 Open a Contact

Actual contacts are stored in the middle of the window. You can change the appearance of this display, but the operation is essentially the same regardless of how you configure the display: Double-click a contact to open it. You may not yet have any contacts in your copy of Outlook; we'll discuss how to add them in the following task, "How to Create a New Contact."

Double-click

## 6 View a Contact

After double-clicking a contact, the Contact window opens to display all the information stored about this individual. The window has multiple tabs in which you can store a wealth of information. To close the contact, click the **Close** button in the top right of the title bar.

## How-To Hints

### Keep Contacts in Outlook

Surprisingly, many Outlook users don't store their contact information in Outlook, but instead keep it in another address book (Netscape, Eudora, or some other program). Keeping all your contact information in Outlook makes it easier to send email and also makes it possible to do mail-merge operations with Office applications, to track documents and messages, as well as to use Outlook maps and phone dialing. Even if you have to import a lot of contacts from another program, it's worth your while to use Outlook as your address book.

## Task 2

# How to Create a New Contact

Although there are some automated ways to create contact entries (discussed in Part 3, Tasks 6 and 7), the most common way to create a contact is by opening a new Contact window and manually transcribing the data—probably from a business card. Thankfully, Outlook provides more fields for data than you are ever likely to need.

## Begin

### 1 Create a New Contact

To create a new contact, click the **New** button in the toolbar. This action opens a new Contact window.

Click

### 2 Enter the Contact's Name

Type the name, title, and company for the new contact. You can change the way Outlook displays the contact name after you enter this information. By default, Outlook shows the contact's name in Last, First format. Click the **File As** list arrow to choose a different format if you want.

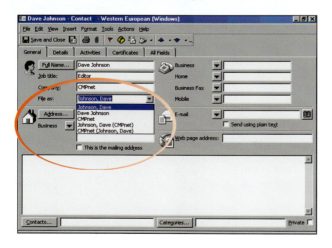

### 3 Enter Phone Numbers

Continue entering contact information for this new individual. When you enter the phone number, don't worry about adhering to a particular format with dashes and parentheses. You can type a string of numbers such as 2125551212; when the cursor leaves the phone field, the number is converted automatically to (212) 555-1212 for you.

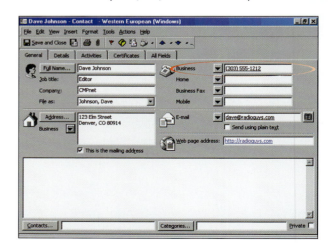

## 4 Change Field Labels

The Contact window is quite flexible. For example, if you have phone numbers different from those the Outlook fields provide, click the **list arrow** for the field you want to change. Select the phone number description you want to use and then enter the number in the field.

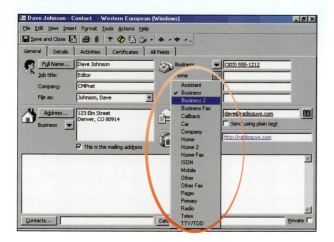

## 5 Enter More Details

You can enter as much or as little information about a contact as you want. You can stop right after the name and email address, for instance, or you can click the **Details** tab and enter more business information, spouse data, and birthdays and anniversaries.

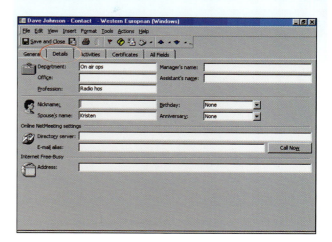

## 6 Save Your New Contact

When you are done entering contact information about this individual, click the **Save and Close** button in the toolbar. The entry appears in the Contacts view. Double-click the entry to open the Contact window again.

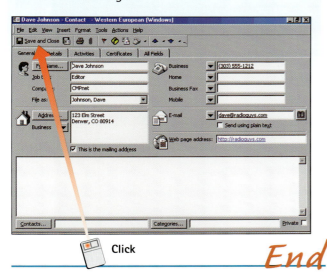

Click

*End*

## How-To Hints

### Use the Notes Field

If you have information—driving directions, a gift list, or the names of all nine of your friend's cats—that won't fit anywhere else, use the Notes field. The Notes field is the large, freeform region at the bottom of each Contact window; you can type anything you want in this field. The Notes field is also searched when you use the **Find** tool, so it's a handy place to store information about your contacts.

Task 3

# How to Add a Contact from an Email Message

Email addresses have one serious shortcoming: They're easy to mistype and enter incorrectly. You may not even notice until days or weeks later when you finally get around to sending an email message and then get a rejection notice from some remote mail server. To avoid that problem—and to make it just a bit easier to create new contacts—you can convert an email message from your Inbox directly into a new contact—with no typing required.

## Begin

### 1 Open the Email Message

Find a message from someone you want to add to your list of contacts. Double-click the message to open it.

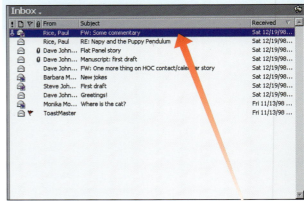

Double-click

### 2 Add Email to Contacts

After the message window is open, right-click the sender's name in the **From** field. Choose **Add to Contacts** from the menu.

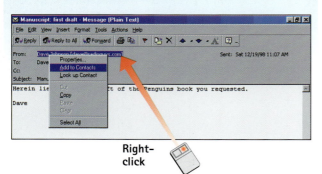

Right-click

### 3 Complete the Contact

Finish filling out the contact information for this individual. Although Outlook can grab the email address from the message, it doesn't know about phone numbers, postal addresses, or any other data—you have to enter that by hand.

118   Part 5: Working with Contacts

## 4 Save Your Contact

When you are done entering contact information about this individual, click the **Save and Close** button in the toolbar.

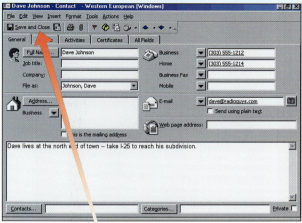

Click

## 5 Resolve Duplicates

If the Contact window closes, you're done. It's possible that the contact already exists in your address book and you have just entered it a second time. If that's the case, Outlook displays the **Duplicate Contact Detected** dialog box. Click the **Open Existing Contact** button to display the original contact with which this new one is in conflict.

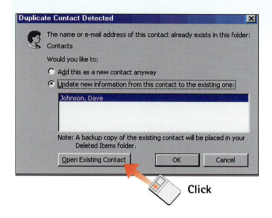

Click

## 6 Update the Old Contact

If the two contacts truly are duplicates, you can click the **OK** button to merge them into a single contact. Do this if you have more information in the **New Contact** window and want to add it to the information that already exists in your address book.

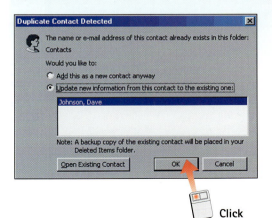

Click

*End*

## How-To Hints

### Trim the Contact Name

Sometimes when you add a contact by using the **Add to Contacts** menu item in an email message, the individual's name appears in the Contact **Full Name** field as something like `Rick Broida [rickb@ibm.net]`. Use the **Delete** key to back over the email address so that this field displays only the person's name, not the name and email information.

## Task 4

# How to Find a Contact by Name

After you acquire a few dozen (or a few hundred) contacts, finding a specific one may not be easy. You can click the **letter tabs** on the right side of the Contacts view to go to that part of the alphabet, but there's a faster solution: Use the **Find** button. This feature is particularly handy if you can remember the person's first name, but not her last.

## Begin

### 1 Display the Find Pane

To look for a contact by name, click the **Find** button in the **Contacts** toolbar.

Click

### 2 Welcome to the Find Pane

The **Find** pane in the Contacts view works much like it does in the Inbox view. Here, however, Find searches text in the Name, Company, and Address fields. It also displays the matching contacts in the bottom pane.

### 3 Enter the Search Word

Type the name you are searching for in the **Look For** field and click the **Find Now** button.

Click

120    Part 5: Working with Contacts

## 4 Review the Matches

Any contacts that match the search word you entered are displayed below the Find pane. Double-click an entry to open it and to display the complete Contact window.

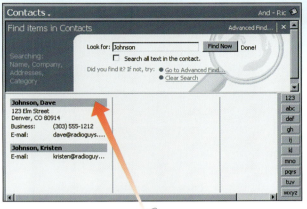

Double-click

## 5 View the Contact

After you find the matching contact, you can edit it, as well as use it to send mail, place a call, and close it when you're done.

## 6 Close the Find Pane

When you are done with your search, click the **Find** button in the toolbar. The search results are replaced with your complete list of contacts.

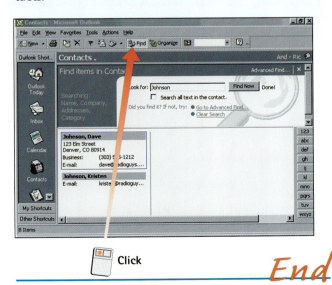

Click

*End*

## How-To Hints

### Keep the Search Simple

When conducting a search, it's usually better to enter too little information in the **Look For** field than too much. If you search for **Eric Beteille**, for example, you could misspell the unusual last name and turn up no results. If you search just for **Eric**, however, you'll get all the Erics in your address book—one of them will be the one you're looking for.

## Task 5

# How to Find a Contact by Keyword

There are situations in which you can't remember (or don't know) the contact's name or company; perhaps you know their job title or some additional text that was embedded in the Contact window's Notes field. At such times, you can search for contacts using a keyword.

## Begin

### 1 Display the Find Pane

To look for a contact using some keyword, begin the same way you did when searching by name: Click the **Find** button in the **Contacts** toolbar.

Click

### 2 Welcome to the Find Pane

The **Find** pane in the Contacts view works much like it does in the Inbox view. Because you're not searching for the contact's name in this case, click **Advanced Find** to access some additional options.

Click

### 3 Enter the Search Word

In the **Advanced Find** dialog box, type the word you want to search for in the **Search for the Word(s)** field.

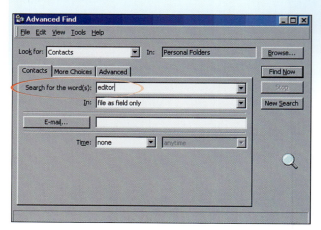

## 4 Expand the Search

Click the **arrow** next to the **In** list box and select **Frequently-Used Text Fields**. This option tells Outlook to look for the keyword in all the fields in which you usually type information for your contacts.

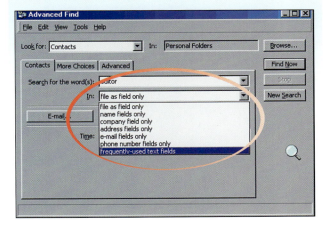

## 5 Start the Search

Click the **Find Now** button in the **Advanced Search** dialog box. Outlook starts searching through your contacts for the word or phrase you entered. The search can take some time, depending on how many contacts you have.

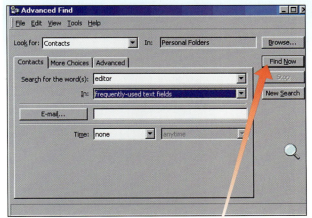

Click

## 6 Review the Matches

When the search is complete, all the contacts that match the search criteria are listed at the bottom of the **Advanced Find** dialog box. Double-click entries to open them.

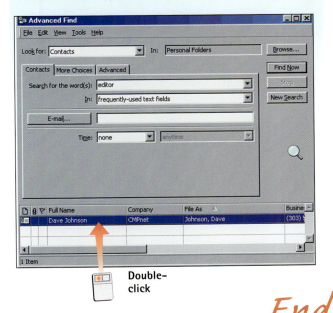

Double-click

## How-To Hints

### Search Everywhere at Once

If you're on a hunt for information, you may appreciate the capability to search everywhere in Outlook at once. If you want to find every instance of the words *99 budget*, for example, you'll want to look in the Contacts view, in your email messages, and in other views as well. To conduct such a search, click the **arrow** next to the **Look For** field in the **Advanced Find** dialog box and choose **Any Type of Outlook Item**.

*End*

How to Find a Contact by Keyword  **123**

## Task 6

# How to Find a Contact from Any View

You don't have to be in the Contacts view to find a contact. In fact, you may frequently want to open a Contact window without actually leaving the Inbox view, where you are working on new messages. Outlook includes a handy way to search for contacts that you can use in every view throughout the program.

## Begin

### 1 Welcome to Find a Contact

The **Find a Contact** field is available from the toolbar in every view in Outlook. Using this field, you can enter a name and have Outlook find the appropriate contact without changing views.

### 2 Enter a Search Name

To use the **Find a Contact** field, just type a name in the field. You can enter part of a name or the entire name—it's your choice. After you type the name, press the **Enter** key.

### 3 Complete the Search

Outlook immediately searches for the name you typed. If it finds only one match, the program opens the appropriate Contact window.

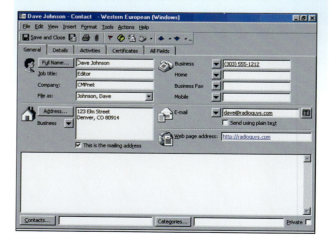

## 4 Search Results Display Multiple

In some cases, Outlook may find more than one match for the name you enter. In this example, I've entered a common name that will result in two or more matches with my list of contacts.

## 5 Choose the Correct Match

If there is more than one match, Outlook displays the **Choose Contact** dialog box. Look for the name you were trying to locate and double-click it. The Contact window for that individual opens.

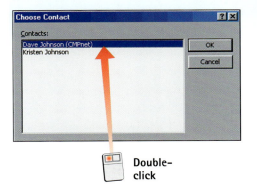

Double-click

## 6 Reuse Search Results

After you search for a name in the **Find a Contact** field, the name is saved to the field in the form of a list box. Click the **list box arrow** and choose the name you want to find. The Contact window for that contact opens immediately.

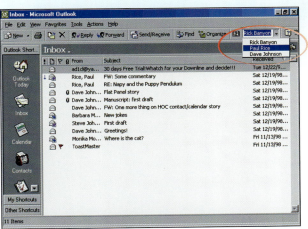

# How-To Hints

## Finding More Than Names

As useful as the **Find a Contact** field is, it is quite limited in that it can help you locate contacts by name only. If you want to find a contact by company, address, or some other keyword, you must switch to the Contacts view and use the **Find** button in the toolbar, as explained in Task 5, "How to Find a Contact by Keyword."

*End*

HOW TO FIND A CONTACT FROM ANY VIEW   125

## Task 7

# How to Find Someone Using the Internet

You always knew the Internet was good for something other than reading *Robotman* comics, right? Did you also know you can use Outlook to search the Internet for people whose email address you don't know? This kind of Internet search relies on a standard called Lightweight Directory Access Protocol (LDAP). You don't have to know how LDAP works, all you have to do is configure Outlook to conduct Internet searches for business associates, long-lost friends, and family members.

## Begin

### 1 Check Directory Services

Your copy of Outlook may already have a slew of LDAP servers installed. To find out, choose **Tools, Accounts** from the menu bar and click the **Directory Service** tab. If there's anything on this tab, continue with step 4. If not, you have to add at least one server before you can search.

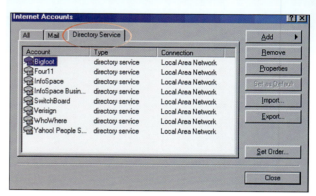

### 2 Add a Directory Service

If you have no directory services installed, you can add this common one: **bigfoot.com**. This is a commercial people-search Web site. Click the **Add** button and then click **Directory Service**.

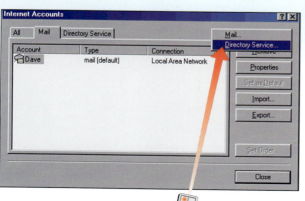

Click

### 3 Complete the Wizard

Follow the wizard's instructions to add the directory service to Outlook. Type **ldap.bigfoot.com** in the Internet Directory (LDAP) Server field. Click **No** when Outlook asks whether you want to check addresses using this directory service. Finish the wizard.

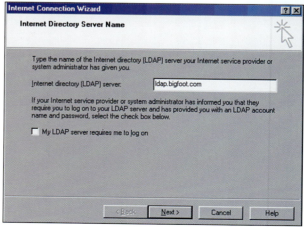

## 4 Search the Internet

After you configure at least one LDAP server, you're ready to search the Internet for people. Choose **Tools, Address Book** from the menu bar. The Address Book opens, displaying your contacts from the Contact view in abbreviated format.

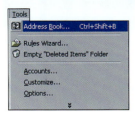

## 5 Find People

Click the **Find People** button in the menu bar of the **Address Book** window.

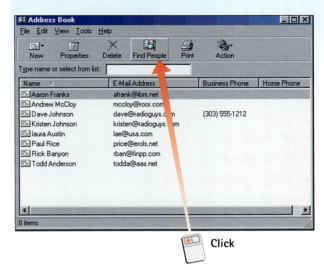

Click

## 6 Perform the Search

When the **Find People** dialog box appears, select an LDAP server from the **Look In** list box. Type the name of the person you are searching for in the **Name** field and then click the **Find Now** button. The search results, which you can add to your contacts list if you want, appear at the bottom of the dialog box.

## How-To Hints

### Try Different Directories

If at first you don't succeed, try a different directory server. Different services maintain sometimes radically different databases, so if one server doesn't have a record of the person you're looking for, another might. In addition, different LDAP servers maintain different kinds of information. Some list postal addresses and phone numbers, while others have just email addresses.

Here is a list of some common LDAP servers you can add to Outlook:

- ✓ `ldap.bigfoot.com`
- ✓ `ldap.four11.com`
- ✓ `ldap.infospace.com`
- ✓ `ldap.switchboard.com`
- ✓ `ldap.whowhere.com`

## Task 8

# How to Create a Distribution List

Do you frequently need to send the same group of people the same email message? Suppose that you send a weekly report to several co-workers every Monday morning. One way to send that weekly message more efficiently is to create a *distribution list*, also known as a *mailing group*. The list contains the addresses of all the people you normally send the message to, so that you can send the message to a single entry—the list or group—instead of adding several names to the **To** field.

## *Begin*

### *1* Open the Address Book

Mailing groups are created in the Outlook address book. To open it, choose **Tools, Address Book**.

### *2* Create a New Group

To create a new group, click the **New** button in the toolbar of the **Address Book** window and choose **New Group**. The My Team **Properties** dialog box opens.

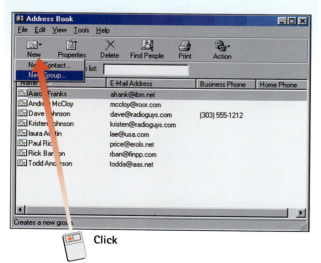

Click

### *3* Name the Group

You can set up as many groups as you like, so give each group a unique name. Type the name you want this group to have in the **Group Name** field.

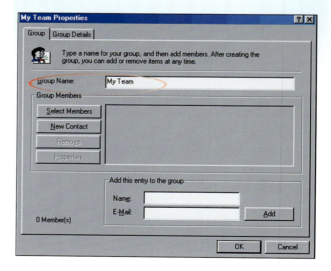

128   Part 5: Working with Contacts

## 4 Add Members to the Group

Click the **Select Members** button to add contacts to your group. The **Select Group Members** dialog box appears.

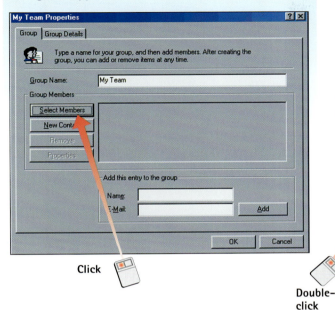

Click

## 5 Choose Contacts for Group

To add contacts to your new group, double-click the desired names in the left pane of the **Select Group Members** dialog box. After you double-click an entry, that entry moves to the right pane. The right pane contains the contacts that will be part of the group. To remove a contact, right-click the name in the right pane and choose **Remove** from the menu.

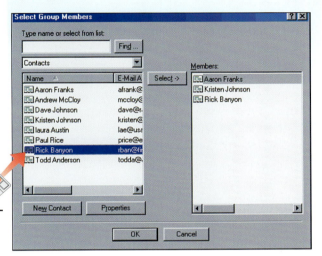

Double-click

## 6 Send a Message to the Group

After you've created the group, you can use it to email messages to everyone in the group at once. Just enter the name of the group in a message window's **To** field to send a message to everyone in the group.

## How-To Hints

### Add New Names to a Group

If you want someone who is not currently in your contacts list to be part of your group, you have two choices:

✓ Add a name to a group without making the individual part of your contacts list. **Use the Add This Entry to the Group** section of the **My Team Properties** dialog box.

✓ Create a new contact during the group-creation process. Click the **New Contact** button on the **My Team Properties** dialog box. The information you enter here is stored in your contacts list.

How to Create a Distribution List  **129**

## Task 9

# How to Use the Organize Button

Just as it does in the Inbox view, the **Organize** button makes it easy to organize and manage your contact data. The only difference is that the **Organize** button is optimized for contacts when you click it from the Contacts view.

## Begin

### 1 Open the Organize Pane

To open the **Organize** pane for your contact information, make sure that you are in Contacts view and click the **Organize** button from the toolbar.

Click

### 2 Welcome to the Organize Pane

The **Organize** pane in the Contacts view has three tabs: **Using Folders**, **Using Categories**, and **Using Views**. The pane always starts in the **Using Categories** view because it is a common task. More information on using this tab is found in the next task, "How to Organize Contacts."

### 3 Move Contacts to Folders

Click the **Using Folders** tab. Click a contact to select it and then choose a folder from the **Move Contact Selected Below To** list box; click the **Move** button. The contact is placed in the selected folder. If you choose the Inbox folder, the contact isn't moved; rather, it is used to start a new mail message. Likewise, you can move a contact to the Calendar to start an appointment with that contact.

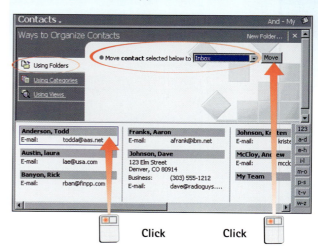
Click     Click

130   Part 5: Working with Contacts

## 4 Change Contact Views

Click the **Using Views** tab to switch to that organizing mode. Change the Contacts view by selecting an option from the **Change Your View** list box. If you want to switch back to the original Contacts view, choose **Default**. Different views have different advantages, so experiment and see which one you like best.

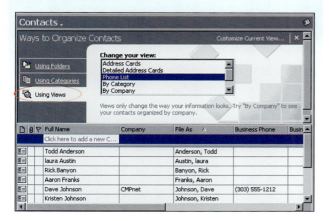

## 5 Make Advanced Changes

You can make a slew of changes to the Contacts view as well. Click the **Customize Current View** button in the Organize pane to see the additional options in the **View Summary** dialog box.

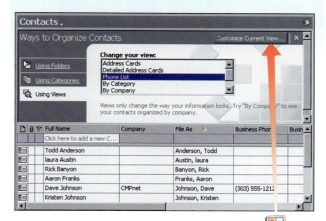

Click

## 6 Change the View

The **View Summary** dialog box has a column of buttons you can use to modify the display of your contacts list. The **Fields** button, for example, lets you add, remove, and reorder the fields in the Contact window. The **Sort** button lets you change the way the display is sorted; the **Other Settings** button allows you to change fonts used to display your contacts.

### How-To Hints

#### Emailing Contact Info

In Part 3, Task 6, "How to Send Contact Info in Messages Automatically," you saw how you can use vCards to email contact information to people who use Outlook. If you have to email contact information to someone who uses an incompatible mail program, you can still do the job without a lot of typing. Here's how:

1. Drag the contact to the Notes icon in the Outlook bar.
2. Close the new note and switch to the Notes view.
3. Drag the new note from the Notes view to the Inbox icon in the Outlook bar. All the contact information appears in a new message window, ready to email.

*End*

# Task 10

## How to Organize Contacts

Although the Category tool can be convoluted when you're in the Inbox view, it's quite easy to use in the Contacts view. The difference is that support for categories is built into the contact's Organize pane, which means that you can organize and view your contacts by category with just a few simple steps. Categories are great for putting your contacts in logical groups that reflect the way you work. If you manage several projects, for example, you can place your contacts into groups that reflect those projects, making them easier to find.

## Begin

### 1 Open the Organize Pane

To work with your contacts in categories, make sure that you are in the Contacts view. Then open the **Organize** pane by clicking the **Organize** button in the toolbar.

Click

### 2 Create a Category

If you want to view your contacts by categories, you must first assign your contacts to categories. To do that, click the **Using Categories** tab in the **Organize** pane and type the name of a new category in the **Create a New Category Called** field. Click the **Create** button to make the category permanent.

### 3 Assign the Category

After you have created a few categories that describe your various contacts, you must assign the contacts to the appropriate categories. Select one or more contacts and choose the category to which you want to assign them using the **Add Contacts Selected Below To** list box. Click the **Add** button to assign the category to the contacts.

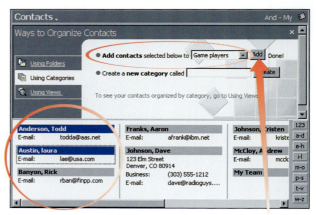

Click

132  Part 5: Working with Contacts

## 4 Change the View

After all your contacts are assigned to specific categories, you can change the view so that you can see your contacts organized into those categories. Click the **Using Views** tab on the Organize pane.

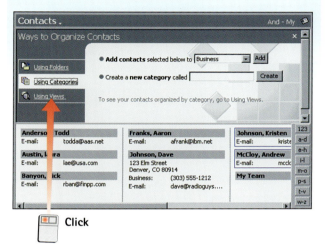
Click

## 5 Select the Category View

Choose **By Category** from the **Change Your View** list box. The view changes to show you all your contacts organized into categories. Click the **plus sign** next to the category labels to expand the groups and show you the actual contacts.

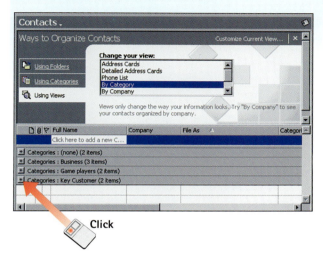
Click

## 6 Drag and Drop New Contacts

After you assign most of your contacts to categories, it's easy to add new contacts to those categories. Simply drag and drop unassigned contacts into the groups that represent the categories you want to assign them to.

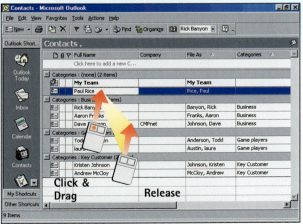
Click & Drag   Release

# How-To Hints

### Categories Are Universal

Any category you create in the Contacts view is available elsewhere in Outlook. Although you can add categories using the **Edit, Categories** menu item from other views such as the Inbox, it's generally easier if you simply create your categories in the Contacts view. The categories are always available anywhere else in the program that you happen to need them.

*End*

HOW TO ORGANIZE CONTACTS  **133**

## Task 11

# How to View a Map to a Contact's Home or Office

Thanks to the Internet, you may never have to whip out a paper atlas again to find your way to a friend's or client's location. Outlook includes a tool that displays a detailed, street-level map of any contact's address. The only caveat is that you have to know the street address to begin with; Outlook can't generate a map based on someone's email address or phone number.

## Begin

### 1 Open the Contact

Start by finding the contact you want to visit. Double-click the entry to open the Contacts window.

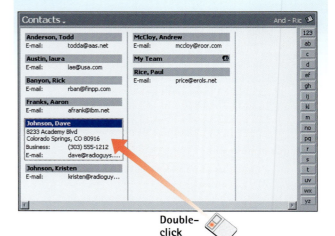

Double-click

### 2 Launch the Map Display

Make sure that you are connected to the Internet and that you've already entered the contact's postal address in the **Address** field. Click the **Display Map of Address** button in the toolbar. Your Web browser will open.

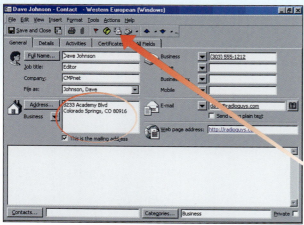

Click

### 3 Welcome to Expedia Maps

Your Web browser displays the contact's local map, along with a push pin that indicates the exact location of the address.

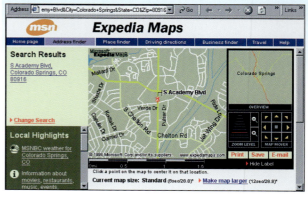

**134** Part 5: Working with Contacts

## 4 Zoom and Pan the Map

The right side of the map includes buttons for panning around the map as well as for zooming in and out. A red line in the **Zoom Level** box shows how aggressively the map is currently zoomed. Redefine the view until it shows exactly what you want to see.

## 5 Print and Mail the Map

When you are satisfied with what you see on the screen, you can send it to your local printer by clicking the **Print** button. You can also email the map to someone by clicking the **E-mail** button. Click the **Save** button to store a link to the map on the Expedia home page—that way you can create a library of locations you can access from your Web browser.

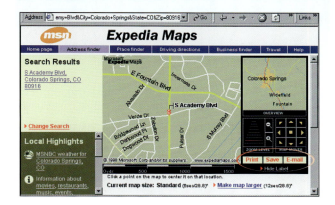

## 6 Get Local Information

The lower-left side of the map page contains links to local information about the selected locale. You can get up-to-date weather information, as well as restaurant listings and other services.

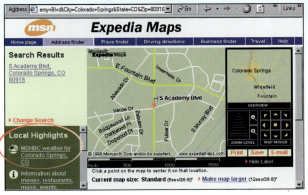

*End*

## How-To Hints

### Complete Driving Directions

If you want complete, turn-by-turn driving directions from one city to another, click the **Driving Directions** link at the top of the Expedia Web page.

If you do a lot of driving between places you've never been before, you may want to invest in a satellite navigation system that provides turn-by-turn directions. Two excellent packages are TravRoute's Copilot Door-to-Door and Magellan's Map 'n Tracker.

TASK *12*

# How to Place a Call to a Contact

If you have a modem attached to your PC, you can use Outlook to dial your phone and record a log of the call with specific contacts. This feature makes dialing easier and gives your PC a taste of the features found in high-end computer telephony software. Use this feature if you spend a lot of time on the phone and want to keep better track of your time.

## *Begin*

### *1* Choose a Contact

Choose the contact you want to call. Click the contact to select it and then click the **Dial list arrow** in the toolbar to choose from among the contact's phone numbers. (If you know that you want to dial the contact's primary phone number, click the **Dial** button.)

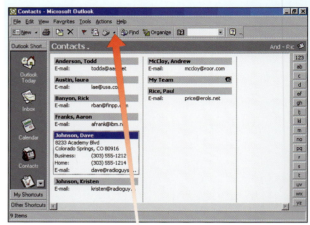

 Click

### *2* Choose a Phone Number

Select the number you want to dial from the **Dial** list.

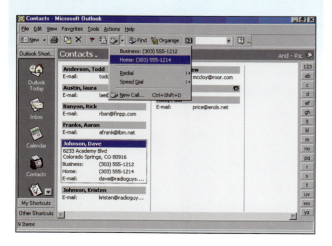

### *3* Set Call Options

The **New Call** dialog box appears. Odds are good that you want to record details about the call while you're on the phone, so click the **Create New Journal Entry When Starting New Call** option.

**136** PART 5: WORKING WITH CONTACTS

## 4 Start the Call

When you are ready to place the call, click the **Start Call** button on the **New Call** dialog box. This action triggers your modem to dial out and place the call. As soon as the number has been dialed, Outlook tells you to pick up the telephone receiver and wait for the other party to answer.

Click

## 5 Record the Journal

When the call begins, Outlook opens a **Phone Call** window that is part of the Journal system. The Journal is explained in Part 7, Task 6, "How to Find Your Way Around the Journal." In essence, the system is a log of your activities taken while using the program. Record any notes about the phone call in this document window and click the **Save and Close** button when you are done. You can later find this log in the **Activities** tab for the contact entry of the person you called.

*End*

## How-To Hints

### Verify Your Modem Settings

To place a call using Outlook, you must make sure that your system is properly configured. First, you must have a modem installed in your PC. Second, the modem cannot be in use when you try to telephone out; if you are connected to the Internet, Outlook can't dial out to your contact.

TASK 13

# How to Link Contacts and Email Messages

Linking contacts and email messages is another way to associate different parts of Outlook to find information more quickly. Suppose that someone sends you an email; the contents of the message relate to a third person who isn't part of the original message exchange. By linking the email to that third person, you'll be able to open the message from that third person's Contact window. This linking feature can save time and help you get organized when you are managing lots of messages and contacts.

*Begin*

### 1 Open the Message

Find the message you want linked to someone in your contact list. Double-click the message to open it.

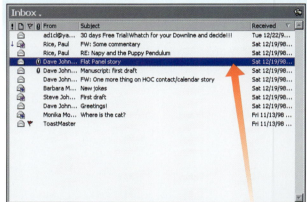

Double-click

### 2 Open the Message Options

Select **View, Options** from the menu bar to open the Options dialog box for the message. It is here that you'll assign the links.

### 3 Link Contacts

Click the **Contacts** button on the **Message Options** dialog box. The **Select Contacts** dialog box opens, allowing you to select individuals to link to the message.

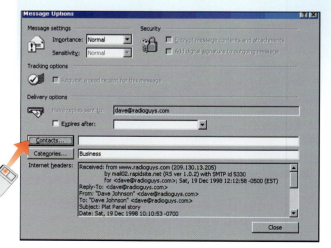

Click

138  PART 5: WORKING WITH CONTACTS

## 4 Choose Contacts to Link

Select any contacts you want associated with the email message. Use the **Alt** or **Shift** key to select more than one contact, if necessary.

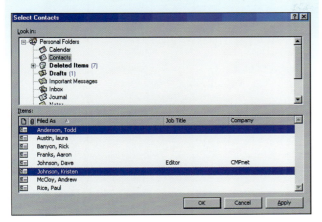

## 5 Save Your Changes

After you add one or more contacts to the **Contacts** field of the message's **Options** dialog box, click the **Close** button to save your changes. The selected names are now associated with the email message; a search of their contact entries should display this email message.

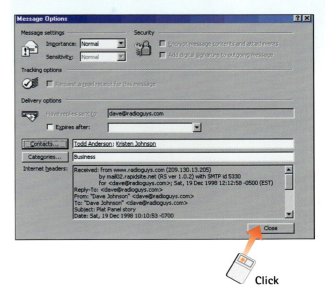

Click

## 6 Open a Contact Window

Open one of the contacts you just associated with the email message. Click the **Activities** tab; this is where Journal information is stored, and this is where you'll see this email message.

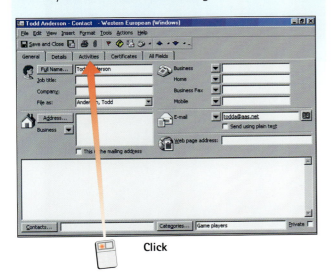

Click

## 7 View the Linked Email

The **Activities** tab shows all the Journal activities for this individual. Select **All Items** from the **Show** list box. You should see the email message you just linked in the Activities list. Double-click the entry to open it.

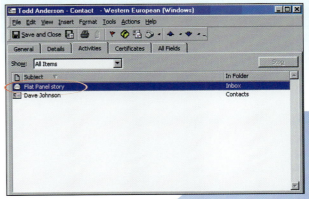

*End*

# Project 2
## Mail Merge Outlook Data

Perhaps the most underused task on the PC today, mail merge allows you to create one letter and automatically insert personal information in it for a hundred or a thousand different recipients.

You can mail merge almost anything: letters, postcards, invoices. In this project, we use Microsoft Word to create an envelope for mailing through the U.S. Postal Service.

### 1 Start the Mail Merge in Word

Open **Word** and choose **Tools, Mail Merge** from the menu bar to open the Mail Merge Helper dialog box.

### 2 Create a Mail-Merge Document

The Mail Merge Helper has three main steps; it's something like a wizard. Start with step 1 and create a new document. Choose **Create, Envelopes**.

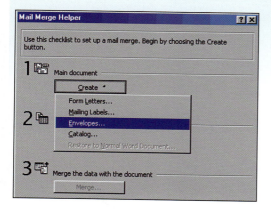

### 3 Start a New Document

Word needs to know whether you want to use the open document (also called the *active window*) or to create a new document. It doesn't really matter, but choose **New Main Document** for this example.

Click

## 4 Get Your Merge Data

With the document created and waiting in the background, the next step is to get the data—the names, addresses, and so on—you'll merge into the document. You want to use Outlook's contact data; choose **Get Data, Use Address Book** in step 2 of the Mail Merge Helper.

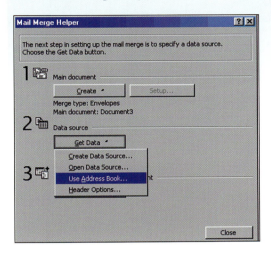

## 5 Import the Outlook Data

Because you specified that you want to use address book data, Word now wants to know what particular address book you want to use. Choose **Outlook Address Book** from the **Use Address Book** dialog box and then click **OK**. Depending on the size of your Outlook contact list, it may take several minutes while Word reads all the data into memory.

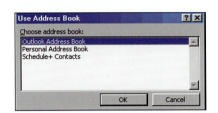

## 6 Set Up Your Document

After Word has grabbed all the contact information from Outlook, it tells you that it's time to set up your envelope. Click the **Set Up Main Document** button on the Microsoft Word dialog box.

Click

## 7 Configure Envelope Options

The Options dialog box you see varies depending on which kind of document you decide to create. For this exercise, you can change the font of the delivery and return addresses, as well as modify the envelope size. All the defaults are fine in this case, so click the **OK** button to move on.

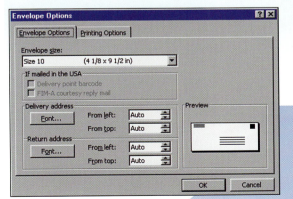

*Continues*

PROJECT 2: MAIL MERGE OUTLOOK DATA  141

*Project 2 Continued*

## 8 Add Merge Fields

Now you've reached the heart of the merge process. In the Envelope Address dialog box, you have to insert the field names that represent the actual Outlook data to be printed. To start, click the **Insert Merge Field** button.

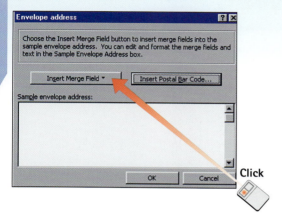
Click

## 9 Select a Field

Because this is an envelope, you have to choose the fields needed by the post office to deliver a letter. Choose **First_Name**, add a space, and then choose **Last_Name**. Press the **Enter** key and add the street address information: **Street_Address**, **City**, and **Postal_Code**.

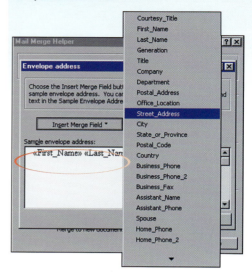

## 10 Complete the Merge Fields

When you have entered all your merge fields, click the **OK** button to return to the Mail Merge Helper dialog box.

Click

## 11 Set Up a Query

You're essentially ready to run the mail merge. Before you do, however, you may want to filter out contacts you don't need. You can tell Word to print specific contacts by almost any criteria. Click the **Query Options** button in step 3 of the Mail Merge Helper dialog box to open the **Query Options** dialog box.

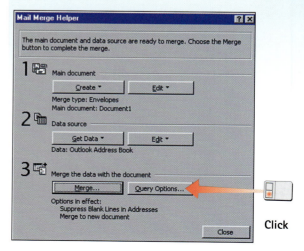
Click

142  PART 5: WORKING WITH CONTACTS

## 12 Define the Query Options

Decide what it is you want to print. In this case, print envelopes only for those in the contact list who have a postal address. Let's filter out contacts without complete addresses. Select **Street_Address** from the **Field** list box. Choose **Is Not Blank** from the **Comparison** field. These options tell Word to use merge data only for records with filled-in addresses. Click the **OK** button.

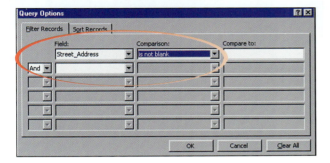

## 13 Start the Mail Merge

Click the **Merge** button in the Mail Merge Helper to start the mail merge.

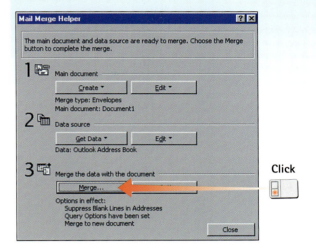

Click

## 14 Launch the Merge

Word displays one last dialog box before starting the mail merge so that you can fine-tune options. For this example, simply click the **Merge** button.

Click

## 15 Print the Results

The first completed mail-merged document appears in a Word window. It may take several minutes for the document to be *fully* generated (that is, for all the envelopes to be generated). The envelopes are fully personalized using the Outlook data—and it took you just a few minutes to create them!

*End*

# How-To Hints

### Format Your Merge Data

Don't be satisfied with the default fonts your application uses with mail-merge data. Mail-merge fields (those with the brackets around them) can be fully formatted with different fonts, point sizes, and colors.

PROJECT 2: MAIL MERGE OUTLOOK DATA    143

# Task

1. How to Find Your Way Around the Calendar  146
2. How to Set an Appointment  148
3. How to Create a Recurring Appointment  150
4. How to Make a Task  152
5. How to Create a Day-Long Event  154
6. How to Invite Someone to a Meeting  156
7. How to Delegate a Task  158
8. How to Change a Scheduled Appointment  160
9. How to Print the Calendar  162
10. How to Share a Calendar  164
11. How to Publish Your Calendar to the Web  166

PART 6

# Working with the Calendar

If you're a typical working professional, you have a busy calendar. Meetings, appointments, and to-do tasks probably litter your daily agenda. If you currently use a paper planner to track your appointments, you can do better. Outlook includes a Calendar that stores all your daily events electronically.

If you use Outlook to track your daily schedule, you can print your agenda and take it with you when you're away from the desk. You can get reminder messages about upcoming meetings before they happen. You can coordinate with other Outlook users to set up meetings that don't conflict with other people's schedules. You can even publish your Calendar to the Web, so that others can see what your day looks like without calling you.

You learn how to do all of these essential tasks by reading this part of the book.

## Task 1

# How to Find Your Way Around the Calendar

Outlook's Calendar view is your one-stop shopping place for managing your schedule. From this view, you can track your daily to-do tasks, schedule appointments and events, and even invite other people to your meetings via email. When you invite other Outlook users to a meeting, both copies of Outlook essentially "talk to each other" by way of email and automatically put the meeting into their respective Calendars. Outlook isn't a standalone program anymore, either: Now you can give other people the ability to modify your appointments, as well as publish your agenda on the Internet.

## Begin

### 1 Switch to Calendar View

You can switch to the Calendar view from anywhere in Outlook by clicking the **Calendar** button in the Outlook bar.

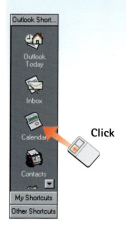

Click

### 2 Welcome to the Calendar

The Calendar view is divided into three major sections: The left column represents today and is for entering and displaying appointments. The top-right side of the display shows a calendar; the right bottom lists any to-do tasks to be completed.

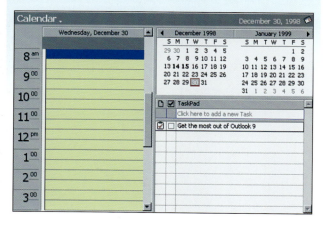

### 3 Using Calendar Toolbars

The Calendar's toolbars are similar to those in other parts of Outlook, although the buttons are optimized for managing your schedule. For example, no matter what date you are currently looking at, you can click the **Go to Today** button to snap back to the current date. You can also use the **Day**, **Work Week**, **Week**, and **Month** buttons to change the view.

**146**   Part 6: Working with the Calendar

## 4 See More of the Year

The Calendar view is configurable; you can drag the borders of each pane around to see more or less of each part of the Calendar. By default, you can see two months in the upper-right corner of the display. Drag the **TaskPad** lower, however, and you can see four months at once.

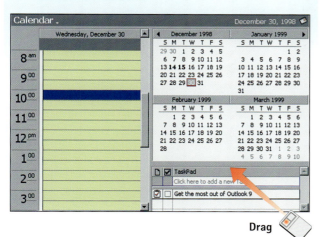

Drag

## 5 View Appointments

The current day's appointments are displayed in the left side of the window. You can use the scrollbar to see appointments earlier or later in the day that don't fit onscreen all at once.

## 6 View Tasks

*Tasks* are unscheduled events of the day that have to occur, but not necessarily at a fixed time. The **TaskPad** displays your tasks; uncompleted tasks "roll over" to the next day.

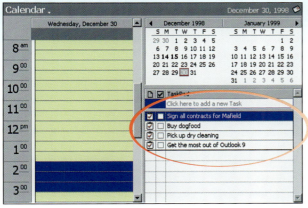

## How-To Hints

### Print the Calendar

Although the Calendar view is great for seeing your day's agenda while you're at the PC, you can also print the Calendar and take it with you when you're on the go. See Task 9 for details on printing the calendar. You can even size the printout to fit popular daily planner notebooks.

*End*

## Task 2

# How to Set an Appointment

To schedule events throughout your day, you have to add appointments to your Outlook calendar. These *appointments* specify where, when, what, and with whom you're doing things throughout the day. An appointment can be as simple as "lunch at noon," or as complicated as a meeting in specific room at a certain time, with a list of other attendees and required action items.

## *Begin*

### *1* Specify a Time Period

Start creating your appointment by dragging a time period in the Calendar view. Just click the start time of your appointment and drag the mouse through the end time. If the meeting lasts for only 30 minutes, just click the appropriate time slot.

### *2* Enter the Appointment

After you specify the duration of the appointment, type the appointment information directly into the appointment box. Press the **Enter** key when you are done.

### *3* Enter Appointment Details

Alternatively, you can enter a lot of details about the appointment. To do so, double-click the time slot in which you want the meeting to begin. This action opens the **Appointment** dialog box.

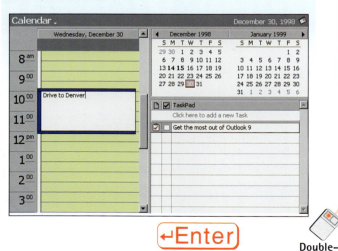

**148**   PART 6: WORKING WITH THE CALENDAR

## 4 The Appointment Dialog Box

The **Appointment** dialog box provides a more comprehensive approach to entering appointment information. You can specify the location and time, enter reminder information, and type freeform notes as well. There's also an **Attendee Availability** tab for inviting others to your meeting (see Task 6).

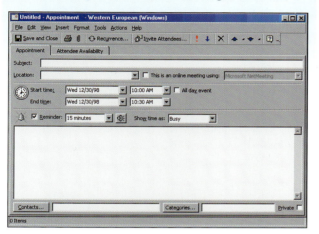

## 5 Enter Appointment Information

Enter the information about the appointment in the **Appointment** dialog box. Make sure that you specify the correct end time for the meeting; enter any additional notes in the **Notes** field. If you want to be reminded about this meeting ahead of time, select the appropriate time from the **Reminder** list box.

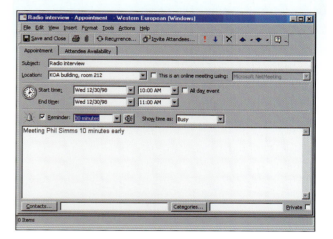

## 6 View Scheduled Meetings

You'll see the scheduled appointment in the Appointment view when you click the **Save and Close** button on the **Appointment** dialog box toolbar. To edit the appointment, double-click the entry.

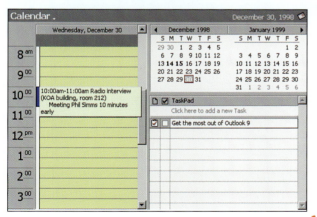

## How-To Hints

### Record Meeting Details

There's nothing worse than not being able to remember what a scheduled meeting is about. One way to jog your memory is to record details in the **Appointment** dialog box's **Notes** field. You can type information there, or you can copy and paste a relevant email message. Even easier, you can drag an email message to the **Calendar** button in the Outlook bar. This action converts the email into a scheduled appointment.

## Task 3

# How to Create a Recurring Appointment

Some meetings, for better or worse, happen over and over and over again. Outlook allows you to mark specific meetings as recurring—that way, you don't have to re-enter the same appointment in each week or month it occurs. Because your regular appointments are already entered, *recurring appointments* make it easy to plan your calendar out for weeks or even months.

## Begin

### 1 Start a Recurring Appointment

To create a recurring appointment, choose **Actions, New Recurring Appointment** from the menu bar in the Calendar view. The **Appointment Recurrence** dialog box opens.

### 2 Specify the Recurrence

The **Appointment Recurrence** dialog box lets you indicate when the meeting actually occurs. Enter the appointment time at the top of the dialog box and then specify a recurrence pattern in that section of the dialog box. Outlook can handle meetings that occur weekly, biweekly, monthly, or just about any other regular pattern you can imagine.

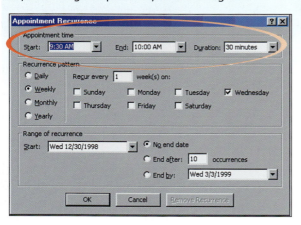

### 3 Specify the Range

In the **Range of Recurrence** section of the dialog box, you can specify that the meetings go on indefinitely; you can otherwise indicate that they terminate at a specific date. After the dialog box is filled out, click the **OK** button.

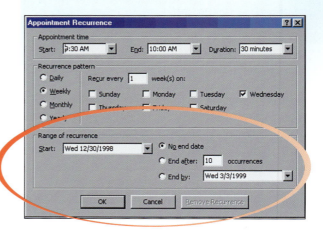

150   Part 6: Working with the Calendar

## 4 Create the Appointment

Now enter the actual appointment details. Specify the meeting subject, location, or any other desired information and click the **Save and Close** button in the toolbar.

Click

## 5 View the Appointment

In the Appointment view, your meeting should appear on all the scheduled dates. You can tell the meeting is a recurring appointment because of the recurring symbol (a pair of revolving arrows) next to the appointment subject.

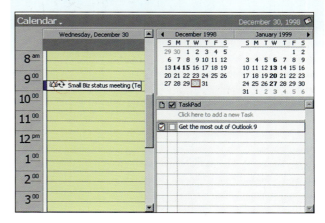

## 6 Edit the Meeting

To change the meeting details, double-click the appointment entry in the Appointment view. The **Open Recurring Item** dialog box appears. Select whether you want to open just the occurrence you selected or to modify all the meetings in this series. Click **OK** to open the **Appointment** dialog box and make your changes.

## How-To Hints

### Making a Single Meeting Recur

If you've already entered a single appointment and later decide to make it a recurring event, double-click the appointment entry in the Appointment view. Click the **Recurrence** button in the **Appointment Recurrence** dialog box's toolbar. You can then turn this meeting into any kind of repeating event you want.

How to Create a Recurring Appointment    151

## Task 4

# How to Make a Task

Not all your daily agenda items have to be scheduled. Simple to-do tasks—"buy bread on the way home," "sort the files today," and "sign the invoices," for instance—are things that can be done at any time. They're just *tasks*. You can use Outlook to list your tasks that await completion. As you complete the tasks, you can cross them off the list just as if they were written on note paper.

## Begin

### 1 Create a New Task

Tasks are displayed in Outlook's **TaskPad**, a small display region under the calendars in the Calendar view. To create a new task, start by clicking the **blank line** at the top of the TaskPad.

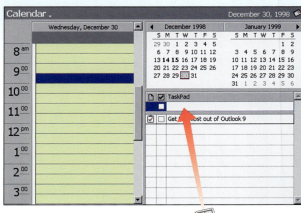

Click

### 2 Name the Task

Type the subject of your new task and press the **Enter** key.

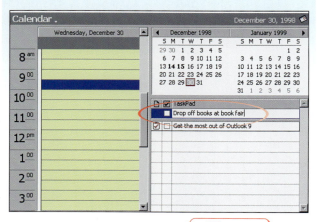

↵Enter

### 3 View Your Tasks

The task appears in the TaskPad task list. When you complete a task, click the **box** to the left of the task to indicate that it is done.

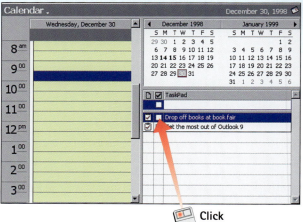

Click

## 4 Enter Task Details

Another way to create a task is to open the **Task** dialog box. Like the **Appointment** dialog box, this dialog box allows you to specify more details for your task. To open the dialog box, double-click any **empty line** in the TaskPad task list.

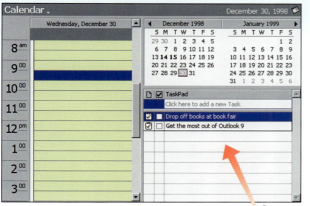

Double-click

## 5 Enter Task Information

When the **Task** dialog box opens, enter the subject and any other information you need—due date, priority, and any notes. You can also request a reminder on a specific date and time.

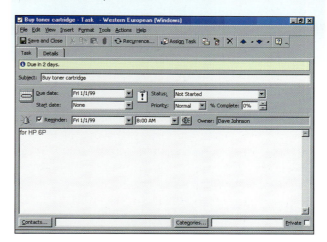

## 6 Save the Task

When you have entered your task information, click the **Save and Close** button in the toolbar. The task appears in the TaskPad task list, just like the others you created using steps 1 and 2.

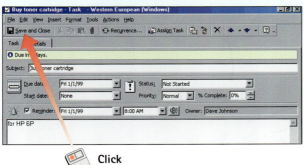

 Click

*End*

## How-To Hints

### Appointment or Task?

Should you make something on your to-do list an appointment or a task? If you have something to do that has no specific scheduled time, make it a task. That gives you a little more scheduling flexibility as your day fills up with meetings and other events. If it's important and it's due on a specific day, consider making it an appointment. Days that have appointments appear in **bold** on the calendar; days with tasks only appear in normal text. If you want to see that next Tuesday includes an important task, schedule it as an appointment.

## Task 5

# How to Create a Day-Long Event

There is one more kind of activity you can schedule in Outlook: the *event*. Events are like appointments, but they are scheduled to take all day. You can mark days with events to indicate holidays, special events (such as a casual day at work), or some other activity you want to be reminded of that is not time specific.

# Begin

## 1 Create a New Event

Events are displayed immediately below the date and date in the Calendar view. To create an event, click the **empty space** above the appointment list.

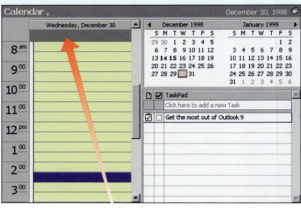

 Click

## 2 Enter the Event

Type the subject of the event and press the **Enter** key.

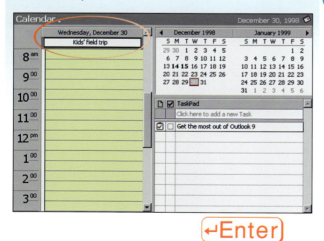

↵Enter

## 3 Start an Event from the Menu Bar

Another way to enter a new event is to use the menu bar. Choose **Actions, New All Day Event** to open the **Event** dialog box.

154  PART 6: WORKING WITH THE CALENDAR

## 4 Enter the Event Details

Enter the information about this event in the **Event** dialog box. Type the subject, location, and any notes. Notice that you can make an event span more than one day by choosing a different end time from the **End Time** list box.

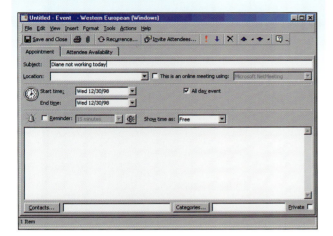

## 5 Save the Event Information

When you are done entering information in the **Event** dialog box, click the **Save and Close** button in the dialog box's toolbar to save the data and display the information in the Calendar view. Events appear at the top of the Appointment pane.

 Click

## 6 View Events

Note that you can have more than one all-day event scheduled for each day. Also note that events do not cause the date to turn bold in the Calendar—only appointments do that.

### Convert Events to Meetings

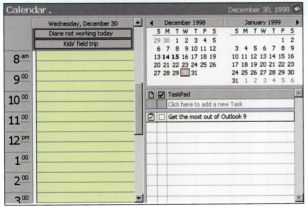

*End*

## How-To Hints

If you need to turn an event into a scheduled appointment, just open the event by double-clicking the entry in the Appointment pane. Click the box to turn off the **All Day Event** option. The **Event** dialog box immediately changes into an **Appointment** dialog box, allowing you to schedule the event at a specific time during the day.

How to Create a Day-Long Event 155

## Task 6

# How to Invite Someone to a Meeting

Appointments needn't be a solitary affair. If you're responding to someone else's meeting request, you probably have little reason to ask others to join you. If you're initiating a meeting, you probably want to invite some people to participate in your event.

If that's the case, you can use Outlook to invite the participants. It's even easier if your invitees also use Outlook: Outlook sends an email invitation to each invitee; the recipient can click to accept, adding his name to your meeting roster automatically. Outlook also updates the recipient's schedule automatically as well, so that he won't forget the appointment.

## Begin

### 1 Create a New Meeting

Start by creating the meeting. To do so, double-click the time at which you want the meeting to start in the Calendar view's Appointment pane.

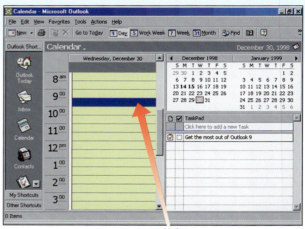

Double-click

### 2 Fill Out Meeting Details

Enter any appropriate meeting details in the **Appointment** dialog box. Make sure that the meeting information includes location and action items—you're inviting others to the meeting. When you're done, click the **Invite Attendees** button to convert the meeting into an email message.

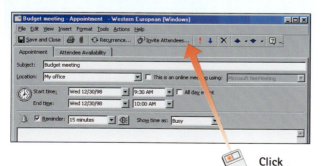

Click

### 3 Add Attendees

The meeting has been converted into a variation of the Outlook email message window. The next step is to invite the meeting participants: Click the **To** button to open the **Select Attendees and Resources** dialog box.

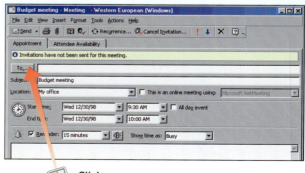

Click

156  Part 6: Working with the Calendar

## 4 Choose the Participants

You may recognize the **Select Attendees and Resources** dialog box; it looks suspiciously like your address book. Double-click a **name** in the left pane to add that person to your recipients list in the right pane (the people you want to invite to the meeting). Click the **OK** button when you have added all the appropriate names.

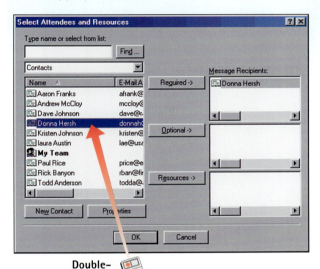

Double-click

## 5 Send the Invitation

When you have finished the meeting invitation—including adding all the appropriate names to the invitation list—click the **Send** button in the dialog box's toolbar. The message is sent to everyone listed in the **To** field.

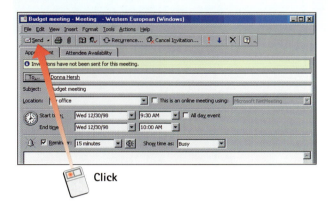

Click

## 6 Respond to Invitations

When the recipients get your message, they only have to click the **Accept** button in the message's toolbar. This action places the meeting in their own Outlook Calendar view and updates your meeting entry with their positive response. Of course, they may opt to tentatively accept the invitation or to decline by clicking the appropriate button. They can click the **Calendar** button to display their schedule and see whether there's a conflict. (Outlook also warns recipients if they try to double-book their time.)

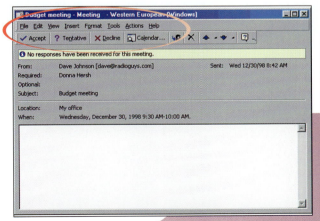

## How-To Hints

### Take a Poll with Outlook

Have you ever wanted to take a quick poll of your co-workers? You can use Outlook to ask your office members a simple yes or no question, such as "Who wants to go to the basketball game Tuesday?" or "Who wants to buy popcorn?" Just create an appointment and invite the office members, but make the poll question the meeting's subject. Those who accept the invitation agree; those who decline do not. Outlook displays all those who accept (or answer yes) in your appointment entry!

*End*

## TASK 7

# How to Delegate a Task

Not every task is something you need to personally accomplish yourself. Many tasks, especially in an office environment, can be delegated to others. When you delegate a task, Outlook lets you choose the recipient and get status reports from the delegate as he works toward accomplishing the project. All this is accomplished through email, much as appointment invitations are (see the preceding task, "How to Invite Someone to a Meeting").

## Begin

### 1 Create a Task

Start the process by creating a task: Click in the **TaskPad** and type the subject of the task you want to delegate. When you're done, press the **Enter** key.

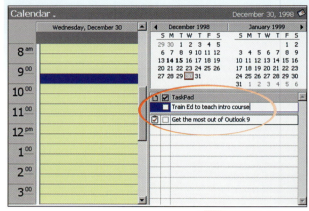

### 2 Open the Task Dialog Box

After you create the task, double-click the task entry in the **TaskPad** list. The **Task** dialog box opens.

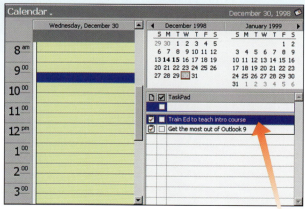

Double-click

### 3 Assign the Task

The **Task** dialog box displays the task details. To assign the task to someone else, click the **Assign Task** button in the dialog box's toolbar.

Click

158   PART 6: WORKING WITH THE CALENDAR

## 4 Choose the Recipient

The **Task** dialog box is converted into an email message window. Indicate who is being assigned to the task by clicking the **To** box to choose from your address book entries.

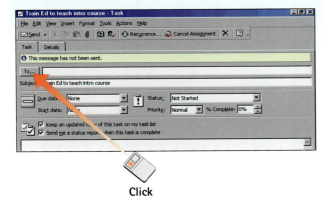

Click

## 5 Pick the Task Recipient

The **Select Task Recipient** dialog box opens, listing the names of everyone in your address book. Double-click the name of the person to whom you want to send the task. That name appears in the **Message Recipients** list on the right. Click the **OK** button when you are done.

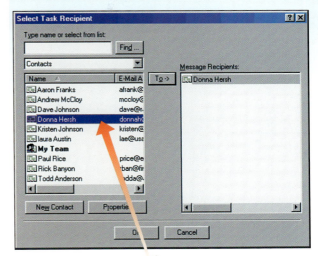

Double-click

## 6 Send the Task

When you're finished with the task, click the **Send** button in the message window's toolbar to forward the task delegation to the intended recipient. That person receives an email message with the task delegation; he can then accept or decline the task the same way he can a meeting invitation.

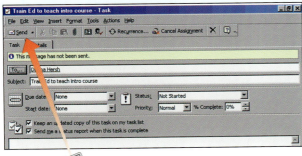

 Click

*End*

## How-To Hints

### Track Your Task Status

Don't let your boss accuse you of slouching off on your task assignments—you can report progress on delegated tasks. Just open the task by double-clicking it; change the task status in the **% Complete** list box and click the **Send Status Report** button in the **Task** dialog box's toolbar.

How to Delegate a Task    **159**

# Task 8

## How to Change a Scheduled Appointment

After you enter appointments, you may occasionally have to change their details. If your meeting time is adjusted or the location changes, for example, it's easy to make the necessary changes.

## Begin

### 1 Edit the Meeting Details

To change appointment details—such as the location, invitees, and so on—start by double-clicking the entry in the **Appointment** pane.

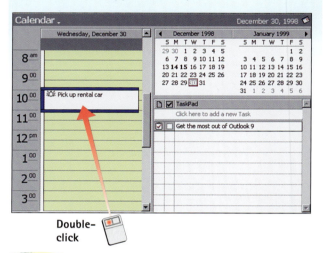

### 2 Change the Meeting

The **Appointment** dialog box should be familiar to you. Make any necessary changes to the information in this dialog box and click the **Save and Close** button in the dialog box's toolbar to save the new data.

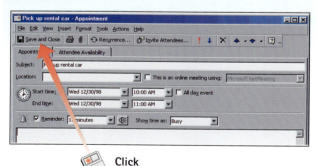

### 3 Change the Duration

It's easy to change the duration of an appointment without opening the **Appointment** dialog box. Just position the mouse pointer on the border of the appointment entry in the Appointment pane. The mouse pointer changes to a two-headed arrow. Click and drag the task edge until it conforms to the new duration.

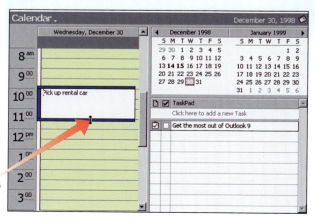

160  PART 6: WORKING WITH THE CALENDAR

## 4 Change the Start Time

You can easily move a meeting to a new time. Move the mouse pointer over the left border of the appointment entry in the Appointment pane. The pointer changes to a four-headed arrow. Click and drag the appointment up or down to the new start time.

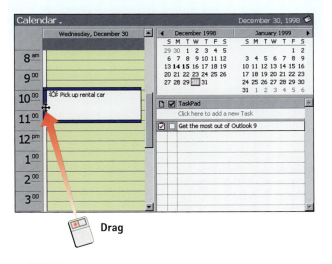

Drag

## 5 Change the Subject

If you want to change the subject of your appointment, don't bother opening the **Appointment** dialog box. Just click the appointment entry in the Appointment pane and type any necessary information or corrections. Press the **Enter** key when you are done.

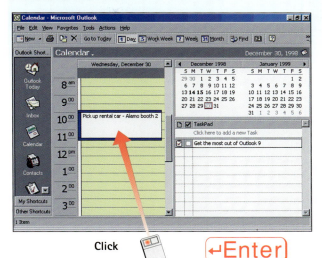

Click   ↵Enter

## 6 Delete an Appointment

If you have to delete an upcoming appointment from your calendar, just click the border to select the appointment. Then press the **Delete** key to remove it.

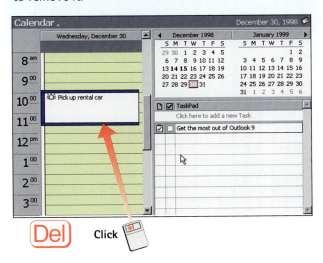

Del   Click

## How-To Hints

### Move a Meeting to a New Day

You can move your meeting to a new day without opening the **Appointment** dialog box. Just click the left border of the appointment (the mouse pointer changes to a four-headed arrow) and drag to a new date in the calendar on the right side of the **Calendar** view. The meeting is automatically rescheduled for the same time on the new day.

*End*

HOW TO CHANGE A SCHEDULED APPOINTMENT  161

## Task 9

# How to Print the Calendar

Microsoft understands that as great as Outlook is, you can't stay chained to your desk all day reading your Calendar. You have to leave your desk at times, but you still need access to your day's agenda. It's easy to print your Calendar in Outlook, and you can even make the printout compatible with many popular daily organizer books.

## Begin

### 1 Quick-Print the Calendar

The fastest way to print your Calendar is to click the **Print** button in the Calendar view's toolbar. This action opens the **Print** dialog box, which is discussed in step 4.

 Click

### 2 See the Print Preview

If you want to see what the Calendar will look like when printed, choose **File, Print Preview** from the menu bar. The **Print Preview** dialog box appears, showing you exactly what is about to be printed. If you approve, click the **Print** button to proceed.

### 3 Open the Print Dialog Box

Numerous options are available for printing your Calendar. Start in the Calendar view and choose **File, Print** from the menu bar. The **Print** dialog box appears.

## 4 Select the Print Style

Select the appearance of your paper calendar from the **Print Style** list box. If you want to double-check the paper's actual appearance, click the **Preview** button after making a selection. If you want to print on a special size paper (to fit in a daily planner book, for instance), select the paper type by clicking the **Page Setup** button.

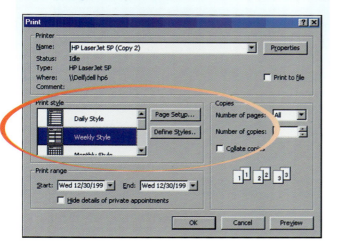

## 5 Select the Range

The default timescale for your printout is determined by the print style you choose: The Daily Style prints just one day, while the Weekly Style prints a week. You can modify that default range, however, by changing the **Start** and **End** list boxes in the **Print Range** section.

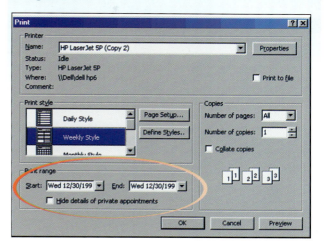

## 6 Print the Calendar

When you are ready to print, click the **OK** button in the **Print** dialog box. The **Printing** dialog box appears momentarily, and the printer does its thing.

## How-To Hints

### Customize Print Styles

If you often print the same kind of calendar page and find yourself always modifying the paper type or some other option, create your own style. On the **Print** dialog box, and click the **Define Styles** button. Double-click the style you want to modify and make your changes. You can also select your favorite style and click the **Copy** button; that allows you to change its options under a different name without changing the original style at all.

# Task 10

## How to Share a Calendar

If you are self-employed and work alone, you may not care about Calendar sharing. Just about everyone else, however, should be keenly interested in this capability. Outlook lets you make your Calendar available to others in their own copies of Outlook. If you share your calendar, co-workers can view your schedule and, if you give them permission, make changes that are automatically updated in your copy of the program.

## Begin

### 1 Enable Calendar Sharing

To give others access to your Calendar data, start by choosing **File, Share, Calendar** from the menu bar. The **Net Folder Wizard** opens to help you set up your Calendar for sharing.

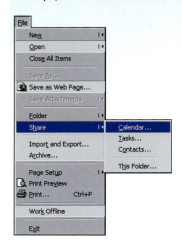

### 2 Start the Wizard

The **Net Folder Wizard** walks you through the process of sharing your Calendar with others. To continue, click the **Next** button.

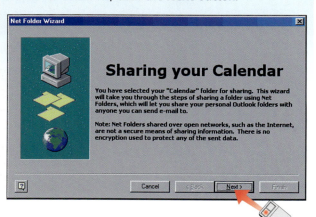

Click

### 3 Create Your Sharing List

You can share your Calendar with one other person or with an army of co-workers. No one has to be physically connected to the same local area network, either, because Outlook keeps everyone connected via email messages. Click the **Add** button to choose names.

Click

**164** Part 6: Working with the Calendar

## 4 Choose Whom to Share With

The **Add Entries to Subscriber Database** dialog box appears. Double-click names in the left pane to add them to the database list in the right pane. When you are done adding names, click the **OK** button.

Double-click

## 5 Change Permissions

Outlook provides a number of choices when it comes to how much control others have over your Calendar data. To inspect—and change, if necessary—the permission levels, select the member you want to work with and click the **Permissions** button.

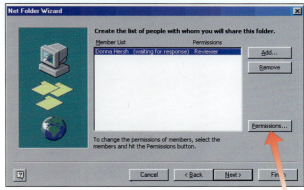

Click

## 6 Set Permissions

Click the option for the level of control you want this person to have over your calendar. A **Reviewer**, for example, can read your Calendar but cannot change it. A **Contributor** can add appointments and tasks, and an **Author** can also delete items he or she adds. An **Editor** can add, change, and delete anything in your Calendar. When you are done, click the **OK** button.

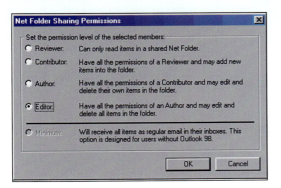

## 7 Invite Subscribers

When you complete the wizard, Outlook sends email messages to the people you added to your subscriber database. If they agree to working with your Calendar by clicking the **Accept** button, Outlook synchronizes their copies of Outlook with yours.

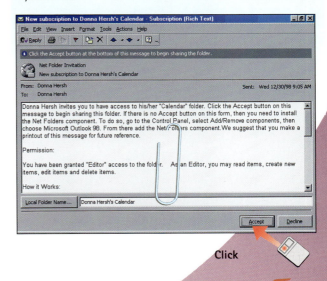

Click

*End*

HOW TO SHARE A CALENDAR  **165**

## Task 11

# How to Publish Your Calendar to the Web

Calendar sharing is a great way to let your co-workers know what's going on in your schedule, but Outlook has even more Calendar publishing tools under the hood. What if you are on the road without a laptop and have to check your Calendar? If you've published your Calendar on the Internet as a Web page, all you have to do is surf to the proper page on someone else's PC; you can get an instant schedule update from there. Combine Calendar sharing with Web publishing, and you can always stay on top of your appointments.

## Begin

### 1 Save as a Web Page

Saving your Calendar as a Web page is very easy. Make sure that you are in the Calendar view and choose **File, Save as Web Page** to get started.

### 2 Set Web Page Options

The **Save as Web Page** dialog box lets you fine-tune your Calendar page. Specify the dates in the **Duration** section and check the option for **Include Appointment Details** if you want to see more than just the appointment subject line on the page.

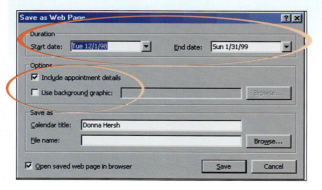

### 3 Name Your Web Page

You have to give your Web page a name. Click the **Browse** button to open the **Calendar File Name** dialog box, which you use to specify where and with what name you want to save the page.

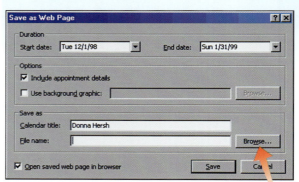

Click

**166**   PART 6: WORKING WITH THE CALENDAR

## 4 Choose the Location

Specify the location and name of your Calendar file. If your office has a *staging server* where you can place files to be posted automatically to the Internet, save it there. Otherwise, you may have to manually place the Calendar on the Web server using FTP software.

## 5 Save the Web Page

When you are ready to create your Calendar Web page, click the **Save** button. If you selected the **Open Saved Web Page in Browser** option, your browser opens and shows you the completed page.

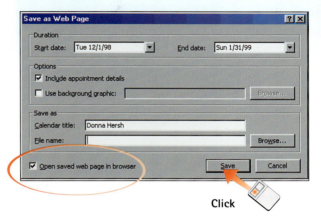

Click

## 6 View the Page on the Web

After your Web page has been published to the Internet, you can retrieve your schedule from any Internet-compatible PC anywhere in the world. Click the **yellow arrow** under an appointment in the Calendar view to see more information about that meeting on the right side of the display.

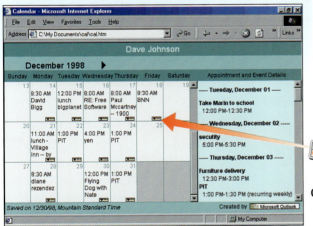

Click

## How-To Hints

### Calendar Isn't Automatic

Unlike some personal information managers, Outlook can't keep your Web page constantly updated, so you should ask someone to do that for you if your schedule changes while you're on the road. Another alternative is to use a macro program that has been trained to save your Calendar as a Web page and automatically post it to the Internet on a regular basis.

HOW TO PUBLISH YOUR CALENDAR TO THE WEB

# Task

1. How to Create a Note  170
2. How to Convert Notes into Email and Back Again  172
3. How to Modify the Look of a Note  174
4. How to Organize Your Notes  176
5. How to Turn On the Journal  178
6. How to Find Your Way Around the Journal  180
7. How to View Journal Entries  182
8. How to View the Journal in Contacts  184
9. How to Track Your Activities  186

## PART 7

# Managing Your Day with Notes and the Journal

Outlook does a lot of things to simplify the way you collect and use information during the day. *But*, as they say on television, *there's more!* You can take freeform notes, for example, and store them in files that look just like Post-It notes.

Outlook's Journal makes it possible for you to track your work activities and to easily find details about your day . If you bill clients by the hour, for instance, you can use the Journal to document how long you worked on specific projects. You can also locate all the times you corresponded with a specific person—using either email or telephone—on a certain day. The Journal is the most intimidating aspect of Outlook, but it can be a rewarding tool if you need its capabilities.

The tasks in this part of the book show you everything you need to know to make the most of both Notes and the Journal.

## Task 1

# How to Create a Note

If you're like most people, you have those ubiquitous yellow sticky notes tacked up all over your desk, computer monitor, cubicle wall, and even perhaps on the family dog. Outlook offers you a more flexible and environmentally sound alternative: the Notes view. Here, you can create freeform notes that look just like sticky notes, but are electronic and are thus easier to manage than a stack of paper.

## Begin

### 1 Switch to Notes

To see your notes, you need to switch to the Notes view. You can click the **Notes** button in the Outlook bar from any view.

Click

### 2 Welcome to the Notes View

The Notes view is one of the simplest views in Outlook. Think of this view as a sort of electronic bulletin board with all your random thoughts, notes, and messages-to-self tacked up in a freeform manner.

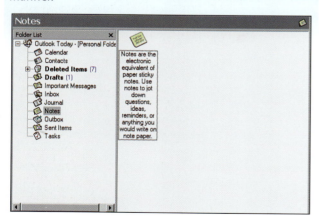

### 3 Create a New Note

To create a new note, double-click any open space in the Notes view's right pane. A blank note appears, ready for you to type into it.

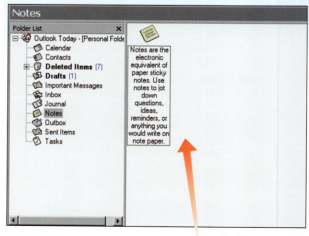

Double-click

**170** Part 7: Managing Your Day with Notes and the Journal

## 4 Use the Blank Note

When the new blank note appears, you can just start typing. Notice that the note is *time stamped* to indicate when it was created.

## 5 Type Your Note

Create your note. You can type as much as you like, but notes don't allow for any fancy formatting. When you're done, click the close box (the **X**) in the upper-right corner of the box. Notes are automatically saved when closed.

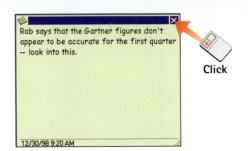

Click

## 6 View the Note in Outlook

After you close your note, it appears in the Notes view. You can read any note's full text just by double-clicking the icon.

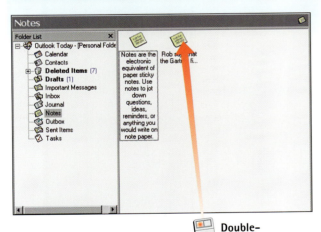

Double-click

---

# How-To Hints

## Take Notes on the Phone

I love the Notes view because it allows me to make freeform notes when I'm in a hurry to record my thoughts—when I'm on the phone, for instance. Before Outlook, I took notes throughout the day on different pieces of scrap paper, many of which would inevitably disappear by the time I needed them days later. Now they're all in the Notes view.

# Task 2

## How to Convert Notes into Email and Back Again

Once you start using the Notes view, you'll quickly get hooked. It's hard to turn a yellow Post-It note on your desk into an email message—it's easy to do if the note is already in Outlook in electronic form. Likewise, you can take an email with important information and convert it to a note, where it can easily be found later.

## Begin

### 1 Convert Email to Note

If you want to discard a message in the Inbox but want to preserve some important information from the email, you can convert it to a note. Select the message and drag it to the **Notes** button in the Outlook bar. The email is a note when you release the mouse button.

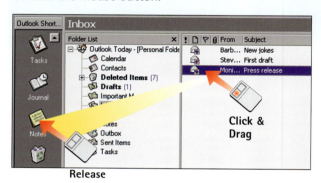

### 2 View the Note

Outlook displays the Note window as soon as the email is converted to a note. Take this opportunity to delete any irrelevant information and then click the **Close** button on the Note window.

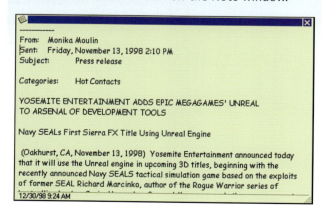

### 3 Switch to the Notes View

Click the **Notes** button in the Outlook bar to see the note you just created from the email message. You can double-click the note to open it.

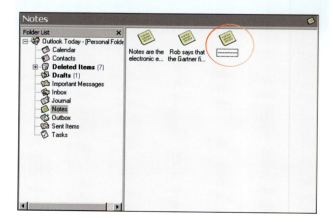

172  PART 7: MANAGING YOUR DAY WITH NOTES AND THE JOURNAL

## 4 Convert a Note to Email

You can go the other way, too: If you wrote a note that you later decide someone else should see, you can convert the note to an email message. Drag the note from the Notes view to the Inbox button in the Outlook bar.

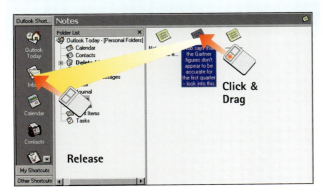

## 5 Edit the Email

After you drop the note in the Inbox, Outlook copies the note into a new message window. You can make changes or additions to the body of the message.

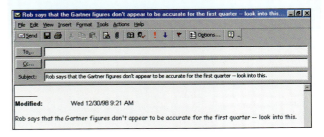

## 6 Send the Email Message

Enter an address for the message and click the **Send** button in the message window's toolbar; the message is sent. Note that this process doesn't remove the note from the Notes view; it simply makes a copy of the note's contents.

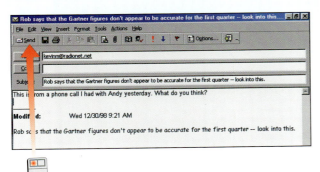

*End*

## How-To Hints

### Naming the Note

You can't exactly give your notes a subject line, but the text that appears under the icon in the Notes view is text taken from the note's beginning. You may want to start your name with whatever text you want visible in the Notes view.

TASK 3

# How to Modify the Look of a Note

Like most views in Outlook, the Notes view is configurable. You can modify its appearance to make things easier to find or for simply aesthetic reasons. You can move notes around, change their color, and even display them in a list format.

## Begin

### 1 Change the Note Icon

You can display your notes with large icons, small icons, or in a list. The large icons are great most of the time, but you may want to experiment with the other view modes. They are all accessed from the toolbar in the Notes view.

### 2 Display Notes as a List

If you want to see all your notes in a list, click the **List** button in the toolbar. Notes are arranged alphabetically; the icons are small so that you can display lots of notes at once. To switch back to the default view, click the **Large Icons** button in the toolbar.

Click

### 3 Change the Note Color

Although notes default to a standard yellow icon and background color, you have five color choices. You can categorize your notes by color or display them all in the same shade. To get to the color menu, right-click a **note icon** to display a menu.

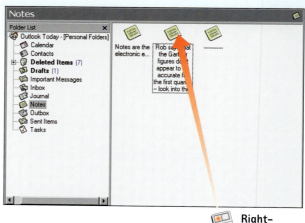

Right-click

174   PART 7: MANAGING YOUR DAY WITH NOTES AND THE JOURNAL

## 4 Choose a Note Color

To change the color of the note, choose **Color** from the menu and select the color you want: **Blue**, **Green**, **Pink**, **Yellow**, or **White**.

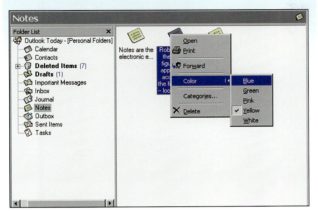

## 5 Move Notes Around

Don't like where your notes are displayed? You can move them around in both in the Large Icons and Small Icons views. Just click and drag the note where you want it to appear.

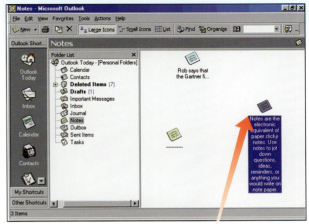

 Click & Drag

## 6 Change the Current View

You have several other ways to view notes. To access these options, select **View, Current View**. One of the most useful views is the Notes List, which shows the first few lines of each note, not unlike the Inbox's AutoPreview mode.

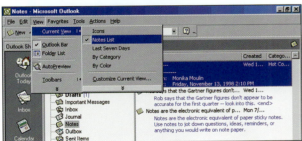

 *End*

### How-To Hints

#### Permanently Changed Color

If you want your notes to always appear in a specific color, you can tell Outlook to generate new notes in that color. Open the **Options** dialog box by choosing **Tools**, **Options** and then clicking the **Notes Options** button on the **Preferences** tab. Select the color you like and save your changes.

How to Modify the Look of a Note  **175**

# Task 4

## How to Organize Your Notes

If you have just a few notes in the Notes view, you can probably find just about everything you need without much trouble. In fact, all the notes may fit onscreen at once. As you collect more and more notes—and as the Notes view becomes increasingly cluttered—you'll pine for organization tools. Luckily, the Organize pane (last seen in the Inbox and Contacts views) also has a role in the Notes view.

## Begin

### 1 Open the Organize Pane

To add a sense of structure and organization to your Notes view, you must first open the Organize pane. Do that by clicking the **Organize** button in the toolbar.

Click

### 2 Move Notes to Folders

Just as you can with email and contacts, you can use the Organize pane's **Using Folders** tab to move messages to other folders. If you select a note and move the note to the Inbox folder, the note is converted into an email message, just as you saw in Part 7, Task 2.

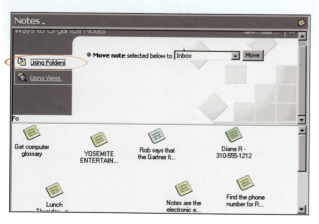

### 3 Change the Notes View

Click the **Using Views** tab to see options for changing the way the Notes view appears. There are five view modes. Click a view; the display automatically changes to reflect your selection.

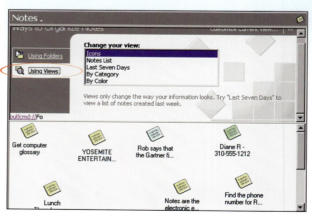

176  PART 7: MANAGING YOUR DAY WITH NOTES AND THE JOURNAL

## 4 Choose the Notes List

Notes List is a good all-around way to work in the Notes view because it shows you the note contents (not unlike AutoPreview mode in the Inbox). Click the **Notes List** option in the **Change Your View** list box to select it. To revert to the default view, click **Icons**.

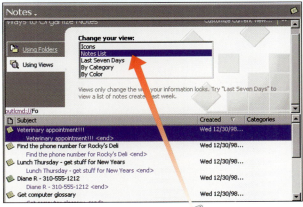

 Click

## 5 Find a Specific Note

Are you looking for a note and remember only a word or phrase from somewhere in it? You need the Find Items pane. Click the **Find** button in the toolbar to open it.

Click

## 6 Searching for a Note

When the Find Items pane opens, type the search word or phrase in the **Look For** field and click the **Find Now** button. The matching notes are displayed in Notes List format at the bottom of the screen.

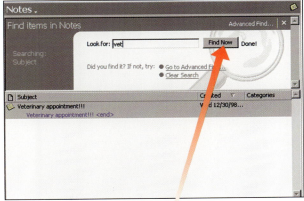

Click

*End*

## How-To Hints

### Other Organization Tools

If you really like to experiment and customize, you should know that there are a wealth of other tools hiding under the right mouse button. Just right-click any unoccupied space in the Notes view to see a menu of additional easy-to-use search and filter tools.

### Experiment with the Mouse

I always recommend that new users experiment with the right mouse button. Click everything and anything with the right mouse button to see what options are available in the inevitable pop-up context menu. Microsoft built Windows and Office with the right mouse button in mind, so there are lots of things you can accomplish easily just by right-clicking.

## Task 5

# How to Turn On the Journal

The Journal is a sophisticated tracking and logging system that allows Outlook to keep track of how you work—automatically and in the background. It can log all your phone calls, email messages, appointments, and the time spent working in Office applications such as Word and Excel.

The Journal is turned off by default when you install Outlook. It's turned off because the Journal is a memory and hard-disk hog and because most users don't really need it. If you have to track your activities on the computer, however, the Journal is a powerful and easy way to do it.

## Begin

### 1 Switch to the Journal

You can switch to the Journal view from anywhere in Outlook by clicking the **Journal** button in the Outlook bar.

### 2 Activate the Journal

If the Journal has not yet been turned on, Outlook displays a dialog box asking whether you want to turn the Journal on. Most of the Journal's tracking features are available without actually turning on the Journal. Answer **Yes** only if you want to track the time you spend on Microsoft Office documents created in applications such as Word and Excel.

### 3 Set Journal Options

If you clicked **Yes**, Outlook displays the **Journal Options** dialog box. Here you can specify what the Journal should track. Click the check boxes for any options you want Outlook to record for later reference.

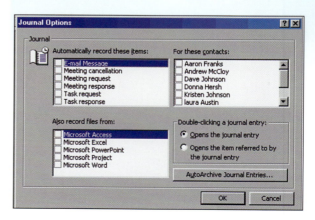

178  PART 7: MANAGING YOUR DAY WITH NOTES AND THE JOURNAL

## 4 Save the Journal Options

After you configure the Journal to record your activities, click the **OK** button to save your options. Outlook displays the Journal view.

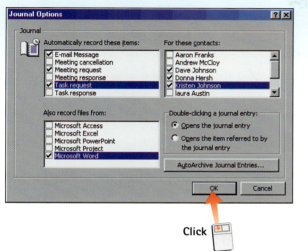

Click

## 5 Welcome to the Journal

By default, the Journal view displays your activities in a timeline format, which you can scroll along in order to look for activities on specific days—and minute-by-minute within each day. You can find an email you sent by looking at a particular day's time, or you can prepare an account to a client for the amount of time you worked on a document in the month of February.

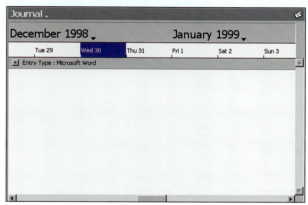

*End*

# How-To Hints

### Use Contacts Instead

Microsoft encourages you to use the Contacts view to find Journal information instead of using the Journal itself to find that information. Why? The Journal slows down Outlook and uses a lot of disk space. You can use the Contacts view to see almost everything the Journal can report (with the exception of document usage, such as how long you worked on a given Word file). Consider whether you really need the Journal before you turn it on.

### How to Turn the Journal Off

If you decide that you don't want the Journal to hog your system's resources, you can turn its tracking capabilities off. Select **Tools, Options** from the menu bar; select the **Preferences** tab from the Options dialog box and click the **Journal Options** button. Clear the check boxes for all the contacts and click **OK** to close the dialog boxes.

TASK 6

# How to Find Your Way Around the Journal

The Journal uses a clever timeline interface to help you locate and view documents, messages, and other kinds of events you have worked on in the past. Your work day is an open book with the Journal—a good thing if you're in a line of work where tracking your time is necessary.

## *Begin*

### *1* Switch to the Journal

Switch to the Journal view from by clicking the **Journal** button in the Outlook bar.

### *2* View Events in the Journal

Depending on the kinds of records you told Outlook to track while you worked (see the preceding task), you'll have different entry types in the timeline. The entries are hidden from view until you click the **plus sign** that's next to an entry type header. Hide the entries by clicking the **minus sign**.

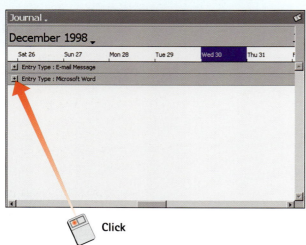

### *3* Scroll to Find Entries

If you've recently worked on the kind of records shown in the display (in this example, email and Word documents), you'll see some entries in the display as soon as you click the **plus signs**. If not, scroll left to see entries you made in the past. Remember that the Journal keeps no record of activity until you turn it on (see the preceding task).

## 4 Change the Zoom Factor

The default view in the Journal is Week, which shows a time period nearly that long simultaneously on the display. You can change the view using the buttons on the toolbar to see more or less on the screen at once.

## 5 Select the Day View

Click the **Day** button in the toolbar to zoom to a single day. In this view, you can see approximately one eight-hour workday onscreen. You can see more precisely when you performed specific activities.

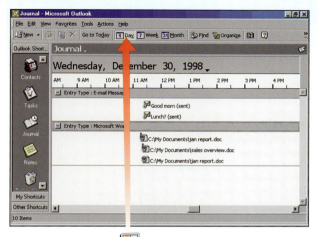

Click

## 6 Change the View

You're not stuck with the timeline view. Click the **Organize** button in the toolbar and then select the **Using Views** tab. From here, you can change the view dramatically. Click the **Entry List** option in the **Change Your View** list box to see Journal entries listed chronologically in a table format.

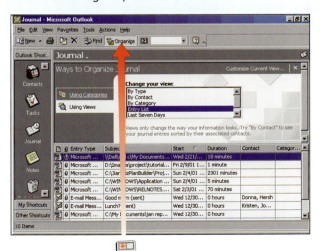

Click

*End*

### Don't Trust the Numbers

In the 1960s, the watchword was "Don't trust anyone over 30." In the Journal, it's "Don't trust the hours Outlook says you worked." Remember that Outlook doesn't know how long you actually *typed* into a Word document, it simply knows how long the document *was loaded* in Word. For all Outlook knows, you worked on the document constantly—or you loaded the document and played Space Invaders all afternoon. Be careful about how literally you accept the work hours Outlook reports.

HOW TO FIND YOUR WAY AROUND THE JOURNAL  **181**

## Task 7

# How to View Journal Entries

Sure, it's great that the Journal can track your activities—but it can do more than that, too. You can open the entries in the Journal view and see notes about an event or open the document in question itself. How you use the Journal depends on what you're trying to learn when you look up an entry.

## Begin

### 1 Locate the Journal Entry

Switch to the Journal view and locate the entry you want to open. Use the scrollbar to move through the Journal. Click the **minus sign** for any entry type you aren't interested in order to free some onscreen real estate.

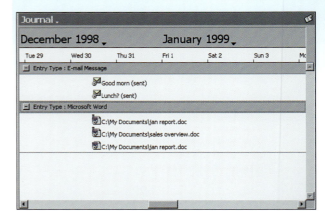

### 2 Open the Journal Entry

When you find the Journal entry you want to see, right-click the entry and choose **Open Journal Entry** from the menu.

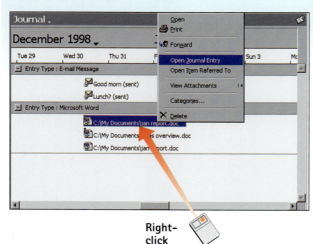

Right-click

### 3 View the Journal Entry

The **Journal Entry** dialog box appears with information about the event. If it's a document entry, you can see the total time the document was open, along with the document's filename and location. You can open the document by double-clicking the **shortcut icon**, or you can type notes and save them as part of the entry by clicking the **Save and Close** button in the toolbar.

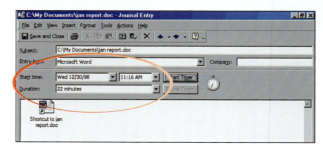

182    PART 7: MANAGING YOUR DAY WITH NOTES AND THE JOURNAL

## 4 Open the Journal Item

If you're interested in opening the document itself—and not the Journal entry—right-click the entry and choose **Open Item Referred To** from the menu.

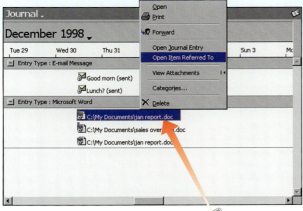

Right-click

## 5 Open the Document

Outlook displays the **Opening Mail Attachment** dialog box if you're trying to open an Office document (such as a Word or Excel file). It offers the opportunity to open or save the attachment. Select the **Open It** option and click the **OK** button to see the document.

## 6 Finding a Specific Entry

The timeline is often a handy way to find documents and events, but sometimes it isn't enough. To look for an entry by keyword, click the **Find** button in the toolbar and enter the search word or phrase in the **Look For** field. Click the **Find Now** button; the results appear at the bottom of the display.

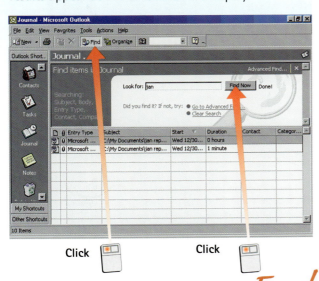

Click          Click

*End*

## How-To Hints

### Search the Contacts View

If you know that you have to find a document or email message associated with a specific contact, it may be easier to look for the document in the **Activities** tab of the appropriate **Contact** dialog box. See the next task, "How to View the Journal in Contacts," for details.

TASK 8

# How to View the Journal in Contacts

Most Journal activities are actually associated with other contacts in your address book. For example, you send email messages and make phone calls to your contacts. In those situations, it's often easier to search for Journal entries in the Contacts view than in the Journal view. Even if you never turned the Journal on, you can still perform these kinds of searches from the Contacts view.

## *Begin*

### *1* Open the Contact

If you have to find an email message or some other kind of Journal entry for a specific person, switch to the Contacts view and double-click the appropriate contact entry.

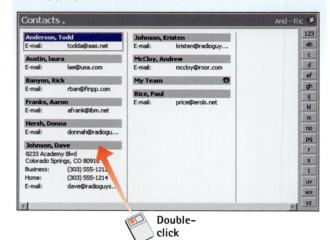

Double-click

### *2* Open the Activities Tab

Click the **Activities** tab when the **Contact** dialog box opens for the individual you selected in step 1. This is the place where all the Journal data is stored for each contact.

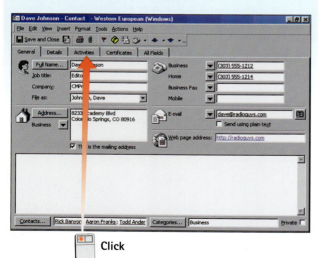

Click

### *3* Welcome to Activities

The **Activities** tab lists all the related entries for this contact. It stores email messages, phone calls, other contacts, appointments, and tasks that the contact has been involved with.

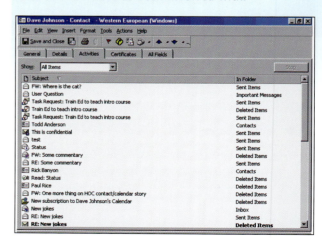

PART 7: MANAGING YOUR DAY WITH NOTES AND THE JOURNAL

## 4 Filter the Activities

You may be staring at dozens or hundreds of entries—a lot to wade through. Click the **arrow** next to the **Show** list box and then select the type of entry you are looking for. In this case, you can see that there are only a few email messages amid all the other activity entries.

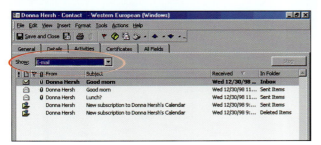

## 5 Show Calendar Entries

Click the **arrow** next to the **Show** list box and choose **Upcoming Tasks/Appointments**. This filter divides the display into two areas so that you can see all the appointments and tasks at the same time. When you find the entry you are looking for, double-click it.

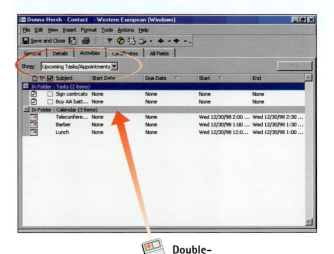

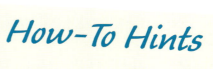
Double-click

## 6 Open the Journal Entry

Outlook immediately opens a double-clicked entry (in this case, an **Appointment** dialog box).

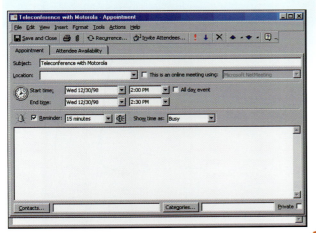

*End*

## How-To Hints

### Sort the Activities Tab

Trying to find a specific entry can sometimes be like locating a particular needle in a stack of needles. To ease the search, use Outlook's sorting tools. As entries appear in the **Activities** tab, click the **Sort by Icon** column header to arrange entries by the kind of record—email, Word document, and so on. Click **Start** to sort by date; click **Subject** to sort by the document subject.

## Task 9

# How to Track Your Activities

The Journal is only as good as the way you configure it. In other words, you may want to track all your interaction with Microsoft Word documents, but Outlook never records any Word sessions at all unless you turn that feature on. You may want to occasionally review your Journal settings and modify them so that they better reflect the way you're currently using the program.

## Begin

### 1 Review Your Needs

Take a look at what the Journal is reporting. Does it capture the kind of records you need in order to track your time or your activities? If not, open the Journal options and change them.

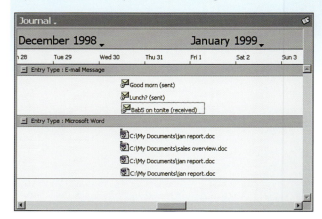

### 2 Open the Options Dialog Box

Choose **Tools, Options** from the toolbar to modify the Journal settings.

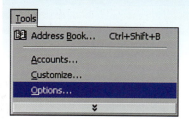

### 3 Open the Journal Options

Click the **Journal Options** button, which is in the **Options** dialog box. This opens the **Journal Options** dialog box, where you'll make the necessary changes to your Journal settings.

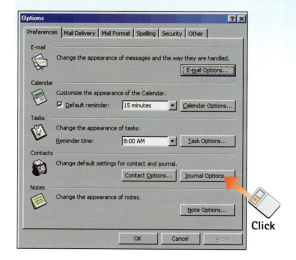

186 Part 7: Managing Your Day with Notes and the Journal

## 4 Select Items and Contacts

Select the check box for each item you want Outlook to record data for, such as email messages, meetings, and tasks. Also decide which contacts you want to track—this is definitely a category you should revisit occasionally as you add new contacts to your address book.

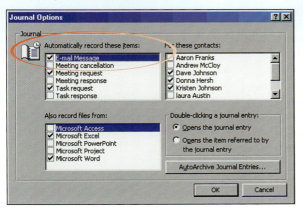

## 5 Select Applications

Also select the check box for any program for which you want to track document usage. Outlook can monitor any Office application you have installed, including Word, Excel, or PowerPoint.

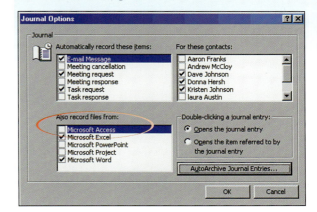

## 6 Configure the Archive

The Journal uses a lot of disk space, so it's a good idea to relegate older entries to the *archive* (a compressed file that takes up less space on your hard disk). In the **Journal Options** dialog box, click the **AutoArchive Journal Entries** button. On the **AutoArchive tab** of the **Journal Properties** dialog box, specify how often Outlook should archive your data. Three to four months is a good value, depending on how often you access very old entries.

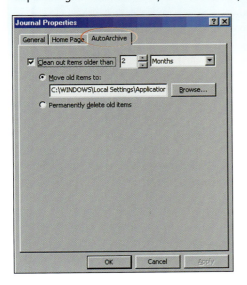

## How-To Hints

### Archiving Your Data

After using Outlook for a year or so, you'll probably find that you've developed quite a collection of email messages and other data. All that takes up a lot of room. A modest Outlook data file can exceed 100MB! To control the growth of Outlook on your hard disk, be sure to activate the AutoArchive tool (explained in Part 10, Task 8, "How to Archive Old Mail").

*End*

**How to Track Your Activities**  187

## Task

1. How to Create a Rule  190

2. How to Disable a Rule  192

3. How to Create an Autoresponder  194

4. How to Create a Rule That Moves Mail  196

5. How to Create a Rule That Assigns Messages to Categories  198

6. How to Avoid Junk Mail Without Reading It  200

# PART 8

# Automating Your Email

As much fun as email can be, you might sometimes wish that it just took care of itself. Well, it can to some degree. Using Outlook's array of *rules*, you can easily "program" Outlook to deal with certain kinds of email in a certain way without your constant direct input.

What does that mean? Consider junk mail: Outlook can move mail that looks like junk to a special folder, which you can review and delete at your leisure. If you're out of town, you can tell Outlook to respond to all mail in your absence with a special "out of town" message. You can even move all messages from a specific person to a special category or folder. It's up to you.

No matter what your needs are, you can almost certainly find a way to use Outlook's rules. The tasks in this part of the book teach you how to create and use rules.

# Task 1

## How to Create a Rule

Did you ever wish your holiday greeting cards could mail themselves? That's an advantage to email—you can automate some tasks, saving time and effort. Outlook uses a library of *rules* to decide how to process mail messages. You can program Outlook to reply to mail with an automated response, to file mail from certain people in a specific way, or to discard specific kinds of messages unopened.

Creating a rule isn't like programming a computer. Outlook provides a wizard that steps you though the process. In this task, you create a simple rule that prints each email as it arrives in your Inbox.

## Begin

### 1 Open the Rules Wizard

Open the **Rules Wizard** by choosing **Tools**, **Rules Wizard**.

### 2 Create a New Rule

The **Rules Wizard** displays all the rules you've already created and lets you generate new ones. To start your first rule, click the **New** button.

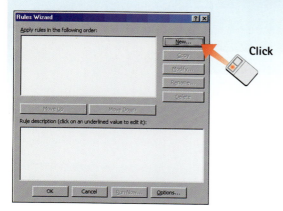

Click

### 3 Choose a Rule

Outlook's Office Assistant may offer additional help the first time you open the **Rules Wizard**. If you want, click **Yes, Please Provide Help**. You can disable the option later, after you're used to the wizard. Click **Check Messages When They Arrive**. This option tells Outlook to act on each message as it is received in the Inbox. Click the **Next** button.

## 4 Choose a Condition

Select the conditions Outlook should check for when executing your rule. Click the **Sent Only to Me** option. Notice that the condition appears in the bottom of the dialog box. Click the **Next** button.

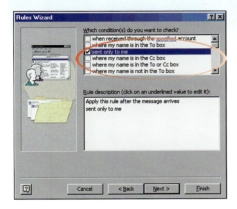

## 5 Choose an Action

Now tell Outlook what to do with the message if it meets your conditions. Select the **Print It** option; click the **Next** button.

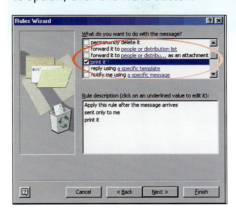

## 6 Make Exceptions

Every rule can have its exceptions, and you can identify any conditions under which you don't want this rule to execute. Because you don't have any exceptions, click the **Next** button.

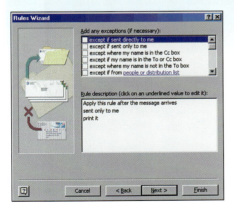

## 7 Name the Rule

Finally, give this rule a distinctive name. Type the name in the **Please Specify a Name for This Rule** field. Click **Finish** to save.

*End*

## Task 2

# How to Disable a Rule

Rules aren't always permanent things; you often need to use them only for a short time. For example, you may want to establish a rule to process messages about a time-sensitive project, or to respond to messages when you're away from your desk. It's a good thing you can disable or delete rules at any time. If you disable a rule, keep in mind that you can always use it again later without re-creating it from scratch.

## Begin

### 1 Open the Rules Wizard

Open the **Rules Wizard** by choosing **Tools**, **Rules Wizard**. This is where you can modify, disable, or delete your existing rules.

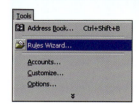

### 2 Select the Rule to Disable

Find the rule you want to disable and click the check box to remove the check mark. Without the check mark, you can leave the rule in Outlook and it won't have any effect on your mail.

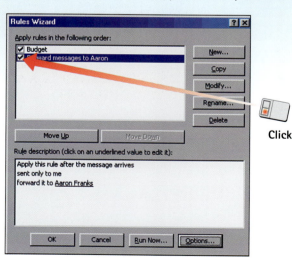

Click

### 3 Save Your Changes

After you disable the rule, click the **OK** button to close the **Rules Wizard** dialog box and save your rules changes.

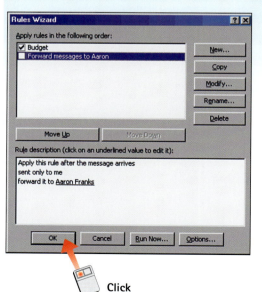

Click

192    PART 8: AUTOMATING YOUR EMAIL

## 4 Delete a Rule

If you're sure that you'll never need a rule again, you can delete it. Open the **Rules Wizard** dialog box, select the rule you want to delete, and click the **Delete** button.

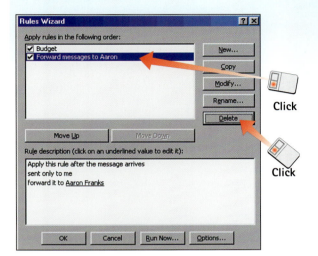

## 5 Confirm the Deletion

Outlook displays a dialog box to make sure that you want to delete the rule. Click the **Yes** button to proceed.

## 6 Close the Wizard

With the rule deleted, click the **OK** button to leave the **Rules Wizard** and return to Outlook.

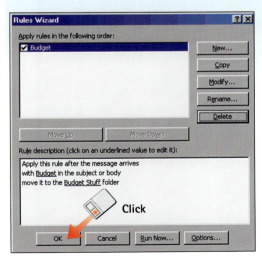

*End*

## How-To Hints

### Make New Rules Easily

If you have to create a new rule that is very similar to an existing one, select the rule in the **Rules Wizard** dialog box and then click the **Copy** button. Click **Modify** to customize the copied rule for the job you have in mind. Save it with a new name (delete the **Copy Of** text from the name) and you're done.

How to Disable a Rule  193

# Task 3

## How to Create an Autoresponder

Outlook has a special kind of rule called an *autoresponder*. You've almost certainly encountered this rule. If you send an email and get an immediate reply that says something like, "We'll get to your email as soon as possible," you know that the company's mail software autoresponded to your message—no human intervention. You can do the same thing with Outlook. This feature is particularly handy if you want to let people know you're out of town for a day or two. The caveat? Your PC must be left running and connected to your mail server so that Outlook can check for mail and respond to messages.

## Begin

### 1 Create the Reply Message

You must first create an email message that Outlook can send as part of its automatic response. Save this file as a template. See Part 10, Task 10 for details on creating an email template.

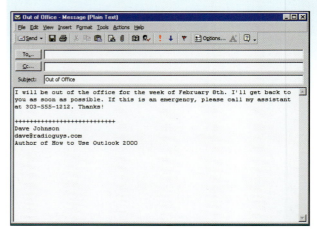

### 2 Create a New Rule

Open the **Rules Wizard** by choosing **Tools**, **Rules Wizard** and clicking the **New** button.

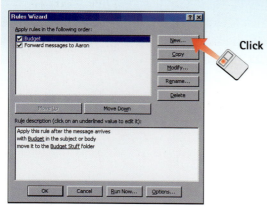

### 3 Select the Rule

This rule should act on new messages as they arrive in your **Inbox**, so select **Check Messages When They Arrive**. Click the **Next** button.

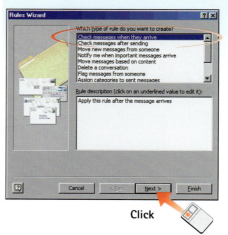

194   Part 8: Automating Your Email

## 4 Specify Conditions

For this example, you want to auto-respond to all mail that arrives in your Inbox from a particular account. Click the **When Received Through the Specified Account** option. In the bottom of the dialog box, click the word **Specified** and select your mail account. Click the **Next** button.

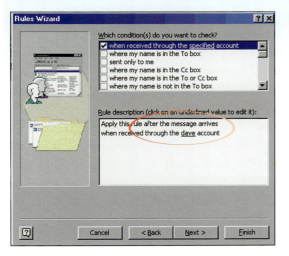

## 5 Process the Message

Now you have to decide what to do with messages that meet the conditions you specified. Because you want to create an autoresponder, click the **Reply Using a Specific Template** option.

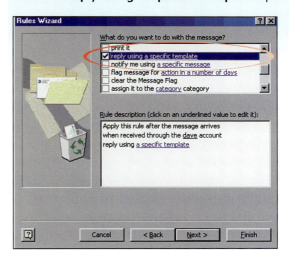

## 6 Specify the Template

In the bottom of the dialog box, click the phrase **a specific template** and choose the email template you created earlier from the dialog box that appears. Click **OK** to close the wizard.

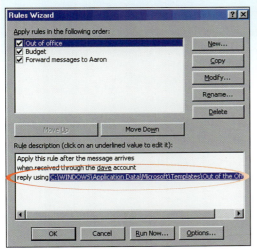

# How-To Hints

## Using Exceptions

Autoresponders are great, but they can be misused. We didn't make use of the wizard's **Add Any Exceptions** page in this example, but you should use it in a real situation to skip replying to certain kinds of messages. In particular, avoid replying to any mailing lists you happen to belong to. You don't want to send your "out of town" email to a mailing list every day. It will be automatically posted to the list, wasting the time of everyone else who subscribes.

## Task 4

# How to Create a Rule That Moves Mail

Although you generally want new mail to arrive in your Inbox, one way to manage your messages is to let Outlook file them for you as they arrive. You can send messages to specific folders based on the sender, keywords, subject, or almost any other criteria you can imagine. I get questions from readers and automatically store them in a special folder that I read from and answer each weekend. That way, those messages don't get mixed up with messages from editors or accidentally lost in my sometimes too-cluttered Inbox.

## *Begin*

### 1 Create Storage Folders

Start by creating all the folders into which you want Outlook to move your messages. Refer to Part 10, Task 7 to see how to add folders to the Folder List.

### 2 Create a New Rule

Open the **Rules Wizard** by choosing **Tools**, **Rules Wizard**. Click the **New** button to begin building the rule.

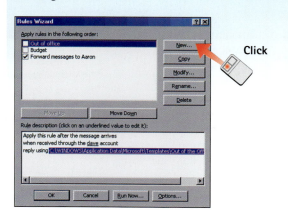

### 3 Choose the Rule

This rule will move messages from specific people on a project team into an Important Messages folder unless the sender marks the message with the Low Importance flag. Click **Move New Messages from Someone**. To choose whose messages will be moved, click the phrase **people or distribution list** that's in the bottom of the dialog box.

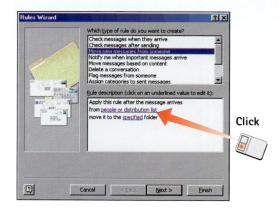

196   Part 8: Automating Your Email

## 4 Choose Names

The **Rule Address** dialog box opens, displaying all the contacts in your address book. Double-click any names you want to include in the rule and then click the **OK** button. Select the folder you want to move the messages to and click the **OK** button.

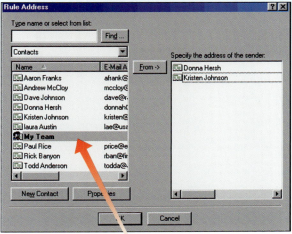

Double-click

## 5 Add Exceptions

You don't want to invoke this rule if the specified people send the message with low importance. Click the **Except if It Is Marked as Importance** option. In the bottom of the dialog box, click the word **Importance** and select **Low Importance**. Click the **Next** button.

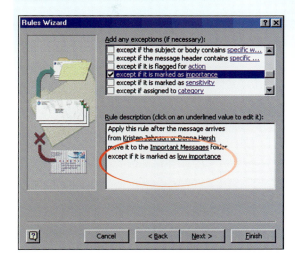

## 6 Name the Rule

Provide a name for the rule in the **Please Specify a Name for This Rule** field and click the **Finish** button to save your new rule.

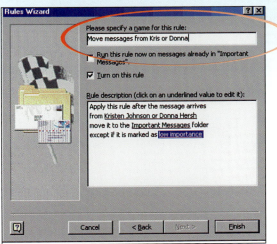

# How-To Hints

## Combining Rules

If you're adventurous, you can combine more than one rule to accomplish complex actions. Suppose that you want to file a message based on category. Incoming messages don't yet have a category, but you can run a rule to assign categories based on message content or the sender's name. Then run another rule to file the message based on category. Just make sure that you arrange the rules in the correct order in the **Rules Wizard** dialog box.

End

## Task 5

# How to Create a Rule That Assigns Messages to Categories

Another handy rule to have is one that assigns messages to categories on-the-fly, as they arrive in your Inbox. Properly applied, you can use such a rule to put many of your incoming messages in categories for easy filing or searches.

## Begin

### 1 Create Categories

Before you start the rule, make sure that you create all the categories you want to use. Choose **Edit**, **Categories** to open the **Categories** dialog box.

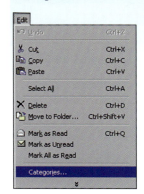

### 2 Open the Master Categories

Click the **Master Category List** button to edit Outlook's categories.

Click

### 3 Add Categories to List

When the **Master Category List** appears, you can add or delete categories. Type the name of your new category in the **New Category** field and click **Add**. When you're done creating categories, click **OK** on both dialog boxes to return to Outlook.

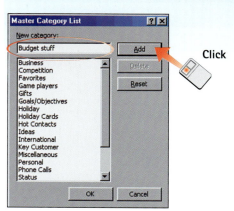

Click

**198**  Part 8: Automating Your Email

## 4 Create a New Rule

When you're ready to create the rule, click **Tools, Rules Wizard**. The **Rules Wizard** dialog box opens. Click the **New** button to start a new rule.

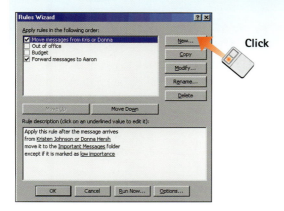

## 5 Select a Rule Type

Assign messages to categories based on words in the message by clicking **Assign Categories Based on Content**. Click the phrase **specific words** in the bottom of the dialog box and prepare to enter the search words.

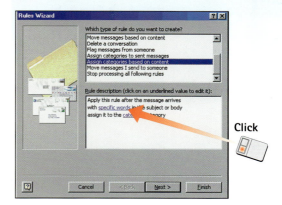

## 6 Enter Search Words

Type a search word in the **Add New** field and click **Add**. If you have several words to look for, type another word and click the **Add** button until all words are entered. Click **OK** to go back to the wizard.

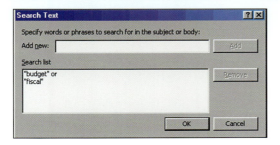

## 7 Select the Category

Click the word **category** in the bottom of the dialog box; type the name of the category to which you want to assign messages that match at least one of the words specified in step 6. Click **OK** to finish the wizard. Your rule is complete.

*End*

How to Create a Rule That Assigns Messages to Categories   199

TASK 6

# How to Avoid Junk Mail Without Reading It

One of the realities of the Internet is that junk mail is cheap. Heck, it's virtually free—for the sender, that is. Some people send massive quantities of messages about everything and anything, much of which eventually finds its way into your Inbox. These messages, called *spam*, are a pain. Responding to the messages usually generates more mail, so the best solution is often to delete it. You can tell Outlook to automatically delete junk mail. The "delete junk mail" feature is a kind of rule, but it's a rule you don't have to create—you simply have to turn it on.

## Begin

### 1 Open the Organize Pane

The rules for junk mail are stored in the Organize pane. To open this pane, start in the Inbox view and click the **Organize** button in the toolbar.

Click

### 2 View Junk Email Settings

The Organize pane helps you manage and sort messages in your Inbox. This pane is explained thoroughly in Part 4, Task 6. Click the **Junk E-Mail** tab to switch to the junk mail settings.

Click

### 3 Move the Messages

The Junk E-Mail rule gives you two options: You can identify offending messages by color or you can move them as they arrive into a junk mail folder. Do the latter: Click the **down arrow** and choose **Move** for both Junk mail and Adult Content mail.

## 4 Turn On the Rule

Click the **Turn On** button for both Junk mail and Adult Content mail. If the Junk E-Mail folder doesn't already exist, Outlook confirms that you want to create it. When the rules are turned on, click the **Organize** button in the toolbar again to close the Organize pane. New junk mail is placed automatically in the Junk E-Mail folder so that it won't take up space in the Inbox.

Click

## 5 Add Addresses to Junk Mail

Outlook comes with a database of email addresses and tell-tale patterns it uses to determine what mail to move to the junk drawer. If you get messages from a specific address that you want to identify as a junk sender, however, right-click the message in the Inbox. Choose **Junk E-Mail**, **Add to Junk Senders List** from the menu. Mail from that sender is automatically processed as junk.

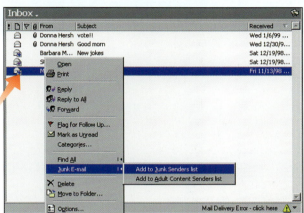
Right-click

## 6 Check and Delete Junk

Outlook doesn't automatically discard junk mail for you. It's always possible that valid mail found its way into your junk folder, and Outlook lets you inspect it first. Get in the habit of looking in the Junk E-Mail folder every few days and saving any useful mail accidentally placed there. Delete the real junk messages to save disk space.

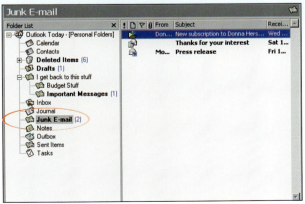

## How-To Hints

### Valuable Mail Alert

Microsoft faced court action last winter from an electronic greeting card company that claimed Outlook was preconfigured to place its email greetings in the Junk E-Mail folder. Microsoft responded that its own email cards are discarded by default in the same way. This illustrates that the junk mail rule's logic isn't perfect. Check the junk folder before you delete its contents to make sure that you don't throw away good, unread mail.

*End*

# Task

1. **How to Import Mail from Another Computer 204**

2. **How to Synchronize Outlook with Another PC 206**

**Project 3: Synchronize Outlook with a Palm PC 208**

# PART 9

# Using Outlook with Other Computers

As Simon and Garfunkel so eloquently pointed out in the 1960s, no computer is an island. As a result, you'll often have to share information with other Outlook users—or with yourself, on another PC.

You can configure Outlook to synchronize your Calendar and contacts with those of another PC, so that you and your co-workers can collaborate more effectively. With additional software, you can also synchronize Outlook with handheld PCs such as the very popular 3Com Palm PC. You learn how to do all these things by following the tasks in this part.

## Task 1

# How to Import Mail from Another Computer

New PCs are always a challenge to set up. Even after all the hardware is installed, you still have to transfer your applications and data files from your old computer to the new one. Just as with your word-processing files and spreadsheets, you certainly don't want to lose your old mail and contact data from Outlook. Thankfully, it's all stored in a single file you can copy to the new PC.

## Begin

### 1 Verify the Location

Open Outlook on the old computer and determine where your data file is stored. Its location can vary depending on who installed Outlook and when it was done. Right-click **Personal Folders** in the **Folder List**.

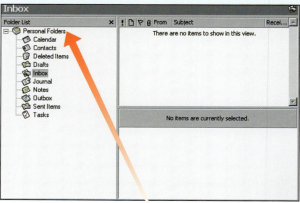

Right-click

### 2 Review the Properties

The context menu for Personal Folders appears. Choose **Properties for "Personal Folders"** to open the **Personal Folders Properties** dialog box.

### 3 Display the Path

Click the **Advanced** button, which is located at the bottom of the **General** tab in the **Personal Folders Properties** dialog box. This action opens another dialog box that includes the data file's path and name.

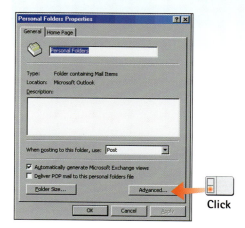
Click

## 4 Note the Filename

In the **Personal Folders** dialog box, check the **Path** field for the file's complete name. Write it down; you'll have to remember this name later.

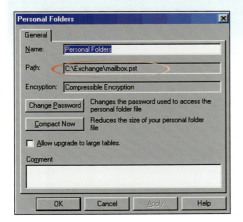

## 5 Copy the File

Close Outlook and then open the appropriate folder to get to the data file. Copy this file to the new PC using a floppy disk, a Zip disk, or the local area network. In most cases, the file is quite large and won't fit on anything smaller than a Zip disk. Now find the Outlook data file on the new PC and close that copy of Outlook. Copy the file from your Zip disk to that location.

## 6 Open Outlook

You can open Outlook on the new PC after you copy the data file to your new computer. (You've copied it where the new copy of Outlook expects to find its own data, right?). Outlook recognizes the data from your old copy of Outlook as if it were its own.

# How-To Hints

## Zip It Up!

If you are trying to copy a large Outlook data file, you can compress the file using a program such as PKZip. I always use WinZip to make files smaller before I copy them because WinZip uses the PKZip compression scheme but has a convenient graphical interface.

## Open Multiple Data Files

You can open different sets of personal folders in much the same way as the steps in this task: Right-click **Personal Folders** in the **Folder List** and choose **Open Personal Folders File** from the menu. Select the file to open; you can have more than one set of mailboxes and contact information at your disposal. This technique is most commonly used to access archived mail.

HOW TO IMPORT MAIL FROM ANOTHER COMPUTER   **205**

## Task 2

# How to Synchronize Outlook with Another PC

These days, a tremendous number of people telecommute and regularly use more than one PC. In the past, it wasn't easy to maintain a single Inbox and a single set of contacts with more than one computer, but Outlook 2000 simplifies the process significantly. With Outlook 2000 you can synchronize two PCs so that you can use the same data no matter where you are—at work, at home, or on the road.

## Begin

### 1 Save Your Data

Click **Tools**, **Synchronize Other Computer**, **Save File** from the menu bar. This action opens a dialog box that allows you to save your data and transfer it to another PC.

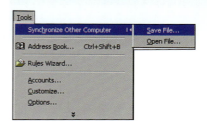

### 2 Set Up Your PC

Use the **Save Synchronization File** dialog box to specify the synchronization options. Because this is your first time using the feature, click the **New** button to get started.

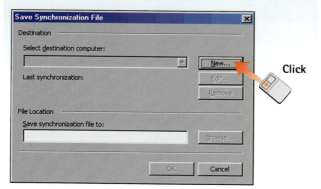

Click

### 3 Choose Folders

The **Synchronize Other Computer** dialog box allows you to choose which folders from your current PC you want to synchronize on the remote computer. Type names for the remote and local PCs in the appropriate fields at the top of the dialog box and click the check boxes for each folder you want to synchronize. Click **OK** when you are done.

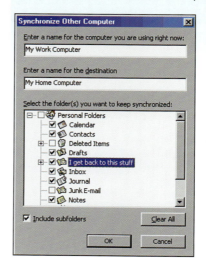

## 4 Select a File Destination

Enter a filename for the synchronization file in the **Save Synchronization File To** field. If you're using a local area network, you can save the file to a hard disk that both PCs have access to. If not, you will probably have to save the file to a Zip disk or to some other removable media large enough to hold the data you are synchronizing. Click **OK** to save the file.

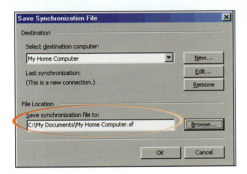

## 5 Synchronize Outlook

On the other computer, choose **Tools**, **Synchronize Other Computer**, **Open File**. This action opens the dialog box that allows you to import and synchronize the data from the other PC.

## 6 Deal with Conflicts

The **Open Synchronization File** dialog box appears. Select the location of the synchronization file from the **Synchronization File Location** list box; click the option that states how Outlook should deal with data conflicts. In the event of a conflict, you can choose to use the data from the other PC (the synchronization file), use whatever data is dated most recent, use the data on the current PC, or ask for a resolution. When it is fully configured, click the **OK** button to synchronize.

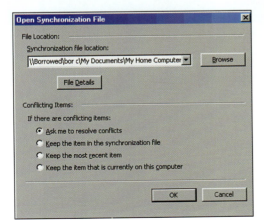

# How-To Hints

## A Note About Synch

The technique in this task is intended for people who want to keep the data on two PCs up-to-date. If you want to share data with other users, it's recommended that you use the Net Folder Wizard instead, as explained in Part 6, Task 10, "How to Share a Calendar."

## I Don't Have That Menu Item!

If you can't find the **Synchronize Other Computer** menu item in the **Tools** menu, the feature was not installed on your copy of Outlook 2000. You can visit the Microsoft Office Web site at
`http://www.microsoft.com`
and download this component. After you install it, the menu item appears and you can synchronize your data with another PC.

# Project 3
## Synchronize Outlook with a Palm PC

With about three million PalmPilots in people's hands, odds are good you have one of these ubiquitous little handheld computers. If you do, you probably want to synchronize your Pilot's data with Outlook so that you always have your contacts and schedule information—even when you're on the road. Outlook can synch with your Pilot, but not right out of the box. Instead, you need one of several Outlook connectivity tools for the Pilot. This project demonstrates synchronizing the Pilot with the most popular of these tools, a program called PilotMirror, from Chapura Software.

### 1 Configure Conduits

When you install PilotMirror, you can decide which kinds of Outlook data you want to synchronize. If you want all the components—Calendar, Contacts, Tasks, and Notes—click the check boxes for all the options and complete the PilotMirror installation.

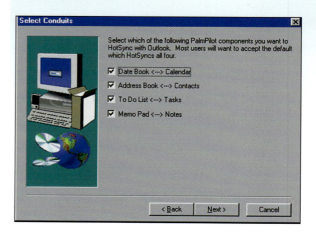

### 2 Configure for First Use

The first time you synchronize Outlook with your Pilot, double-check the settings so that you don't accidentally overwrite data in either Outlook or the Pilot. In **Outlook**, choose **Tools, PilotMirror Settings**.

### 3 Select a User

The **PilotMirror User Settings** dialog box displays all the Pilot users in the PalmPilot desktop's settings. Select the one that represents your PalmPilot (you'll probably only have one entry anyway) and click the **Settings** button.

Click

## 4 Set Your Preferences

Use the **Change Synchronization Preferences** dialog box to tell PilotMirror how to exchange data between the Pilot and Outlook. You can set PilotMirror to overwrite either the Pilot or Outlook; alternatively, you can set it to ask you for conflict resolution. You can also set the default behavior and how PilotMirror will behave on the very next synch.

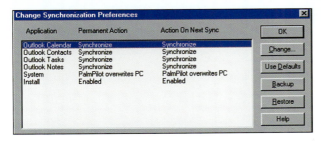

## 5 Change a Setting

To change the way Calendar conflicts are resolved, double-click the **Outlook Calendar** field in the **Change Synchronization Preferences** dialog box. The **Outlook Calendar Properties** dialog box appears.

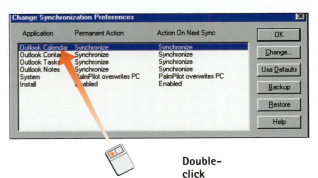

Double-click

## 6 Set PilotMirror Actions

In the **Outlook Calendar Properties** dialog box, set the default action for PilotMirror in the **Permanent Action** section; click the option for the **One-Time Action of Next HotSync** section. If this is the first time you're using PilotMirror, you may want to let Outlook overwrite all Pilot data; afterwards, always **Synchronize** the data so that you get the changes as they occur in both locations.

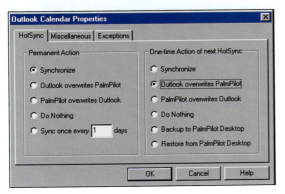

## 7 Set Exceptions

Click the **Exceptions** tab. If you schedule many recurring appointments in Outlook—and exceptions to those regular appointments—the synchronization process may be slowed down significantly. To minimize the synchronization time, tell Outlook to look no more than a certain number of days ahead when synchronizing. Type a number in the **Look Ahead** field (30 days is a good compromise). Click **OK** when you're done.

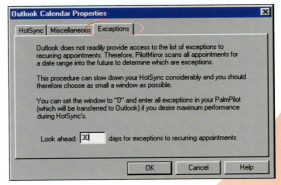

*Continues*

*Project 3 Continued*

## 8 Finish Settings

Double-click all the other items in the **Change Synchronization Preferences** dialog box, setting the synchronization settings for each to reflect the way you want the data to be transferred. Beware of setting the **PalmPilot Overwrites PC** option; you could lose valuable Outlook data if you enable that option.

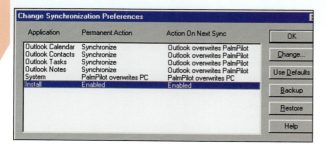

## 9 View the HotSync Status

If your PalmPilot software is properly installed, you should see the **HotSync** status icon in the System Tray. This icon displays the last time you performed a HotSync. (Hold the mouse pointer over the icon.) It can also be used to change your synchronization's settings.

## 10 Open the Sync Settings

Right-click the **HotSync** icon in the System Tray. If you're synchronizing your Pilot using the docking cradle, **Local** should be checked. Choose **Setup** from the menu to open the **Setup** dialog box.

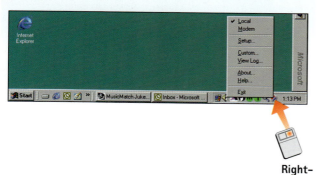

Right-click

## 11 Verify the COM Port

The **Setup** dialog box displays the current settings for your Pilot's HotSync. Click the **Local** tab and verify that the Pilot is configured to use the correct COM port. Click the **OK** button when you are done.

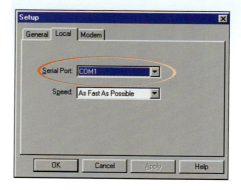

210  PART 9: USING OUTLOOK WITH OTHER COMPUTERS

## 12 Verify Conflict Settings

You can check the conflict settings you made earlier one last time before starting the HotSync. Right-click the **HotSync** icon in the System Tray and choose **Custom** from the menu. The **Custom** dialog box displays the very next action that PilotMirror will take. Click the **Done** button to close.

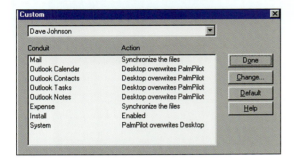

## 13 Synchronize Your Pilot

Place the Pilot in its cradle and press the cradle's **HotSync** button. The synchronization process begins and lasts several minutes, depending on how much information must be transferred. If you're synchronizing for the first time, the process will take longer than subsequent HotSyncs.

## 14 View the HotSync Log

You may sometimes encounter the *HotSync Log* (which appears automatically when the synchronization is complete). This text file records any errors that occurred while synchronizing your data. The most common problem is a note in a contact entry that exceeds the PalmPilot's allowed maximum length. This error isn't catastrophic; it just means that the entire note didn't make it into your Pilot.

*End*

## How-To Hints

### Getting PilotMirror

PilotMirror from Chapura Software is a popular PalmPilot accessory. It's available in many retail stores. You can also purchase it from **www.pilotgear.com**, the largest Web-based distributor of Palm software

PROJECT 3: SYNCHRONIZE OUTLOOK WITH A PALM PC   211

# Task

1. How to Customize Menus and Toolbars 214
2. How to Add Groups to the Outlook Bar 216
3. How to Add a File to the Outlook Bar 218
4. How to Configure Outlook to Find People 220
5. How to Switch Between Internet-Only and Corporate Mail Settings 222
6. How to Add a Corporate Mail Account 224
7. How to Add Folders to the Folder List 226
8. How to Archive Old Mail 228
9. How to Discard Old Mail 232
10. How to Create a Mail Template 234
11. How to Use a Mail Template 236
12. How to Detect and Repair Outlook 238

# PART 10

# Customizing Outlook

Outlook is an extremely customizable program. That's great if you're the kind of person who likes to tweak all the little buttons and valves, but it can be intimidating if you don't like to mess around under the hood very much.

Whether or not you like to tweak your software, the tasks in this part of the book should prove very valuable. You learn how to change the program's appearance, archive old mail to save disk space, change the program's mail format, and more.

## Task 1

# How to Customize Menus and Toolbars

Like most of the other applications in the Microsoft Office 2000 family, Outlook 2000 employs new features called *Personalized Menus* and *Personalized Toolbars*. These toolbars and menus "learn" which commands you use most often and make them more accessible. The commands you rarely use are hidden and out of the way. This system makes it easier to find exactly what you're looking for without being bogged down by menus and icons you never need.

## Begin

### 1 Access Common Menus

The menu commands you use frequently are readily visible when you click the menu bar. Click **Tools** to see the ordinary menu items. Notice the arrow at the bottom of the menu; it expands the menu to show infrequently used items. Click the **arrow** to see all the options available in the Tools menu.

Click

### 2 View Hidden Menu Items

The menu items you don't use often are displayed in light gray; the menu items you usually see are shown in dark gray. If you choose a hidden item, it is displayed in the menu the next time you open it. If you don't use the item for a while, it finds its way back to the hidden menu.

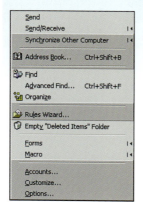

### 3 View Hidden Toolbars

The toolbars in Outlook work much the same way the menus do. Each toolbar has an arrow that, when clicked, displays infrequently used toolbar icons.

**214** PART 10: CUSTOMIZING OUTLOOK

## 4 Choose a Hidden Icon

If you want to access a hidden toolbar button, click the **arrow** at the end of the toolbar and then click the **hidden button** you want to use. The command runs; the button is moved to the toolbar. (Outlook assumes that it's a feature you plan to use a again soon.) If you don't use the button again soon, Outlook moves the button back to the hidden region under the arrow.

Click

## 5 Edit the Toolbar Buttons

Outlook makes it easy to manually add or remove buttons from the toolbars. Click the **arrow** at the end of the toolbar and then click the **Add or Remove Buttons** option. The toolbar editor opens.

Click

## 6 Turn Buttons On and Off

The toolbar editor displays a list of all the possible buttons on the toolbar. If the button has a check mark, it is displayed in the toolbar. No check mark indicates that the button is found in the hidden menu. To change the status of a button, click the option to turn the check mark on or off. You can also choose **Reset Toolbar**, which returns the toolbar to the default settings it had when you installed Outlook.

*End*

## How-To Hints

### Open and Close Toolbars

In many of the Outlook views, you can display additional toolbars to provide fast access to some common commands and features. You can turn entire toolbars on and off by right-clicking the **toolbar**. The resulting menu shows all the toolbars you can display. Click the **toolbar name** to enable or disable it, depending on your needs.

HOW TO CUSTOMIZE MENUS AND TOOLBARS   215

## Task 2

# How to Add Groups to the Outlook Bar

The Outlook bar is a convenient way to switch among the different views within Outlook—and it does so much more. You can launch other applications, display documents and Web pages, and so on. Most importantly, you can customize the bar by making use of groups. Each *group* can contain certain kinds of buttons, so that you can organize it like a set of folders. There's almost no limit to how you can customize the Outlook bar.

## Begin

### 1 Using the Outlook Bar

No doubt, you recall how easy it is to switch among views using the Outlook bar. Most of the time, you stay in the **Outlook Shortcuts** group, which contains the Outlook view buttons. As you get more familiar with the program, you'll no doubt want to make your own groups and put your own buttons in them.

### 2 Create a New Group

To create a new group in the Outlook bar, right-click any part of the Outlook bar that doesn't include a button. Choose **Add New Group** from the menu.

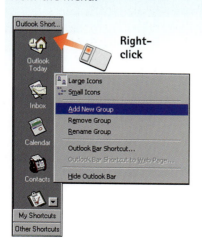

### 3 Name the New Group

The new group appears at the bottom of the Outlook bar. Type the name you want the new group to have and press the **Enter** key.

**216** PART 10: CUSTOMIZING OUTLOOK

## 4 Display the Group

You can begin using your group after you create and name it. You can add documents, applications, and Web pages to the group so that you can launch them from Outlook. Click the new group to switch to it.

Click

## 5 Using the New Group

You can now edit the group contents. (See the next task, "How to Add a File to the Outlook Bar," for details.) You can edit the group itself—rename or delete it, for example. Do so by right-clicking the group name.

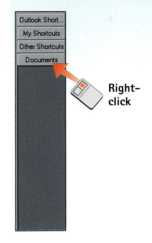

Right-click

## 6 Modify the Group

From the menu, choose the action you want to perform on the group. Choose either **Rename Group** or **Remove Group**. Remember that a group is like a folder; if you delete it, you delete any shortcuts stored in the group as well.

### How-To Hints

#### Changing Icons

The Outlook bar can show its buttons as large icons—which is the default—or as small buttons—handy if you put a lot of items in a single group. To change the icons' size, right-click in a group and choose **Small Icons** from the menu.

*End*

TASK 3

# How to Add a File to the Outlook Bar

After you create some custom groups in the Outlook bar, you'll no doubt want to fill the groups with files—documents, Web pages, and so on. You can then use Outlook as a sort of quick-launch manager for your favorite programs. If you spend a lot of time in Outlook, you'll find the Outlook bar even more convenient after you load it with file shortcuts.

*Begin*

### 1 Working with Groups

You can place file shortcuts in any group—existing or new. To get started, click the name of the group in which you want to place the shortcut to a file. You switch immediately to that group.

### 2 Choose the File

Find the file you want to place in the Outlook bar. Open the Windows folder that contains the file. (Look in the My Documents folder for a document file; in the Program Files folder for an application.) You can also open the C:\Windows\Favorites folder to find a Web page. You may find it convenient to resize the folder so that you can fit both it and Outlook on the screen at the same time.

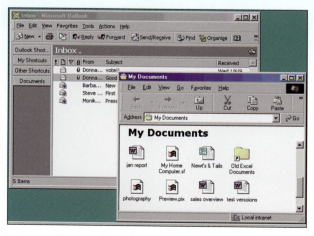

### 3 Drag and Drop the File

Drag the file from the folder and drop it into the Outlook bar. Notice that you've created a shortcut that points back to the original file; you didn't really move the original file.

Release          Drag

## 4 Arrange Shortcut Icons

You can control the arrangement of files in the Outlook bar. Click a file and drag it higher or lower in the bar to rearrange the icons. When you drag a new file into the Outlook bar, you can place it between existing files: Simply drop the file when you see a black divider icon indicating that the file will appear in that location.

## 5 Delete a Shortcut

After you add a file to the Outlook bar, you can always rename or delete it. To delete a file shortcut, right-click it and choose **Remove from Outlook Bar** from the menu.

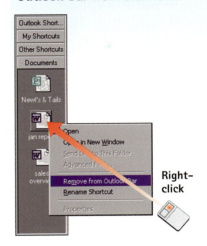

Right-click

## 6 Open a File

To open a file, start a program, or display a Web page that has been stored in the Outlook bar, click the button. The shortcut launches the original file.

Click

### How-To Hints

#### Adding Outlook Buttons

You can add buttons to the Outlook bar that represent views of anything in Outlook. For example, you can create a button for a folder you previously added to a folder view. To do that, right-click the **Outlook bar** and choose **Outlook Bar Shortcut** from the menu; select the item you want from the **Add to Outlook Bar** dialog box.

*End*

## Task 4

# How to Configure Outlook to Find People

Outlook 2000 is compatible with an Internet protocol called *Lightweight Directory Access Protocol* (*LDAP*). LDAP servers allow you to find contact information for people over the Internet as if you were looking them up in the local phone book. You may have to configure Outlook before you can use LDAP servers. To actually find people on the Internet, see Part 5, Task 7, "How to Find Someone Using the Internet."

## *Begin*

### *1* Start Setting Up Accounts

LDAP server information is stored in the same place as your personal email account settings. Start by choosing **Tools**, **Accounts**.

### *2* View Your Accounts

The **Internet Accounts** dialog box displays all the accounts you have established, both for email and LDAP. To see your LDAP accounts, click the **Directory Service** tab. You may not have any accounts built yet, in which case this tab will be blank. To create a new account from any page in the dialog box, click the **Add** button.

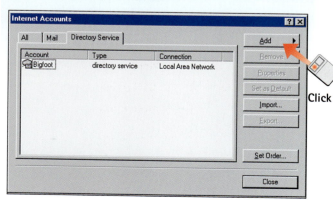

### *3* Create a Directory Account

Click **Directory Service** from the menu that appears when you click the **Add** button. This action opens the **Internet Connection Wizard** dialog box.

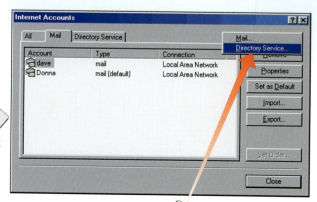

## 4 Define Your Directory

If you know the name of a directory you want to add to Outlook, type it into the **Internet Directory (LDAP) Server** field. Your company, for instance, may have provided you with the name of a local LDAP server. Otherwise, type `ldap.bigfoot.com` (a popular commercial server). Click the **Next** button.

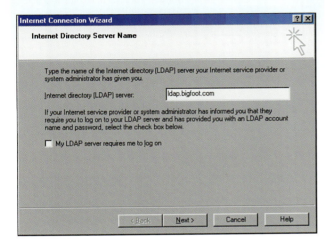

## 5 Finish the Wizard

Complete the wizard. Outlook asks whether you want to check email addresses using this directory service. In general, you should choose **No**; this significantly slows down the process of sending email.

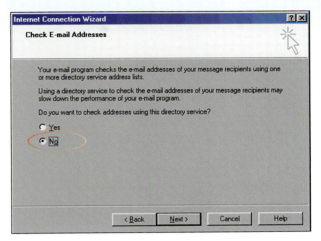

## 6 Adding Other Servers

Add as many servers as you like. Often you can find a specific person's name only by searching several different LDAP servers. When you're done, click the **Close** button.

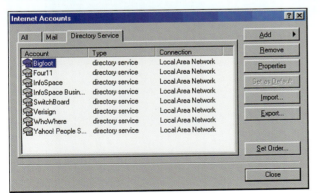

### How-To Hints

#### Popular LDAP Servers

Here are a few LDAP servers I recommend you add to your Outlook settings. If you're looking for a long-lost friend, one of these services may very well put you back in touch:

- ✓ `ldap.bigfoot.com`
- ✓ `ldap.four11.com`
- ✓ `ldap.infospace.com`
- ✓ `ldap.switchboard.com`
- ✓ `ldap.whowhere.com`

## Task 5

# How to Switch Between Internet-Only and Corporate Mail Settings

Outlook is really two very different programs, and you can use whichever one is appropriate to your work environment. Using the simple Internet-only mail interface, you can work with a large number of mail accounts and LDAP servers. Switch to the corporate mail configuration, where you can add lots of different kinds of mail systems as services to Outlook.

## Begin

### 1 Open Outlook Options

To change Outlook's mail configuration, you must first open the **Options** dialog box. Choose **Tools**, **Options** from the menu bar.

### 2 Mail Delivery Options

When the **Options** dialog box appears, click the **Mail Delivery** tab. This is where you can configure many of Outlook's mail options, including its behavior when connecting to the Internet.

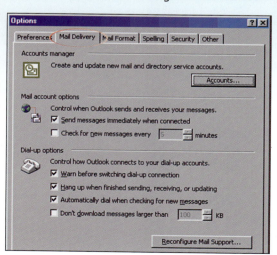

### 3 Reconfigure the Mail

To actually reconfigure your mail, click the **Reconfigure Mail Support** button at the bottom of the dialog box. Now you can choose which Outlook interface you want to use.

Click

222  PART 10: CUSTOMIZING OUTLOOK

## 4 Select a Configuration

The **Outlook 2000 Startup** dialog box appears. Click the option for the mail configuration you want to use and then click the **Next** button. You can always switch back if you want to.

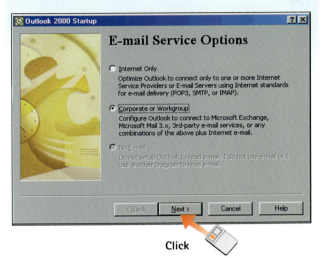
Click

## 5 Commit to the Change

Outlook has to shut down and load some new files to make the change. To commit to this modification, click the **Yes** button on the **Outlook 2000 Startup** dialog box.

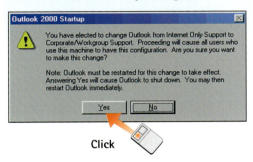
Click

## 6 Install New Files

Outlook requests the Outlook or Office CD-ROM. Insert the appropriate disc in your CD-ROM drive and click the **OK** button. When the installation is complete, you can restart Outlook in the new mode.

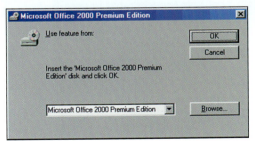

*End*

## How-To Hints

### Understanding Mail Support

Outlook behaves very differently depending on whether you use the traditional corporate mail settings or the newer Internet-only mail mode. In the corporate mail configuration, remember that message accounts are called *services* and the settings for them are found in **Tools**, **Services** from the menu bar. When you change mail settings in Corporate mode, you must restart Outlook before the changes take effect. In addition, it's much more difficult to send mail using a specific Internet account. Internet-only mail is a much better solution for most users.

## Task 6

# How to Add a Corporate Mail Account

If you set up Outlook to use the corporate mail configuration, you can install services for a large variety of message types, including cc:Mail, faxes, Microsoft Mail, and more. The interface, however, is quite different than what you've seen in Internet-only mail. You should familiarize yourself with this procedure.

## Begin

### 1 Open the Services Options

In Internet-only mail, you access your accounts using the **Tools**, **Accounts** menu option. In Outlook's Corporate Mail mode, however, that menu item doesn't even exist. Instead, choose **Tools**, **Services**.

### 2 Add a Mail Service

Use the **Services** dialog box to add, remove, and edit your various message accounts. The **Services** tab displays all the accounts you've created. To add a new account, click the **Add** button.

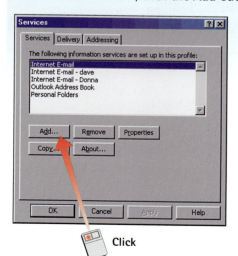

Click

### 3 Choose a Type of Service

Because Outlook lets you choose from all sorts of message formats, you have to specify what kind of mail you want to add. If you're adding Internet email, for instance, click **Internet E-Mail** and then click the **OK** button.

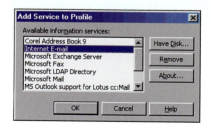

224   PART 10: CUSTOMIZING OUTLOOK

## 4 Configure Your Mail

The **Main Account Properties** dialog box opens. Enter the details of your account, such as your name and email address in the **General** tab.

## 5 Complete the Mail Settings

Click the **Servers** tab and enter your POP3 and SMTP server names, as well as your username and password. When you finish adjusting your mail settings, click the **OK** button to close the dialog box.

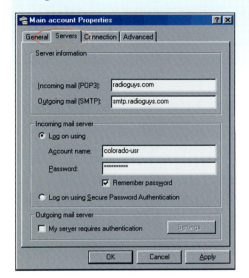

## 6 Set Mail Priority

Click the **Delivery** tab on the **Services** dialog box. You can specify which email account is responsible for sending mail by arranging the order of the accounts. Remember that you can't direct Outlook to send mail from an account other than the one with the highest priority on this tab; that is, unless you reorder the accounts on this tab and then close and restart Outlook.

### How-To Hints

#### Using Profiles

If you use the corporate mail configuration, you can create multiple profiles. A *profile* represents all the settings Outlook uses to send and receive mail. You can create profiles for different users of the same PC, for example, or you can create different profiles for different email accounts if you have more than one. When you load a particular profile, you can be sure that the account in that profile will be used to send your mail. Ask the Office Assistant for help in creating multiple profiles in Outlook.

*End*

How to Add a Corporate Mail Account   225

## Task 7

# How to Add Folders to the Folder List

The *Folder List* is a great time-saver and organizational tool. It allows you to keep your old mail structured so that it's easy to find. Most people know the danger of discarding important messages: You have to refer to them soon afterwards.

Outlook allows you to add an unlimited number of folders to the Folder List; you can even nest folders, putting related folders inside others.

## Begin

### 1 View the Folder List

You can display the Folder List in any Outlook view by choosing **View, Folder List**. Switch to any folder by clicking it; its contents are displayed in Outlook's right pane.

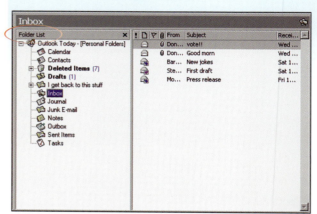

### 2 Create a New Folder

To create a new folder, right-click the folder you want to nest the new folder within. To place the folder *in the root* of the Folder List (to give it equal footing with the Inbox), right-click **Personal Folders** at the top of the **Folder List**. Choose **New Folder** from the menu.

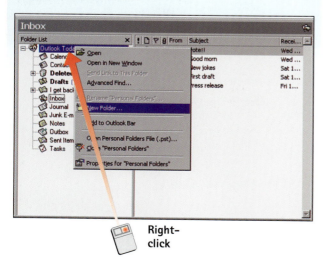

Right-click

### 3 Name the New Folder

The **Create New Folder** dialog box appears. Type the name of the new folder in the **Name** field. You can also specify the location of the folder in the **Select Where to Place the Folder** field. (If you right-clicked the appropriate location to create the folder, the location is already determined.) Click the **OK** button.

226  PART 10: CUSTOMIZING OUTLOOK

## 4 Add Shortcut to the Outlook Bar

Outlook offers you the option of adding a shortcut to this folder to the Outlook bar. If you plan to access this folder frequently, it can be convenient to place a shortcut there. Click **Yes** or **No** depending on your preference. If you decide to add the shortcut later, see the How-To Hint in Part 10, Task 3 for details.

## 5 View Your New Folder

When your folder is complete, you can view its content by clicking the folder in the **Folder List**. If you added a shortcut to the Outlook bar, you can click that icon to move to the folder.

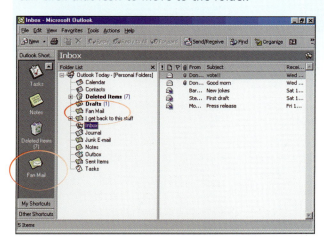

## 6 Drag and Drop Folders

You can reorganize your folders by dragging and dropping. If you want to nest a folder you just created within a folder you had already added to Outlook, just click and drag the folder. Move it over the other folder and drop it there. The folder automatically moves to the new location. You can hide subfolders by clicking the **minus** button to the left of the folder name.

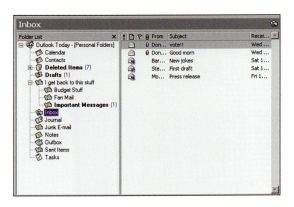

## How-To Hints

### Get the Most from Folders

After you create a folder, you can drag and drop files from the Inbox or other folders into it for long-term storage. You can also create a rule (see Part 8, Task 1) to automatically move specific kinds of new mail into the folder. Don't forget that you can right-click a folder in the **Folder List** to see more options. You can move, rename, and delete folders (for instance), and you can nest new folders within it. You can consider the Folder List an electronic filing cabinet.

## Task 8

# How to Archive Old Mail

As you accumulate more and more email, so grows the hard disk space Outlook needs to store it. After a year of ordinary use, your combined mailbox can consume as much as 100MB of space on your computer.

One way to control the rate at which your Inbox eats space is to archive old mail. When you archive, Outlook compresses the mail in a way that saves a lot of storage space. It's a good idea to archive mail after a period of time (perhaps every three months). If you use the procedure in this task, you can still access that archived mail as if it were sitting in Outlook's ordinary mail file.

## Begin

### 1 Set Outlook Options

Archiving can occur automatically after you configure it. First you have to set it up. The controls for mail archiving are found in the **Options** dialog box. To get started, choose **Tools**, **Options** from the menu bar.

### 2 Open AutoArchive

Click the **Other** tab on the **Options** dialog box. (This is where Microsoft put all the options that didn't fit anywhere else.) Click the **AutoArchive** button.

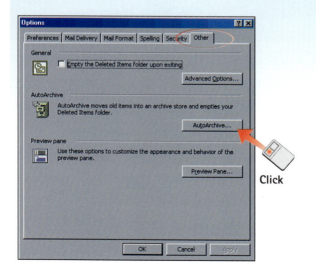

### 3 Set AutoArchive Options

The **AutoArchive** dialog box contains all the global settings for archiving your Outlook data. Click the check box for **AutoArchive Every** and then set a time period. This setting specifies how often Outlook tries to archive old items. If you want to be warned before Outlook starts the archiving process, select the **Prompt Before AutoArchive** option. Click **OK**.

## 4 Set Local Properties

After you set the global options for archiving, you must set the local archiving properties for each folder in Outlook that you want to archive. Any folder for which you don't set archive options is not archived. Right-click the **Inbox** in either the **Folder List** or the Outlook bar.

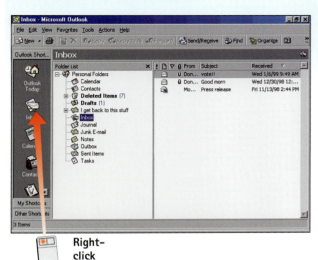

Right-click

## 5 Open Folder Properties

Choose **Properties** from the context menu that appears. The archive properties are accessed from the **Properties** dialog box for each folder.

## 6 Viewing Folder Properties

The **Inbox Properties** dialog box has several tabs. (You'll probably never have to mess with anything on the **General** or **Home Page** tabs.) Click the **AutoArchive** tab.

## 7 Enable Archiving

Click the check box for **Clean Out Items Older Than** to turn AutoArchive on. Set the time period you want to leave mail in the Inbox before archiving. Make sure that the tab is set to move old items to the archive file, not to permanently delete the old items. Click **OK** to close the dialog box. Repeat steps 4 through 7 for every folder you want to AutoArchive.

*Continues*

## How to Archive Old Mail Continued

### 8 Archive Mail Now

After you configure Outlook for AutoArchiving in the **Options** dialog box, it activates with no input from you. If you want to trigger archiving manually, you can do that as well. Choose **File**, **Archive** from the menu bar.

### 9 Set Archive Options

The **Archive** dialog box lets you archive your data immediately. If you want to archive all the folders for which you have set archive options, choose **Archive All Folders According to Their AutoArchive Settings**. If you want to archive a specific folder, choose **Archive This Folder and All Subfolders**. Click **OK** to start the process.

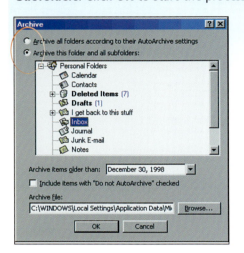

### 10 View Archived Items

Unfortunately, an item is no longer part of the Personal Folders once that item has been archived, and is therefore not visible from Outlook. There's an easy way around that problem, however: Add a new Personal Folders group to the Folder List and make the archived mail part of that folder set. You can then read archived mail as easily as if it were still in your Inbox. To start, right-click **Personal Folders**.

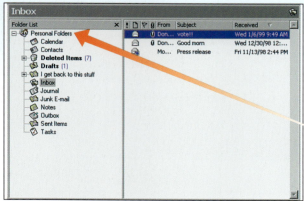

### 11 Open New Personal Folders

Choose **Open Personal Folders File (.pst)** from the menu.

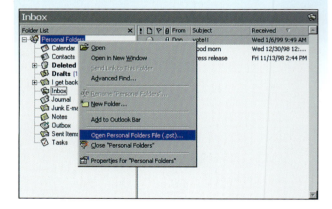

Right-click

230   PART 10: CUSTOMIZING OUTLOOK

## 12 Choose the Archive File

The **Open Personal Folders** dialog box appears. Choose the archive file to which Outlook has been saving all your archive data. You may have to refer to the **Options** dialog box to check the file and path specified in the **AutoArchive** tab. Click **OK** to close the dialog box.

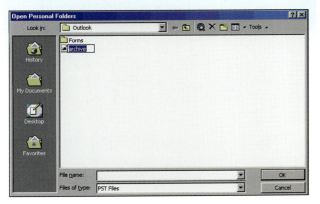

## 13 View the Archive Folder

Look for the new folder in the Folder List called **Archive Folders**. This folder contains all the archive data Outlook has been generating based on your AutoArchive settings. Click the **plus sign** to see the folder's contents.

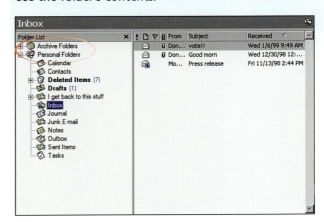

## 14 Read Archived Email

The **Archive Folders** contain folders for all the archived items you specified, including mail, notes, and the Calendar. To read a message or old calendar event, click the folder as you ordinarily do. The entry appears in the appropriate Outlook display. You can even move items by dragging and dropping them from the archive to your ordinary personal folders, and vice versa.

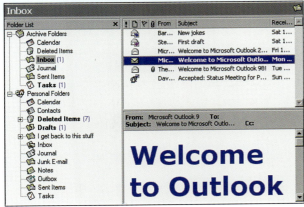

*End*

## How-To Hints

### Striking the Right Balance

You may have to tweak your archive settings over time to get them just right. You don't want to archive too often; the archive process ties up Outlook for several minutes. If you make the interval between AutoArchives too long, your Inbox becomes overburdened with old mail and the archive process will take a very long time when it finally does occur.

Also select the right age at which mail should be archived. If you routinely refer to mail that's six months old or more, take that into account when deciding on your archive settings. Others may get by just fine by archiving mail after just four weeks.

How to Archive Old Mail

## Task 9

# How to Discard Old Mail

Outlook conveniently provides a **Deleted Items** folder in which you can discard unwanted mail. When you delete a message, it ends up in the **Deleted Items** folder but items aren't deleted right away, you can set Outlook to empty the trash automatically every day, or at some other a specific interval.

## Begin

### 1 View Deleted Items

To see the contents of the Deleted Items folder, click it in the **Folder List**. Even if you've been using Outlook for only a short time, you may be surprised to find a lot of mail hiding in there. That's because when you delete a message, it isn't really deleted; it is simply moved to this folder, awaiting further action.

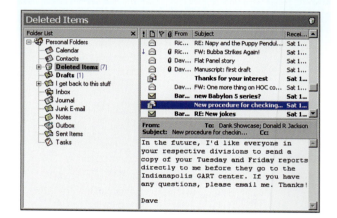

### 2 Empty Mail Manually

If you've accumulated some mail in the Deleted Items folder and want to discard it permanently, right-click **Deleted Items** and choose **Empty "Deleted Items" Folder** from the menu. That mail is gone and can't be recovered, so be sure that you really want to delete it.

### 3 Set Options for Deleting

Many people prefer to have their deleted items disposed of automatically. To set that option, choose **Tools**, **Options** from the menu bar.

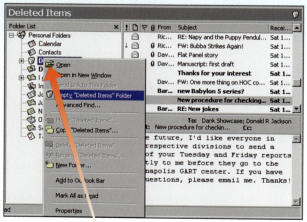

Right-click

232  PART 10: CUSTOMIZING OUTLOOK

## 4 View the Options

When the **Options** dialog box appears, click the **Other** tab to switch to the Deleted Items settings.

## 5 Automate Your Trash

Select the **Empty the Deleted Items Folder Upon Exiting** option. This option tells Outlook to delete your trash every time you quit Outlook. Click the **Advanced Options** button to see more trash settings.

## 6 Turn Off the Warning

If Outlook deletes your trash every time you quit the program, the convenience is eliminated if Outlook also asks your permission to do so each time; I suggest that you turn off the **Warn Before Permanently Deleting Items** option. Click **OK** to exit the dialog box. Your discarded mail is now deleted automatically when you exit Outlook; it won't accumulate.

# How-To Hints

## Be Careful with Trash

Although I highly recommend letting Outlook delete your unwanted mail for you for convenience's sake, the danger is that you'll end up deleting stuff you really need. Be careful. Don't forget, however, that in many cases you'll have a record of the discarded email anyway—if you reply to it. You can always look in your **Sent Items** folder to find your replies to deleted email. Hopefully you'll have left enough of the original message text in the reply that you'll find what you need.

*End*

## Task 10

# How to Create a Mail Template

Have you ever wished you had a ready-made mail message that all you had to do was address and send it? You might be a store owner who is responding to a request for common information. You might be sending a frequent reply message to another department in your company. If you are out of town, you might want Outlook to automatically send an "out of office" notification to anyone who sends you a message.

You can do any of those things with a *mail template*, which is an email message you save in template format instead of sending to a recipient. You can retrieve the template and use it over and over again. After you create a template, refer to the next task, "How to Use a Mail Template," for details on actually retrieving and using the template.

## Begin

### 1 Create the Template

Start by creating a new mail message: From the Inbox view, click the **New** button in the toolbar.

Click

### 2 Fill Out the Message

Create your message template as if you were writing the email to, and intend on actually sending it to, someone. Leave the **To** and **Cc** fields blank, but enter a subject and fill in the message body.

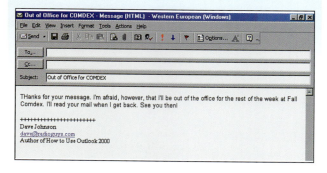

### 3 Save the Template

When you are done creating the message, choose **File**, **Save As** from the menu bar.

**234** PART 10: CUSTOMIZING OUTLOOK

## 4 Choose the Template Format

In the **Save As** dialog box, click the **Save as Type** list arrow and choose **Outlook Template**. Type a name for the file in the **File Name** field.

## 5 Store the Template

Click the **Save** button to save the template you just created to your hard disk.

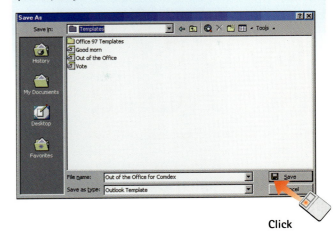

Click

## 6 Close the Message Window

After you save the template, Outlook returns you to the message window for the template you just created. Because you don't actually want to send this message now, click the **Close** button in the message window's title bar; click the **No** button when Outlook asks whether you want to save changes.

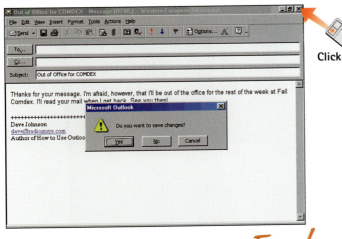

Click

*End*

## How-To Hints

### Templates Can Be Fancy

When you create a template, there's no reason not to make it fancy. If you send HTML messages (Web page-like email with formatting), you can create your template with stationery, fancy text, and even graphics. You can also attach files to template files, so that your template recipients can get a Word document or some other attachment with the email.

How to Create a Mail Template   **235**

## Task 11

# How to Use a Mail Template

After you create a message template (see Part 10, Task 10), you can easily use the template over and over again to send essentially the same message to many different people at different times. One of the most common applications for a template is to use Outlook as an autoresponder, so that it fires off a standard reply to incoming email. See Part 8, Task 3 for details on creating an autoresponder.

## Begin

### 1 Choose a Template

When you have to send a message based on a template you've already created, don't start your message with the toolbar's **New** button. Instead, choose **File**, **New**, **Choose Form** from the menu bar.

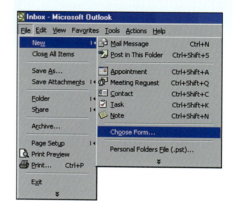

### 2 Choose a Library

Forms and templates are stored in several different folders on your hard disk. By default, all user-created templates are placed in a specific folder so that they're easy to find. In the **Choose Form** dialog box, click the **Look In** list box to select the proper folder.

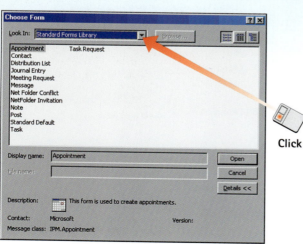

### 3 Open User Templates

Choose **User Templates in File System** from the **Look In** list box. This action displays a list of all the templates you've already created.

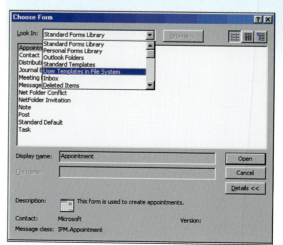

## 4 Select the Template

Double-click the template you want to use to send an email message.

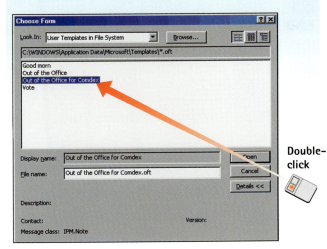

Double-click

## 5 Complete the Message

The selected template opens in a message window. It should look just the same as when you saved it earlier. Complete the message by adding the addressees in the **To** and **Cc** fields and making any necessary changes to the message text.

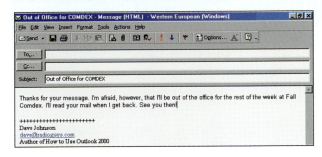

## 6 Send the Message

When you're done tweaking the template, click the **Send** button to deliver the message just like any other email message. The original template, however, remains just as you last saved it—the changes you just made are not a permanent part of the template).

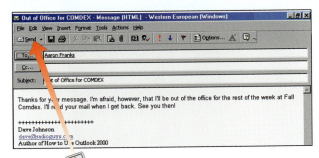

Click

 *End*

## How-To Hints

### The Template Is Unchanged

When you create a new message based on a template, you don't actually change the template stored on the hard disk. Instead, you're opening a *copy* of the template when you create a message. If you want to permanently change the template, you have to save the changed template to your hard disk as described in the preceding task, "How to Create a Mail Template."

How to Use a Mail Template 237

## Task 12: How to Detect and Repair Outlook

Like the rest of the Office 2000 family, Outlook 2000 includes some self-diagnostic and self-repair tools. If Outlook determines that a part of its core files have been damaged or deleted, for example, it recommends that you run a repair program so that it can fix itself. Likewise, if you notice that something is amiss, you can use Outlook's Detect and Repair features to let Outlook fix itself.

## Begin

### 1 Choose Detect and Repair

If Outlook begins to behave oddly or crash unexpectedly, key files may have been damaged. You can let Outlook repair itself by choosing **Help**, **Detect and Repair** from the menu bar.

### 2 Start the Repair

Outlook displays the **Detect and Repair** dialog box. Click the **Start** button to begin the diagnostic process.

Click

### 3 Wait for Outlook

It may take several minutes while Outlook gets ready to perform its diagnostic. Stand by while Outlook readies itself.

## 4 Close Outlook

You may see an unmarked dialog box with one or more programs listed. This dialog box indicates that you have to close the programs before Outlook can proceed. Close the necessary programs and then click the **Cancel** button on the dialog box.

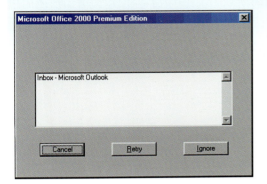

## 5 Insert the CD-ROM

Outlook will probably request the CD-ROM that contains Outlook 2000. Insert that disc in your CD-ROM drive and click **OK** to continue.

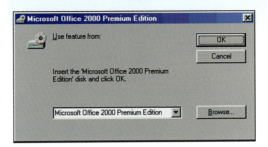

## 6 Outlook Repairs Itself

Outlook reads data from the CD-ROM and makes the appropriate repairs to itself. If there was a problem, Outlook should be as good as new when the procedure is complete.

## How-To Hints

### Add More Components

Not all of Outlook was necessarily installed when you first put Outlook on your hard disk. There may be additional features, help systems, templates, and stationery on the CD-ROM available for use as you prefer. To see what is not fully installed, insert your Outlook CD-ROM and run the Setup program. Look through the installation features for items that are not installed or that are not set to run from the CD. If you have sufficient hard disk space, you can install them now and get extra features from your copy of Outlook.

How to Detect and Repair Outlook    239

# Glossary

**accounts**  Accounts correspond to electronic mailboxes on your ISP's mail server.

**address book**  Outlook's electronic phone book. It's another way to view your contacts (described in Part 5).

**appointment**  An entry in the Outlook Calendar view that describes a scheduled event on your daily agenda.

**archive**  A compressed file that takes up less space on your hard disk than the contents of the file normally would.

**avatar**  A graphical representation of a person or character. Microsoft uses avatars such as dogs, cats, and a fanciful Einstein to give the Help system a friendly face.

**Blind Courtesy Copy (BCC)**  A way to send multiple copies of a message so that no one can see the email address of any other recipient.

**categories**  Specialized labels you can assign to messages, contacts, notes, and other kinds of Outlook information so that you can more easily sort the information later.

**dial-up connection**  A way to access the Internet using an analog modem. A dial-up connection uses a phone number, username, and password to enable you to send email and to surf the Web.

**distribution list**  A group that contains the addresses of all the people you frequently send messages to. You can use the list to send a message to a single entry—the group—instead of listing the individual names of all the recipients in your email message's **To** field.

**email address**  The name you use in the **To** or **Cc** line of an email message so that you can send the message.

**events**  Similar to an appointment, but an event is scheduled to take all day.

**flags**  Visual cues you can add to your email messages. They identify messages that need follow-up or that fit some other criteria you set up.

**group**  In the Outlook bar, a series of buttons that offer shortcuts to the various views in Outlook. You can switch groups using the Outlook bar to access a different set of shortcut buttons.

**Inbox**  The name Microsoft uses to describe the entire email portion of the Outlook program.

**ISP (Internet service provider)**  The company or organization responsible for providing you with access to the Internet. Typically, an ISP provides you with dial-up access and an email account.

**Journal**  A sophisticated tracking and logging system that keeps track of how you work. The Journal can log all your phone calls, email messages, appointments, and so on.

**keywords**  Words or phrases that assist you to search for a specific item.

**mail account name**  The name you're given by your network administrator or Internet service provider. The account name is used in the dial-up connection and as part of your email address.

**mail merge**   The process of combining a mailing list with a document template so that the same letter can be simultaneously sent to many different addressees.

**mailing group**   See *distribution list*.

**message body**   The actual email message.

**message forwarding**   The process of sending a message you received from one person to someone else.

**nested folders**   Folders stored within other folders in a logical order (for example, a main folder called **Budget Stuff** that contains two nested folders: **99 Budget** and **2000 Budget**).

**Office Assistant**   An animated character called an *avatar* that interprets plain-English questions to help you find the answers to common questions about Outlook.

**Outlook bar**   The vertical strip of icons on the left side of the Outlook window. Switch to any of the views by clicking the appropriate icon. See also *group*.

**password**   A secret phrase that, when combined with a username, allows you to access specific and protected data such as a Web page, financial data, or an email account.

**POP3**   The industry-standard protocol for receiving and storing Internet mail. Most ISPs use POP3 mail servers, and most mail software (including Outlook) is POP3 compatible.

**profile**   In the corporate mail configuration, you can create multiple profiles. A profile represents all the settings Outlook uses to send and receive mail.

**read receipt request**   An email option you can set for messages you send; when the recipient opens your message, you get a verification message confirming that your message was opened.

**rule**   A list of criteria Outlook uses to respond to email messages in a quasi-automatic fashion.

**service**   Each of Outlook's services is a different kind of message, such as email, fax, or cc:Mail.

**signatures**   Lines of text at the end of an email message that identify the sender, often provide contact information, and may also say something unique about the sender. Some signatures include witticisms or provide a one- or two-line résumé.

**SMTP**   The industry-standard protocol for sending Internet mail. Most ISPs use SMTP mail servers to send messages, and most mail software (including Outlook) is SMTP compatible. See also *POP3*.

**spam/spammer**   The mass mailing of unsolicited messages is referred to as spamming; undesired mail is spam. The person responsible for sending this mass mailing is a spammer. The origin of the term is lost in Internet obscurity, but the phrase is almost universally understood.

**stationery**   A background image your email message text is layered on top of. The effect is very much like typing on fancy stationery.

**subject line**   In an email message, this is a brief synopsis of the topic of the message; it is located in the header area of the message and can be seen in most views.

**tab**   In a complex dialog box, the tabs are located along the top of the pane. Click a tab to display a separate page within the dialog box.

**task**   An unscheduled event of the day that has to occur, but not necessarily at a fixed time.

**template**   An email message you save in template format instead of sending to a recipient. The template contains boilerplate text and formatting you can retrieve and use repeatedly.

**ToolTip**   The small box that appears next to a toolbar button when you hold the mouse cursor over the button. The box contains a terse explanation of what the toolbar button does.

**vCard**   An industry-standard way to include your name, email address, regular address, phone number, and so on in an email message so that message recipients can save this information into their Outlook Contacts view without having to retype that information.

**view**   Outlook is a single program that has many views. Each view is designed to manage a different aspect of your day (such as email, contacts, appointments, and notes). You switch among these views by clicking the desired view in the Outlook bar.

# Index

## A

**accounts, 6**
   corporate mail accounts, creating, 224-225
   default accounts, 58
   Internet connections, changing, 10-11
   Internet-only accounts, setting up, 6-7
   ISP access numbers, 11
   sending mail from specific accounts, 58-59

**Accounts command (Tools menu), 6, 10, 23, 58**

**actions (rules), selecting, 191**

**Actions menu commands, Resend This Message, 63**

**activities (Journal), tracking, 186-187**

**Activities tab (Contact dialog box), 184-185**

**Add Services to Profile dialog box, 8**

**Add to Outlook Bar dialog box, 219**

**Address Book, 127**
   distribution lists, creating, 128-129
   *see also* contacts

**Address Book command (Tools menu), 69**

**addresses**
   adding contacts from, 118-119
   adding to Contacts automatically, 74-75

**addressing email messages, 42-43**

**Advanced Find dialog box, 98-99, 111, 122-123**

**Advanced Options dialog box, 18, 25**

**Advanced Search dialog box, 111**

**Appointment dialog box, 149, 156, 160**

**Appointment Recurrence dialog box, 150-151**

**appointments, 13**
   comparing to tasks, 153
   converting events into, 155
   creating, 148-149
   deleting, 161
   editing, 160-161
   moving to another day, 161
   recurring appointments
      *creating, 150-151*
      *meeting details, editing, 151*
   viewing, 147

**archive, 187**

**archiving email messages, 228-231**
   reading archived items, 230-231

**ASCII text, 66**

**assigning tasks, 158-159**

**attachments**
   adding to email, 48-49
   opening, 50-51
   printing, 55
   saving, 50-51
   troubleshooting, 49-51
   viewing in Preview pane, 103

**Attachments command (View menu), 103**

**AutoArchive dialog box, 228**

**AutoArchiving, 228-230**

**automated email**
   automated mail checking system, 56-57
   rules, 189
      *actions, selecting, 191*
      *assigning messages to categories, 198-199*
      *Autoresponders, creating, 194-195*
      *combining, 197*
      *conditions, selecting, 191*
      *copying, 193*
      *creating, 190-191*
      *disabling, 192-193*
      *exceptions, selecting, 191*
      *junk mail, avoiding, 200-201*
      *moving mail to folders, 196-197*
      *naming, 191*

**automatic startup, 5**

**AutoPreview, 84-85**
  enabling, 84

**AutoPreview command (View menu), 36, 84**

**AutoPreview mode (email), 36**

**Autoresponders, creating, 194-195**

**avatars, 26**

**Background command (Format menu), 70**

**Background Picture dialog box, 70, 90**

**backgrounds**
  color, changing, 67
  settings, changing, 90
  stationery, 70-71

**Bcc (Blind Courtesy Copy) feature, 46-47**

**Bcc Field command (View menu), 46-47**

**bigfoot.com Web site, 126**

**bulleted text, 92-93**

**buttons, adding to Outlook bar, 219**

**Calendar view, 146-147**
  appointments
    *creating, 148-149*
    *deleting, 161*
    *editing, 160-161*
    *moving to another day, 161*
    *recurring appointments, creating, 150-151*
    *viewing, 147*

events
  *converting into appointments, 155*
  *creating, 154-155*
  meetings, creating, 156-157
  options, setting, 23
  pane borders, resizing, 147
  printing, 162-163
    *print styles, selecting, 163*
  switching to, 146
  TaskPad, 147
  tasks
    *assigning, 158-159*
    *creating, 152-153*
  toolbars, 146

**calendars**
  printing, 162-163
  sharing, 164-165

**calling contacts, 136-137**

**categories, 108**
  assigning messages to (rules), 198-199
  organizing contacts, 132-133

**Categories dialog box, 108, 198**

**centering text, 91**

**Change Synchronization Preferences dialog box, 209-210**

**Choose Contact dialog box, 125**

**Close button, 5**

**closing**
  Find pane (folder windows), 97
  Outlook, 5
  Preview pane (folder windows), 97

**coloring text, 92**

**colors**
  backgrounds, 67, 90
  marking messages by color, 107
  note colors, changing, 174-175

**combining rules, 197**

**commands**
  Actions menu, Resend This Message, 63
  File menu
    *Exit, 5*
    *Print, 14, 54, 162*
    *Print Preview, 162*
  Format menu
    *Background, 70*
    *Font, 92*
    *Paragraph, 67, 91*
  Help menu
    *Hide the Office Assistant, 27*
    *Microsoft Outlook Help, 26*
  Insert menu, File, 48
  Tools menu
    *Accounts, 6, 10, 23, 58*
    *Address Book, 69*
    *Options, 18, 22*
    *PilotMirror Settings, 208*
    *Services, 8*
  View menu
    *Attachments, 103*
    *AutoPreview, 36, 84*
    *Bcc Field, 46-47*
    *Current View, 175*
    *Folder List, 5, 17, 25, 104*
    *Preview Pane, 84, 97*

**completed tasks (Outlook Today view), 13**

**conditions (rules), selecting, 191**

**connections (email accounts)**
  changing, 10-11
  options, setting, 24

**Contact dialog box, 74-75**
  Activities tab, 184-185

**Contact window, 115**
  contacts, creating, 116-117
  field labels, changing, 117
  Notes field, 117

contacts
- adding from email addresses, 118-119
- contact information
  - *adding automatically, 74-75*
  - *vCards, 72-73*
- creating, 116-117
  - *detailed information, adding, 117*
  - *field labels, changing, 117*
  - *name information, 116*
  - *phone number information, 116*
- digital IDs, adding, 79
- display settings, 131
- distribution lists, creating, 128-129
- emailing contact information, 131
- linking to email messages, 138-139
- maps
  - *printing, 135*
  - *viewing, 134-135*
- moving to folders, 130
- opening, 115
- organizing with categories, 132-133
- placing calls to, 136-137
- saving, 117
- searching
  - *Find a Contact field, 124-125*
  - *Internet searches, 126-127*
  - *by keyword, 122-123*
  - *by name, 120-121*
- viewing, 115

**Contacts toolbar, Find button, 120**

**Contacts view, 114-115**
- changing, 131
- contacts, organizing with categories, 132-133
- elements, 114
- Find pane, 120
- letter tabs, 115
- Organize button, 130
- Organize pane, 130-133
  - *Customize Current View button, 131*
  - *Using Categories tab, 132*
  - *Using Folders tab, 130*
  - *Using Views tab, 131-133*
- searching Journal information, 179, 184-185
- switching to, 114
- toolbar, 114

**copying rules, 193**

**corporate mail configuration**
- accounts, creating, 224-225
- multiple profiles, 225
- switching to, 222-223

**Create New Folder dialog box, 104, 226**

**Create New Signature Wizard, 65**

**Current View command (View menu), 175**

**customizing**
- Notes view, 174-175
- Outlook bar
  - *buttons, adding, 219*
  - *file shortcuts, adding, 218-219*
  - *groups, adding, 216-217*
  - *icons, sizing, 217*
- Outlook Today view, 16-17
- print styles, 163

## D

**data files**
- importing from another computer, 204-205
- multiple data files, opening, 205
- synchronizing on PCs, 206-207

**Day view (Journal), 181**

**default accounts (email), 58**

**delegating tasks, 158-159**

**Deleted Items folder, 232**
- emptying, 232
- options, setting, 24-25, 232-233
- viewing contents, 232

**deleting**
- appointments, 161
- email messages, 37, 232
  - *options, setting, 232-233*
- file shortcuts from Outlook bar, 219

**desktop information manager, 3**

**Detect and Repair dialog box, 238**

**Detect and Repair features, 238-239**

**dial-up connection options, setting, 24**

**dialog boxes**
- Add Services to Profile, 8
- Add to Outlook Bar, 219
- Advanced Find, 98-99, 111, 122-123
- Advanced Options, 18, 25
- Advanced Search, 111
- Appointment, 149, 156, 160
- Appointment Recurrence, 150-151
- AutoArchive, 228
- Background Picture, 70, 90
- Categories, 108, 198
- Change Synchronization Preferences, 209-210
- Choose Contact, 125
- Contact, 74-75
  - *Activities tab, 184-185*
- Create New Folder, 104, 226
- Detect and Repair, 238
- Duplicate Contact Detected, 75, 79, 119
- E-mail Options, 82-83
- Edit Signature, 73
- Envelope Address, 142
- Event, 154-155
- Find People, 127

**DIALOG BOXES 247**

Flag for Follow Up, 100-101
Font, 92
Group By, 109
Insert File, 48
Internet Accounts, 6, 10, 58, 220
Internet Connection Wizard, 220
Journal Entry, 182
Journal Options, 178, 186
Mail Merge Helper, 140
Main Account Properties, 225
Microsoft Word, 141
My ISP Properties, 9
My Other ISP Properties, 11
My Team Properties, 128
New Call, 136-137
Open Personal Folders, 231
Open Recurring Item, 151
Open Synchronization File, 207
Opening Mail Attachment, 51, 183
Options, 18, 22
   *Format tab, 71*
   *Mail Delivery tab, 23-24, 56-57*
   *Mail Format tab, 24, 52-53, 64-68*
   *Other tab, 25*
   *Preferences tab, 22-23*
   *Security tab, 76-78*
   *Spelling tab, 44, 80*
Outlook 2000 Startup, 223
Outlook Calendar Properties, 209
Paragraph, 91-92
Personal Folders Properties, 204
PilotMirror User Settings, 208
Print, 14-15, 54-55, 162-163
Print Preview, 162
Print to File, 15
Printer Properties, 15

Query Options, 142
Rule Address, 197
Save Attachment, 51
Save Synchronization File, 206
Select Attendees and Resources, 156-157
Select Folder, 16, 111
Select Group Members, 129
Select Names, 42
Select Task Recipient, 159
Services, 8-9, 224-225
Signature Picker, 64, 73
Spelling, 45
Stationery Picker, 71
status (email), 34-35
Synchronize Other Computer, 206
Task, 153, 158-159
Use Address Book, 141
View Summary, 109, 131

**dictionary, adding words to, 45, 80-81**

**digital IDs**
adding to contacts, 79
encrypted email messages, sending, 78-79
setting up, 76-77
VeriSign, 76-77

**directory services, 126-127**

**disabling rules, 192-193**

**displaying**
all topic-related messages, 110-111
Folder List, 25
messages, 84-85
Office Assistant, 26

**distribution lists, creating, 128-129**

**documents (Word)**
Journal items, opening, 183
mail merging data, 140-143
   *queries, setting up, 142-143*

Drafts folder, 59

**drag and drop technique, moving folders, 227**

**Duplicate Contact Detected dialog box, 75, 79, 119**

# E

**E-mail Options dialog box, 82-83**

**Edit Signature dialog box, 73**

**editing appointments, 160-161**

**email, 31**
accounts, 6
   *corporate mail accounts, creating, 224-225*
   *default accounts, 58*
   *Internet connections, changing, 10-11*
   *Internet-only accounts, setting up, 6-7*
   *ISP access numbers, 11*
   *sending mail from specific accounts, 58-59*
addresses
   *adding contacts from addresses, 118-119*
   *adding to contacts automatically, 74-75*
attachments
   *adding, 48-49*
   *opening, 50-51*
   *printing, 55*
   *saving, 50-51*
   *troubleshooting, 49-51*
AutoPreview mode, 36
Bcc (Blind Courtesy Copy) feature, 46-47
checking mail automatically, 56-57
checking for new mail, 34
contact information, sending, 131
Deleted Items folder options, setting, 24-25

Drafts folder, 59
folders (Outlook Today), showing, 16
Inbox folder, 35
Inbox view, 32-33
message transmission, 34-35
messages
   *addressing, 42-43*
   *archiving, 228-231*
   *converting notes to email messages, 172-173*
   *converting to notes, 172*
   *creating, 42-43*
   *deleting, 37, 232-233*
   *displaying all topic-related messages, 110-111*
   *displaying with AutoPreview, 84-85*
   *displaying with Preview Pane, 84-85*
   *encrypted messages, sending, 78-79*
   *formatting, 66-67, 90-93*
   *forwarding, 40-41*
   *forwarding styles, setting, 83*
   *leaving copies on the mail server, 88-89*
   *linking to contacts, 138-139*
   *mail templates, 234-237*
   *marking as read/unread, 102-103*
   *marking by color, 107*
   *marking with flags, 100-101*
   *moving into folders, 105-107*
   *organizing in folders, 104-105*
   *plain-text format, 68-69*
   *printing, 54-55*
   *read receipt requests, 86-87*
   *reading, 36*
   *replies, formatting, 82-83*
   *replying to, 37-39*
   *resending, 62-63*
   *restoring to unread status, 37*
   *searching by keywords, 97-99*
   *searching by subject/sender, 96-97*
   *sending with mail templates, 236-237*
   *sorting with categories, 108-109*
   *spelling check, 44-47*
   *stationery, selecting, 90*
   *text, formatting, 91-93*
   *writing with Word, 52-53*
options, setting, 22-25
Outbox folder, 34
paper clip icons, 50
security
   *digital IDs, 76-79*
   *encrypted email messages, sending, 78-79*
Send/Receive button, 34
Sent Items folder, 57, 62
services, 8
   *creating, 8-9*
   *Internet email service, adding, 9*
signatures, creating, 64-65
spam, 41, 47
   *avoiding with rules, 200-201*
stationery, 70-71
status dialog box, 34-35
vCards, 72-73

Email view, 13

encrypted email messages, sending, 78-79

entries (Journal)
   archiving, 187
   documents, opening, 183
   opening, 182
   searching by keyword, 183
   viewing, 180-181

Envelope Address dialog box, 142

Event dialog box, 154-155

events
   converting into appointments, 155
   creating, 154-155

exceptions (rules), selecting, 191

Exit command (File menu), 5

Expedia Web site, 134-135

# F

field labels (Contact window), changing, 117

file attachments
   adding to email, 48-49
   opening, 50-51
   saving, 50-51
   troubleshooting, 49-51
   viewing in Preview pane, 103

File command (Insert menu), 48

File menu commands
   Exit, 5
   Print, 14, 54, 162
   Print Preview, 162

files
   data files, synchronizing on PCs, 206-207
   importing from another computer, 204-205
   multiple data files, opening, 205
   printing, 15
   shortcuts
      *adding to Outlook bar, 218-219*
      *deleting from Outlook bar, 219*

Find a Contact field, 124-125

Find button (Contacts toolbar), 120

Find Items pane (Notes view), 177

Find pane (folder windows), 96-98
   closing, 97

**Find People button (Address Book window), 127**

**Find People dialog box, 127**

**Find tool, 96**

**finding**
  contacts
    *Find a Contact field, 124-125*
    *Internet searches, 126-127*
    *by keyword, 122-123*
    *by name, 120-121*
  Journal entries
    *Contacts view, 179, 184-185*
    *by keyword, 183*
  messages
    *by keywords, 97-99*
    *by subject/sender, 96-97*
    *topic-related messages, 110-111*
  notes, 177
  people on the Internet, 220-221

**Flag for Follow Up dialog box, 100-101**

**flags, 100-101**

**Folder list, 5, 32**
  adding folders, 226-227
  displaying, 25, 226
    *in Outlook Today view, 17*

**Folder List command (View menu), 5, 17, 25, 104**

**folders, 5**
  adding to Folder List, 226-227
  contacts, moving to folders, 130
  creating, 104, 226-227
  Deleted Items folder, 232
    *emptying, 232*
    *options, setting, 24-25, 232-233*
    *viewing contents, 232*
  Drafts folder, 59
  email folders (Outlook Today), showing, 16
  files, moving to folders, 105
  Inbox folder, 35
  messages, moving to folders, 106-107, 196-197
  moving, drag and drop technique, 227
  nested folders, creating, 105
  notes, moving into folders, 176
  organizing messages, 104-105
  Outbox folder (email), 34
  selecting, 5
  Sent Items folder, 57, 62
  shortcuts, adding to Outlook bar, 227

**Font command (Format menu), 92**

**Font dialog box, 92**

**Format menu commands**
  Background, 70
  Font, 92
  Paragraph, 67, 91

**Format tab (Options dialog box), 71**

**formatting**
  email messages, 66-67, 90-93
    *backgrounds, 90*
    *colored backgrounds, 67*
    *HTML format, 67, 93*
    *plain-text formatting, 68-69*
    *text, 91-93*
  message replies, 82-83

**forwarding email messages, 40-41**
  forwarding styles, setting, 83

**four11.com Web site, 127**

## G-H

**Group By dialog box, 109**

**groups, adding to Outlook bar, 216-217**

**hard disks, viewing contents, 21**

**Help menu commands**
  Hide the Office Assistant, 27
  Microsoft Outlook Help, 26

**Help system (Office Assistant), 26-27**
  cartoon character, changing, 27
  displaying, 26
  Help topics, searching, 26-27
  hiding, 27
  Microsoft Knowledge Base Web site, accessing, 28-29
  moving, 27

**hidden menus, viewing, 214**

**hidden toolbars**
  buttons, 215
  viewing, 214

**hiding Office Assistant, 27**

**HotSync Log (PalmPilot), 211**

**HotSync settings (PalmPilot), 210-211**

**HTML (Hypertext Markup Language), formatting email messages, 67**

**HTML format, 93**

## I

**icons**
  note icons, changing, 174
  Outlook bar
    *Other Shortcuts group, 21*
    *size, changing, 217*
    *viewing, 20*

**IMAP mail servers, 89**

importing mail from another computer, 204-205

Inbox folder, 35

Inbox view, 32
  AutoPreview, 84-85
    enabling, 84
  Folder List, 32
  message status icons, 33
  Organize pane, 106-107, 110, 200-201
    Using Colors tab, 107
    Using Folders tab, 106-107
    Using Views tab, 107-110
  toolbar commands, 32-33

infospace.com Web site, 127

Insert File button, adding to the toolbar, 49

Insert File dialog box, 48

Insert menu commands, File, 48

installing Outlook, extra features, 239

integrated mail client, 3

Internet Accounts dialog box, 6, 10, 58, 220

Internet Connection Wizard, 6

Internet Connection Wizard dialog box, 220

Internet connections (email accounts), changing, 10-11

Internet email service, adding, 9

Internet searches
  contact searches, 126-127
  people searches, 220-221

Internet-only email accounts, setting up, 6-7

Internet-only mail configuration, switching to, 222-223

inviting people to meetings, 156-157

ISPs (Internet Service Providers), access numbers, 11

Journal, 178-179
  activities, tracking, 186-187
  entries
    archiving, 187
    document entries, opening, 183
    opening, 182
    searching by keyword, 183
    viewing, 180-181
  logging calls to contacts, 137
  options, setting, 178-179, 186-187
  searching Journal information (Contacts view), 179, 184-185
  turning off, 179
  turning on, 178

Journal Entry dialog box, 182

Journal Options dialog box, 178, 186

Journal view, 179
  entries, opening, 182
  switching to, 178

junk mail, avoiding with rules, 200-201

K-L

keyword searches, 97-99
  contacts, 122-123
  Journal entries, 183

Knowledge Base Web site, 29

labels (categories), 108

LDAP servers, 126-127
  accounts, setting up, 220-221
  popular LDAP servers, 221

letter tabs (Contacts view), 115

Lightweight Directory Access Protocol (LDAP), 220

linking contacts and email messages, 138-139

lists, displaying notes as, 174

mail configuration, changing, 222-223

Mail Delivery tab (Options dialog box), 23-24, 56-57

Mail Format tab (Options dialog box), 24, 52-53, 64-68

Mail Merge Helper dialog box, 140

mail merges, 140
  merging data into Word documents, 140-143

mail servers
  IMAP, 89
  leaving copies of messages, 88-89

mail templates
  creating, 234-235
  saving, 234-235
  sending messages, 236-237

mail, see email

mailing groups, creating, 128-129

Main Account Properties dialog box, 225

maps (contact location)
  printing, 135
  viewing, 134-135

meetings, 156-157

menus
  hidden menus, viewing, 214
  hidden toolbars, viewing, 214
  Personalized Menus feature, 33, 214-215

MENUS 251

**merging data into Word documents,** 140–143
    queries, setting up, 142–143

**message status icons (Inbox view),** 33

**messages (email)**
    addressing, 42–43
    archiving, 228–231
    converting messages to notes, 172
    converting notes to email messages, 172–173
    creating, 42–43
    deleting, 37, 232–233
    displaying
        *all topic-related messages, 110–111*
        *with AutoPreview, 84–85*
        *with Preview Pane, 84–85*
    encrypted messages, sending, 78–79
    formatting, 66–67, 90–93
    forwarding, 40–41
        *forwarding styles, setting, 83*
    leaving copies on the mail server, 88–89
    linking to contacts, 138–139
    mail templates, 234–237
    marking
        *by color, 107*
        *with flags, 100–101*
        *as read/unread, 102–103*
    moving into folders, 105–107
    organizing in folders, 104–105
    plain-text format, 68–69
    printing, 54–55
    read receipt requests, 86–87
    reading, 36
    replies, formatting, 82–83
    replying to, 37–39
    resending, 62–63
    restoring to unread status, 37
    searching
        *by keywords, 97–99*
        *by subject/sender, 96–97*
    sending with mail templates, 236–237
    sorting with categories, 108–109
    spelling check, 44–47
    stationery, selecting, 90
    text, formatting, 91–93
    writing with Word, 52–53

**Microsoft Knowledge Base Web site,** 29

**Microsoft Office Web site,** 207

**Microsoft Outlook Help command (Help menu),** 26

**Microsoft Web site,** 29

**Microsoft Word, see Word**

**Microsoft Word dialog box,** 141

**mouse, right-clicking,** 177

**moving**
    appointments to another day, 161
    folders (drag and drop technique), 227
    mail to folders (rules), 196–197
    notes, 175
        *into folders, 176*
    Office Assistant, 27

**multiple data files, opening,** 205

**multiple profiles,** 225

**My Computer view,** 21

**My ISP Properties dialog box,** 9

**My Other ISP Properties dialog box,** 11

**My Team Properties dialog box,** 128

# N

**naming rules,** 191

**nested folders, creating,** 105

**Net Folder Wizard,** 164–165

**New Call dialog box,** 136–137

**note icons, changing,** 174

**Notepad, adding words to spelling dictionary,** 80–81

**notes**
    color, changing, 174–175
    converting email messages to notes, 172
    converting to email messages, 172–173
    creating, 170–171
    displaying as a list, 174
    moving around, 175
    moving into folders, 176
    searching, 177
    viewing, changing views, 175

**Notes field (Contact window),** 117

**Notes List (Notes View),** 177

**Notes view,** 170–171
    customizing, 174–175
    Find Items pane, 177
    notes, creating, 170–171
    Notes List, 177
    Organize pane, 176
    search and filter tools, 177
    switching to, 170
    view modes, selecting, 176

# O

**Office Assistant,** 26–27
    cartoon character, changing, 27
    displaying, 26
    Help topics, searching, 26–27
    hiding, 27

Microsoft Knowledge Base Web site, accessing, 28-29
moving, 27

**Open Personal Folders dialog box, 231**

**Open Recurring Item dialog box, 151**

**Open Synchronization File dialog box, 207**

**opening**
contacts, 115
file attachments (email), 50-51
Journal entries, 182-183
multiple data files, 205

**Opening Mail Attachment dialog box, 51, 183**

**options**
Folder List, displaying, 25
saving, 25
setting, 22
*Calendar view, 23*
*connection options, 24*
*email, 23*
*email options, 22-25*

**Options command (Tools menu), 18, 22**

**Options dialog box, 18, 22**
Mail Delivery tab, 23-24, 56-57
Mail Format tab, 24, 52-53, 64-68, 71
Other tab, 25
Preferences tab, 22-23
Security tab, 76-78
Spelling tab, 44, 80

**Organize button (Contacts view), 130**

**Organize pane**
Contacts view, 130-131
*Customize Current View button, 131*
*Using Categories tab, 132*
*Using Folders tab, 130*
*Using Views tab, 131-133*
Inbox view, 106-107, 110, 200-201
*Using Colors tab, 107*
*Using Folders tab, 106-107*
*Using Views tab, 107-110*
Notes view, 176

**Other Shortcuts group (Outlook bar icons), 21**

**Other tab (Options dialog box), 25**

**Outbox folder (email), 34**

**Outlook**
closing, 5
Detect and Repair features, 238-239
importing mail from another computer, 204-205
installing, extra features, 239
mail configuration, changing, 222-223
options, 22
*Calendar view, 23*
*connections, 24*
*email, 22-25*
*Folder List, displaying, 25*
*saving, 25*
reporting of work hours, 181
searching everywhere in Outlook, 123
starting, 4
*automatically, 5*
*startup views, selecting, 18-19*
synchronizing
*with another computer, 206-207*
*with PalmPilot, 208-211*

**Outlook 2000 Startup dialog box, 223**

**Outlook bar, 4, 20-21**
buttons, adding, 219
file shortcuts
*adding, 218-219*
*deleting, 219*
folder shortcuts, adding, 227
groups, adding, 216-217
icons
*Other Shortcuts group, 21*
*sizing, 217*
*viewing, 20*
items, adding, 21
views
*selecting, 4-5*
*switching, 20*

**Outlook Calendar Properties dialog box, 209**

**Outlook dictionary, adding words to, 45**

**Outlook Today summary, printing, 14-15**

**Outlook Today view, 4, 12-13**
appointments, 13
customizing, 16-17
switching between views, 12-13
tasks, completed tasks, 13

**PalmPilot Gear HQ Web site, 211**

**PalmPilots**
PilotMirror, 208
*configuring, 208-210*
synchronizing with Outlook, 208-211
*HotSync Log, 211*
*HotSync settings, 210-211*

**pane borders (Calendar view), resizing, 147**

**paper clip icons (email), 50**

**Paragraph command (Format menu), 67, 91**

**Paragraph dialog box, 91-92**

**people searches (Internet), 126–127**
   bigfoot.com, 126

**permissions, sharing calendars, 165**

**Personal Folders Properties dialog box, 204**

**Personalized Menus feature, 33, 214–215**
   hidden menus, viewing, 214

**Personalized Toolbars feature, 214–215**

**PilotMirror, 208**
   configuring, 208–210

**PilotMirror Settings command (Tools menu), 208**

**PilotMirror User Settings dialog box, 208**

**PIMs (Personal Information Managers), 3**

**PKZip, 205**

**plain-text messages, sending, 68–69**

**polls, taking, 157**

**Preferences tab (Options dialog box), 22–23**

**Preview Pane**
   folder views, displaying messages, 84–85
   folder windows, 97
      *attached files, viewing, 103*

**Preview Pane command (View menu), 84, 97**

**primary recipients (email), 43**

**Print command (File menu), 14, 54, 162**

**Print dialog box, 14–15, 54–55, 162–163**

**Print Preview command (File menu), 162**

**Print Preview dialog box, 162**

**print styles, 163**

**Print to File dialog box, 15**

**Printer Properties dialog box, 15**

**printing**
   calendar, 162–163
      *print styles, selecting, 163*
   contact location maps, 135
   email messages, 54–55
      *attached files, 55*
   files, 15
   money-saving measures, 55
   Outlook Today summary, 14–15

**profiles, multiple profiles, 225**

##  Q

**queries, setting up (mail merges), 142–143**

**Query Options dialog box, 142**

##  R

**read receipt requests, 86–87**

**read, marking messages as, 102–103**

**reading**
   archived items, 230–231
   AutoPreview mode, 36
   email messages, 36

**recipients**
   adding to email messages, 42–43
   primary recipients, 43

**recurring appointments**
   creating, 150–151
   meeting details, editing, 151

**repairing Outlook (Detect and Repair features), 238–239**

**replies, formatting, 82–83**

**replying to email messages, 37–39**
   Reply to All button, 39

**resending email messages, 62–63**

**resizing Outlook bar icons, 217**

**restoring email to unread status, 37**

**right-clicking (mouse), 177**

**Rule Address dialog box, 197**

**rules, 189**
   actions, selecting, 191
   Autoresponders, creating, 194–195
   combining, 197
   conditions, selecting, 191
   copying, 193
   creating, 190–191
      *assigning messages to categories, 198–199*
      *junk mail, avoiding, 200–201*
      moving mail to folders, 196–197
   disabling, 192–193
   exceptions, selecting, 191
   naming, 191

**Rules Wizard**
   Autoresponders, creating, 194–195
   copying rules, 193
   creating rules, 190–191
   disabling rules, 192–193
   moving mail to folders, 196–197

##  S

**satellite navigation systems, 135**

**Save Attachment dialog box, 51**

**Save Synchronization File dialog box, 206**

**saving**
   contact information, 117
   file attachments (email), 50–51

mail templates, 234-235
options, 25

**search and filter tools (Notes view), 177**

**searching**
contacts
*Find a Contact field, 124-125*
*Internet searches, 126-127*
*by keyword, 122-123*
*by name, 120-121*
email messages
*by keywords, 97-99*
*by subject/sender, 96-97*
everywhere in Outlook, 123
Help topics (Office Assistant), 26-27
Journal entries
*Contacts view, 179, 184-185*
*by keyword, 183*
notes, 177
people on the Internet, 220-221
topic-related messages, 110-111

**security (digital IDs)**
adding to Contacts, 79
encrypted email messages, sending, 78-79
setting up, 76-77
VeriSign, 76-77

**Security tab (Options dialog box), 76, 78**

**Select Attendees and Resources dialog box, 156-157**

**Select Folder dialog box, 16, 111**

**Select Group Members dialog box, 129**

**Select Names dialog box, 42**

**Select Task Recipient dialog box, 159**

**Send/Receive button (email), 34**

**sending email messages**
encrypted messages, 78-79
with mail templates, 236-237
plain-text format, 68-69
read receipt requests, 86-87
resending, 62-63
from specific accounts, 58-59

**Sent Items folder, 57, 62**

**servers**
IMAP, 89
LDAP servers, 126-127
*accounts, setting up, 220-221*
*popular LDAP servers, 221*
leaving copies of messages, 88-89

**services, 8, 223**
Internet email service, adding, 9
mail services, creating, 8-9

**Services command (Tools menu), 8**

**Services dialog box, 8-9, 224-225**

**settings, 22**
Calendar view options, 23
connection options, 24
email options, 22-25
Folder List, displaying, 25
saving, 25

**sharing calendars, 164-165**

**shortcuts**
file shortcuts
*adding to Outlook bar, 218-219*
*deleting from Outlook bar, 219*
folder shortcuts, adding to Outlook bar, 227

**Signature Picker dialog box, 64, 73**

signatures
creating, 64-65
vCard, creating, 72-73

**sizing Outlook bar icons, 217**

**sorting email messages (categories), 108-109**

**spam (email), 41, 47**
avoiding with rules, 200-201

**spelling checker**
aborting, 45
adding words to Outlook dictionary, 45
dictionary, adding words to, 80-81
email messages, checking, 44-47

**Spelling dialog box, 45**

**spelling dictionary, adding words to, 80-81**

**Spelling tab (Options dialog box), 44, 80**

**starting Outlook, 4**
automatically, 5
startup views, selecting, 18-19

**stationery, 70-71**
selecting, 90

**Stationery Picker dialog box, 71**

**status, checking task status, 159**

**status dialog box (email), 34-35**

**styles, changing Outlook Today view, 17**

**switchboard.com Web site, 127**

**Synchronize Other Computer dialog box, 206**

**synchronizing Outlook**
with another computer, 206-207
with PalmPilot, 208-211
*HotSync Log, 211*
*HotSync settings, 210-211*

## T

**Task dialog box, 153, 158–159**
**Task view, selecting, 20**
**TaskPad (Calendar view), 147**
**tasks, 147**
  assigning, 158–159
  comparing to appointments, 153
  completed tasks, 13
  creating, 152–153
  open tasks, 13
  status, checking, 159
**templates (mail templates)**
  creating, 234–235
  saving, 234–235
  sending messages, 236–237
**text**
  ASCII text, 66
  bulleted text, 92–93
  centering, 91
  coloring, 92
  style, changing, 91–93
**toolbars**
  Calendar view, 146
  Contacts toolbar, Find button, 120
  Contacts view, 114
  hidden toolbars, 215
  Inbox view, 32–33
  Personalized Toolbars feature, 214–215
    hidden toolbars, viewing, 214
  turning on/off, 215
**Tools menu commands**
  Accounts, 6, 10, 23, 58
  Address Book, 69
  Options, 18, 22
  PilotMirror Settings, 208
  Services, 8
**ToolTips, 33**

tracking Journal activities, 186–187
**troubleshooting file attachments (email), 49–51**
**turning on/off**
  Journal, 178–179
  toolbars, 215

## U

**unread status (email)**
  marking messages with, 102–103
  restoring, 37
**Use Address Book dialog box, 141**
**Using Categories tab (Organize pane), 132**
**Using Colors tab (Organize pane), 107**
**Using Folders tab (Organize pane), 106–107, 130, 176**
**Using Views tab (Organize pane), 107–109, 131–133, 176**

## V

**vCards, 72–73**
**VeriSign, 76–77**
**View menu commands**
  Attachments, 103
  AutoPreview, 36, 84
  Bcc Field, 46–47
  Current View, 175
  Folder List, 5, 17, 25, 104
  Preview Pane, 84, 97
**View Summary dialog box, 109, 131**
**viewing**
  contacts, 115
  hard disk contents, 21
  Outlook bar icons, 20

**views, 4–5**
  Calendar view, *see* Calendar view
  Contacts view, 114–115
    changing, 131
    elements, 114
    Find pane, 120
    letter tabs, 115
    Organize button, 130
    Organize pane, 130–131
    organizing contacts with categories, 132–133
    searching Journal information, 179, 184–185
    switching to, 114
    toolbar, 114
  displaying messages, 107
  Email view, 13
  Find a Contact field, 124–125
  Inbox view, 32
    AutoPreview, 84–85
    Folder List, 32
    message status icons, 33
    Organize pane, 106–110, 200–201
    toolbar commands, 32–33
  Journal view, 179
    opening entries, 182
    switching to, 178
  My Computer, 21
  Notes view, 170–171
    customizing, 174–175
    Find Items pane, 177
    Notes List, 177
    notes, creating, 170–171
    Organize pane, 176
    search and filter tools, 177
    switching to, 170
    view modes, selecting, 176
  Outlook startup views, selecting, 18–19
  Outlook Today, 4, 12–13
    appointments, 13
    completed tasks, 13

*customizing, 16-17*
*switching between views, 12-13*
selecting, 4-5
switching with Outlook bar, 20
Task view, selecting, 20
Week view (Journal), 181

## W-Z

**Web sites**
bigfoot.com, 126
Expedia, 134-135
four11.com, 127
infospace.com, 127
Microsoft, 29
Microsoft Knowledge Base, 29
Microsoft Office, 207
PalmPilot Gear HQ, 211
switchboard.com, 127
VeriSign, 76-77

**Week view (Journal), 181**

**windows (Contact window), 115**
contacts, creating, 116-117
field labels, changing, 117
Notes field, 117

**WinZip, 205**

**wizards**
Create New Signature Wizard, 65
Internet Connection Wizard, 6
Net Folder Wizard, 164-165
Rules Wizard
*Autoresponders, creating, 194-195*
*copying rules, 193*
*creating, 190-191*
*disabling rules, 192-193*
*moving mail to folders, 196-197*

**Word**
documents, mail merging data, 140-143
email messages, writing, 52-53

**work hours, reporting of, 181**

**Zoom and Pan features (viewing maps of contact locations), 135**

# Get FREE books and more...when you register this book online for our Personal Bookshelf Program

*http://register.samspublishing.com/*

 Register online and you can sign up for our *FREE Personal Bookshelf Program*...unlimited access to the electronic version of more than 200 complete computer books—immediately! That means you'll have 100,000 pages of valuable information onscreen, at your fingertips!

 Plus, you can access product support, including complimentary downloads, technical support files, book-focused links, companion Web sites, author sites, and more!

 And you'll be automatically registered to receive a *FREE subscription to our weekly email newsletter* to help you stay current with news, announcements, sample book chapters, and special events including, sweepstakes, contests, and various product giveaways!

 We value your comments! Best of all, the entire registration process takes only a few minutes to complete, so go online and get the greatest value going—absolutely FREE!

## Don't Miss Out On This Great Opportunity!

Sams is a brand of Macmillan Computer Publishing USA. For more information, please visit *www.mcp.com*

Copyright ©1999 Macmillan Computer Publishing USA

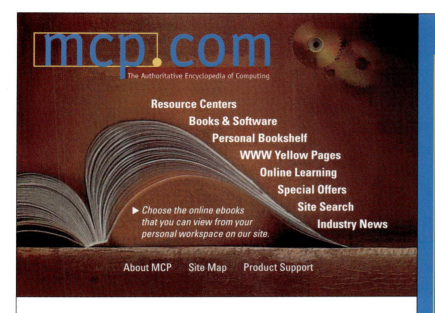

## Turn to the *Authoritative* Encyclopedia of Computing

You'll find over 150 full text books online, hundreds of shareware/freeware applications, online computing classes and 10 computing resource centers full of expert advice from the editors and publishers of:

- Adobe Press
- BradyGAMES
- Cisco Press
- Hayden Books
- Lycos Press
- New Riders
- Que
- Que Education & Training
- Sams Publishing
- Waite Group Press
- Ziff-Davis Press

When you're looking for computing information, consult the authority. The Authoritative Encyclopedia of Computing at mcp.com.

### Get the best information and learn about latest developments in:

- Design
- Graphics and Multimedia
- Enterprise Computing and DBMS
- General Internet Information
- Operating Systems
- Networking and Hardware
- PC and Video Gaming
- Productivity Applications
- Programming
- Web Programming and Administration
- Web Publishing

# How to Use

How to Use *provides easy, visual information in a proven, step-by-step format. This helpful guide uses colorful illustrations and clear explanations to get you the results you need.*

## Other How to Use Titles

### Microsoft Word 2000
*Sherry Kinkoph*
ISBN: 0-672-31531-9
$24.99 US/$37.95 CAN

### Microsoft Excel 2000
*Dan and Sandy Gookin*
ISBN: 0-672-31538-6
$24.99 US/$37.95 CAN

### Microsoft PowerPoint 2000
*Susan Daffron*
ISBN: 0-672-31529-7
$24.99 US/$37.95 CAN

### Microsoft Publisher 2000
*Jennifer Fulton*
ISBN: 0-672-31571-8
$24.99 US/$37.95 CAN

### Microsoft Access 2000
*Jacqueline Okwudli*
ISBN: 0-672-31491-6
$24.99 US/$37.95 CAN

### Microsoft Windows 98
*Doug Hergert*
ISBN: 1-56276-572-8
$24.99 US/$37.95 CAN

### America Online 4
*Elaine Madison and Deborah Craig*
ISBN: 1-56276-543-4
$24.99 US/$37.95 CAN

### Computers
*Lisa Biow*
ISBN: 0-7897-1645-3
$24.99 US/$37.95 CAN

### The Internet
*Mark Walker*
ISBN: 1-56276-560-4
$24.99 US/$37.95 CAN

**SAMS**
www.samspublishing.com

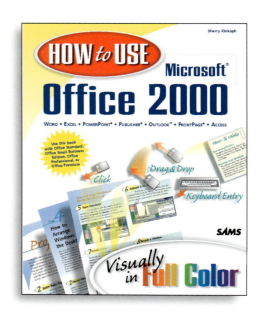

### How to Use Microsoft Office 2000
*Sherry Kinkoph*
ISBN: 0-672-31522-X
$24.99 US/$37.95 CAN

All prices are subject to change.